SCC Library

3 3065 00344 3169

Santiago Canyon College
Library

D0700567

SEEKING CIVILITY

K
184
.J365
2003

SEEKING CIVILITY

COMMON COURTESY

AND THE COMMON LAW

George W. Jarecke and Nancy K. Plant

Northeastern University Press
OCM 51838565
Boston

Santiago Canyon College
Library

Northeastern University Press

Copyright 2003 by George W. Jarecke and Nancy K. Plant

All rights reserved. Except for the quotation of short passages for the purposes of criticism and review, no part of this book may be reproduced in any form or by any means, electronic or mechanical, including photocopying, recording, or any information storage and retrieval system now known or to be invented, without written permission of the publisher.

Library of Congress Cataloging-in-Publication Data

Jarecke, George W., 1953–
Seeking civility : common courtesy and the common law /
George W. Jarecke and Nancy K. Plant.
p.   cm.
Includes bibliographical references and index.
ISBN 1–55553–576–3 (cloth : alk. paper)
1. Law—United States—Anecdotes.   2. Right and wrong.   3. Law and ethics.   4. Civil society.   I. Plant, Nancy K., 1960–   II. Title.
K184.J365   2003
340'.112–dc21   2003005457

Designed by Amber Frid-Jimenez

Composed in Minion by Coghill Composition Company in Richmond, Virginia.
Printed and bound by The Maple Press Company in York, Pennsylvania. The paper is Maple Tradebook Antique, an acid-free sheet.

MANUFACTURED IN THE UNITED STATES OF AMERICA
07 06 05 04 03   5 4 3 2 1

The authors dedicate this book to their parents,
Marc and Gerry Plant and Walt and Jeannette Jarecke.

Road rage threatens mental health and physical safety. People use cell phones in public places with blithe indifference to the tranquillity of others. Smokers, while fairly well vanquished, still have a defiant look about them when they light up outside office buildings, and aren't especially careful about where they blow their smoke. We find ourselves asking, why won't people behave? What can we do to counter their lack of common courtesy?

Sometimes the law and legal system have been asked to intervene. For instance, individuals have brought lawsuits against smokers for endangering their health. State legislatures have begun to pass laws forbidding people from using cell phones while driving. But is the legal system the right means for enforcing good manners? That is one question that we explore in this book.

The discussions are intended as a set of general observations about how the American legal system addresses issues of civility. As in our first book, *Confounded Expectations: The Law's Struggle with Personal Responsibility*, we describe the facts and law of a broad selection of cases for the general reader rather than the legal scholar. We also take up certain quasi-laws and codes enacted by non-governmental institutions.

When matters of pleading or court procedure are important enough to influence the narrative, we explain them as briefly as possible or relegate them to an endnote. Further, we do not intend the text to be an exhaustive review of the law in any particular subject, as our purpose is to consider what the cases say about the relationship of the legal system to civility. However, the cases presented are, at least as of this writing and unless otherwise noted, good law in the state or federal court out of which they came.

In order to avoid using the masculine pronoun *he* to indicate an individual whose gender is not known, we have varied the use of *he* and *she*.

As it did in our first book, the litigious nature of our society requires us to make these disclaimers:

(1) The law is constantly changing, and the specific laws described in this book may have changed. We have presented these cases and statutes to stimulate thought and discussion, however, not to provide legal advice. Anyone with a legal problem or question should consult someone licensed to practice law in his or her state.

(2) The authors make assertions in this book about the motivations, behavior, and strategies of the parties in the cases being discussed. Those opinions are based on the facts of the cases, all of which facts are set forth in the courts' written opinions or gained through the authors' interviews with counsel for the parties. Further, the opinions expressed are the authors' own and do not reflect the opinions, legal theories, or stated positions of their employers or clients, past or present.

The authors wish to acknowledge the invaluable help and advice of Dr. Leroy Rouner, Professor of Philosophy, Religion, and Philosophical Theology at Boston University, and Dr. Elizabeth Hoffman, Professor of Sociology at Purdue University. The authors also thank Bradford Steiner, Esq., Steiner Norris PLLC, Seattle, Washington, for his expert advice and help with respect to matters of trial and appellate procedure, any confusion or mistakes about which, however, are the authors' responsibility only. Finally, the authors extend their gratitude to their editor, Mr. Robert J. Gormley, for his patience and wise counsel.

SEEKING CIVILITY

Miss Carrie Nickerson was about forty-five years old when these events took place, sometime shortly before 1920. The facts described here come from the opinion of the Supreme Court of Louisiana, where the case was eventually decided.[1]

The unmarried Miss Nickerson was eccentric, perhaps, having been an inmate of an insane asylum some twenty years before. But she was energetic, supporting herself as a soap drummer for the California Perfume Company in Webster and the surrounding parishes in the northwestern part of Louisiana.

She was a kinswoman of some degree of Burton and Lawson Deck. There was an old story in that family that the two had buried a pot of gold coins on a place that was now owned by John W. Smith, also in Webster Parish. On a trip to Shreveport, Miss Nickerson chanced to consult with a fortuneteller who confirmed for her that the relatives had indeed buried some gold. He even provided her with a map showing its location, which was on John W. Smith's property.

At this point, Miss Nickerson, a couple of relatives, and a fellow named Bushong, who some said was a suitor of Miss Nickerson's, spent several months digging on Smith's property. Smith not only granted cordial permission, but he let them stay at his house free of charge—perhaps, one might speculate, so that he might claim some commission in respect of whatever they found. They dug everywhere: around the roots of shade trees and the pillars of the house, everywhere.

Finally, three people—Smith's daughter, a Miss Minnie Smith; a man constantly referred to by the court in its opinion in the ensuing litigation as "William or 'Bud' Baker"; and H. R. Hayes—came up with the idea of burying a pot of gold for the prospectors to excavate. They found an old copper bucket, filled it with rocks and dirt, and buried it in an old chimney on the adjacent property. They fastened the pot with two lids, putting between the two a note written by Hayes and wrapped in tin. The note—which was dated either July 1, 1884, or 1784, depending on whom one asked—instructed the finders not to open the lower lid for three days in order that all of the family's heirs could be notified and gathered.

The burial was completed near the end of March. The idea was that the prospectors would find the pot on April 1, making for a great April Fools' joke. Unfortunately the digging wasn't focused in quite the right place, so it was April 14, a Saturday, before the discovery was made. Grady Hayes, H. R. Hayes's brother, perhaps frustrated by their inability to come up with the pot and deciding to get it over with, was helping with the digging and actually made the find. And what a discovery it was.

Everyone rushed to the spot, and even those who were in the know were as excited as Miss Nickerson and her innocent followers. The note was found and read; H. R. Hayes counseled Miss Nickerson to follow its instructions. He suggested having the pot carried to the bank at Cotton Valley, a small town a few miles away (home to a little more than a thousand souls, these days) until the other relatives could be found. They did so, but, at the bank, there was a small glitch. Mr. Gatling, the cashier, refused to give a receipt for "a pot of gold" because it was, after all, still covered by the lower lid, and he had no real way of knowing what was in it. Nevertheless, the pot was left in the bank's safekeeping.

The news spread, of course, and Mr. A. J. Hodges, the bank vice-president, who for some reason hadn't actually been at the bank, showed up and chewed things over with Gatling. They decided that the best course was to examine the pot so that if it did contain gold they might take proper precautions to guard the bank. They opened the lid and discovered the truth. Unfortunately, but inevitably, the truth leaked out, if not from them, then from other sources, so that nearly everyone knew that the pot of gold was a hoax.

In the meantime, Miss Nickerson traveled twenty miles or so to Minden and persuaded Judge R. C. Drew to accompany her back to Cotton Valley on the following Monday to make sure that the pot was properly and ceremoniously opened. According to Judge Drew, he had already heard that it was all a joke, and he tried to convince Miss Nickerson not to count on coming into any fortune. But they were friends, and he felt kindly toward her, so he finally consented to go. Their entourage included about a half dozen other relatives of Burton and Lawson Deck.

Accordingly, a gathering surrounded the bank in Cotton Valley at 11 A.M. on Monday. Among the attendees were H. R. Hayes and Bushong, who, while probably innocent, might still be thought of as something like the original gold digger. Judge Drew, as spokesman for the family, asked Gatling to produce the pot so that they might open it and examine the contents.

Now the facts become unclear, as often happens when a storm hits. Some say that Miss Nickerson could tell that the pot had been tampered with because of the position of a string that had been attached to the pot; others say that it wasn't till after the lid was lifted that Miss Nickerson flew into a rage. In any event, she saw the stones and dirt, and, convinced that she had been robbed of her gold, hurled the lid of the pot at Gatling. For some reason she was also enraged at H. R. Hayes and flew at him with such violence that Hayes had to appeal to Bushong and others to restrain her.

Eventually the scene quieted, and apparently the relatives slinked away. But not Miss Nickerson. She filed suit against H. R. Hayes, "William or 'Bud' Baker," John W. Smith, Miss Minnie Smith, Gatling, and a number of other persons not otherwise identified, but including Mrs. Fannie Smith, A. J. Hodges, R. M. Coyle, Sam P. D. Coyle, and Dr. Charles Coyle. She claimed $15,000 in damages in the form of financial outlay, loss of business, mental and physical suffering, humiliation, and injury to reputation and social standing. Oddly enough, she doesn't appear to have sued them for the theft of the money (which, in common law, her lawyer would have called conversion). In any event, the court record says that, two years after the events, she died, still believing that she had been robbed.

What's clear is that she did feel that she'd suffered mentally, had been humiliated, and had incurred injury to her reputation and social standing. It does seem a tough situation. Cotton Valley was a small community. Everyone seemed to know everyone; word about the hoax spread quickly around the area. Even Judge Drew, twenty miles away in Minden, knew about it. Somehow a half dozen of the Decks' other descendants had been lined up within three days. Minden, the largest town in the parish, is today a city of not much over thirteen thousand. Everyone must have come to find out about Miss Nickerson's humiliation. Had she been a spinster secluded on a family farm, she might well have felt horribly embarrassed. That she traveled about the parish as a representative of the California Perfume Company must have made things all the worse. One might say that the experience literally killed her.

And what of the people who perpetrated the hoax? It seems cruel enough to encourage her to go digging with friends after this purported gold, but then actually to plant it on the property is crueler still. And how much worse to allow the gathering at the bank on that Monday morning. And not to stop the proceedings at the last moment, lead her into the bank away from everyone else, and tell her the truth. There's something malicious about at least some of the people here; maybe the rest were following the mob. Further, it's not beyond speculation that they knew that she had been in an insane asylum and had some sense that she might be susceptible to real anguish as a result of their actions. The court says that it is "for some reason, not clearly explained"[2] that she turned on H. R. Hayes. If she had some inkling that she hadn't been robbed, and that there had been a hoax, and he was its perpetrator, then there's plenty of explanation for her outrage.

The court calls what these people did a practical joke. But under the circumstances, isn't it something worse? Here was a woman known to be emotionally fragile, who is led to believe that a pot of gold—the literal pot of gold at the end of the rainbow—was located on her old relatives' property. Isn't it worse than a practical joke to raise this woman's hopes with the understanding that the point was to embarrass her in front of everyone she knew? And perhaps with the understanding that she had a history of being unable to cope with her emotions? We might say that they behaved badly, immaturely, thoughtlessly. We might say that they acted uncivilly.

How should we, as a society, react to the incivility of the type attributed to the practical jokers in the *Nickerson* case? Can we punish it, or at least control it, through our legal system or through other societal means? Or is incivility an inevitable result of the raucous freedom that we Americans have chosen to afford ourselves, in a culture that values free expression and individual liberty?

Before we begin considering questions of civility and the law, we must define civility, and, hence, incivility. Definitions abound.[3] Some define civility in terms of a citizen's involvement in political or religious life; others may interpret it to require strict adherence to political correctness. We mean neither of those.

Civility is, first, an attitude of respect for the rights, feelings, and thoughts of those other individuals with whom we share space in the world.

Second, civility is an intention to accommodate our own interests to the greater good of the community—even to sacrifice—because, in the end, our best interests are most realized when integrated with those of the community. Of course, we are permitted to expect a fair exchange: We may expect those others in the community to subjugate their individual interests to the greater good of the community as well.

Third, civility is a respect for the rules, whether they be expressed as etiquette, tradition, or even laws by which the community is governed. It is both a willingness to follow those rules and a justified expectation that others will follow them. Or, in those cases in which the rules are wrong, whether because society has outgrown them or because we gradually come to realize that they have always been misguided, civility entails a commitment to change the rules so that they become rules worthy of respect and adherence.[4]

Obviously incivility has always been with us. All we need to do is look at the *Nickerson* case. Further, most of the cases described in this book were litigated before the last twenty years of the last century. It's also true that examples of new sorts of incivility exist and even proliferate. Motorists claim harassment by other angry motorists—road rage, it's called.[5] Rules of etiquette for using mobile phones, even if they weren't obvious common sense, can certainly be found.[6] Still, complaints about people using mobile phones in public places abound, and it's astounding how often this occurs and how private the subject matter is. In fact, the two uncivil acts sometimes combine: One driver shouts furiously at another as the latter drives sixty-five miles per hour while chattering on his mobile phone.

Another example is that, despite the decades-old attempts to raise consciousness about the ability of our speech to offend others, people still do speak offensively, and defiantly—note the baseball pitcher John Rocker's extended tirade in *Sports Illustrated*.[7] As technology advances, so does incivility. There are simple breaches of "netiquette": not including a copy of the e-mail to which one is responding, or not beginning with an address ("Dear Sam"), but only launching into a message. But there is more: The personal computer, the Internet, chat rooms, and user groups have greatly expanded the number of insults and the ways in which we can annoy each other.

Whether or not incivility is actually increasing is difficult to measure, either anecdotally or by true quantitative means. In a recent lecture series sponsored by Boston University, the general consensus among the commentators was that society has grown increasingly uncivil.[8] As we are not social scientists, we are incapable of making that call and so don't purport to. It is possible that the newer forms of incivility are manifestations of behavior that's existed all along.

It is also possible that civility is not in decline at all but is simply evolving, with one area seeming in decline and another on the upswing. Mark Caldwell argues that the decline of the aristocracy, the upward mobility of the other classes, and the simple physical mobility of modern society work against the stability of civility.[9] "With equal participation from everyone, manners never stabilize, but cycle incessantly, worsening or disintegrating in one context, re-forming themselves in another. They may decline at the table, but improve at the gallows, deteriorate at the graveside just as they evolve panache in the on-line chat form."[10]

The problems, some trivial and some not, obviously have not gone unnoticed and, in fact, have generated a number of comments.[11] As a sample of the variety of the opinions that abound, we briefly consider three different views on the subject.

Judith Martin, also known as the syndicated columnist Miss Manners, has authored several books on etiquette.[12] She has weighed in on the subject of civil-ity as well.[13] Miss Manners believes that etiquette matters quite a bit and, in most cases, etiquette ought to serve as the set of rules that governs our behavior. Its sanctions are simply less severe than those of the law. "Our freedoms," she says, "are better served if these matters are mandated by manners."[14] Etiquette is a gentler, more flexible regulatory scheme than the law. To those who scoff at etiquette as a code of snobbish behavior, she retorts that in fact it is the great equalizer—it applies to all. If one followed the code, one wouldn't need so much law. The regulation of life by etiquette would actually create more freedom than the regulation imposed by law.

Miss Manners fears, however, that the law has recently taken over matters better governed by etiquette. She does not agree, for instance, that we ought to have a constitutional amendment prohibiting desecration of the flag. Instead, she says, the flag is a symbol the respect for which should be mandated by eti-quette. Making flag desecration illegal, in all likelihood, won't guarantee the flag's protection. History is made by people who disobeyed the law in order to advance a cause, and often the disobedience was with respect to a symbol, like the flag. The Boston Tea Party is one of this country's most treasured memories of the disrespect shown a symbol.

Yet one of the causes of this invasion of the jurisdiction of etiquette by the law, she suspects, is that people have finally become tired of breaches of etiquette. It was always rude, she notes, to grab women without their permission and to blow tobacco smoke at other people. However, somewhere along the line, the victims became fed up with it and forced their point, and those behaviors have become illegal, in certain contexts.

Miss Manners's main argument, then, is that etiquette is far from the formal, outmoded code that it is made out to be. Instead, it is a gentler, extralegal code, breaches of which are disapproved by the society subject to and supportive of it. But people needn't end up in court, and people needn't go to jail. Were we to embrace etiquette, we wouldn't have to resort to turning manners into matters for the courts.

M. Scott Peck, a psychiatrist who lately has been using less medical means to try to cure society, has a different view. His book, called *A World Waiting to Be Born* and subtitled *Civility Rediscovered*, is in part a description of the work of his nonprofit Foundation for Community Encouragement, which conducts workshops around the country for groups wanting to learn how to create a sense of community. (These can be corporations, churches, or, one supposes, any other sort of group.[15]) He also pursues a slightly different angle in the book, focusing on the corporate organization and how one achieves a measure of civility there.[16] He decries the patterns of self-absorption, the callousness, the crude materialism of contemporary society. We have, he says, a "hole in the mind," an inability to see ourselves as part of a larger whole.[17] Instead, true civility is, he says, "consciously motivated organizational behavior that is ethical in submission to a Higher Power."[18] Thus Peck seems to part ways with Miss Manners in several significant respects, the first being this submission to a higher power, to which Miss Manners makes little reference.

Another significant difference is that he states that "genuine civility is a form of healing behavior that demands often painful honesty and the scalpel of candor."[19] Being polite is uncivil if it means not speaking the truth. One suspects that Miss Manners would opt for the white lie more frequently.

There are, Peck says, three interlocking cornerstones of civility: The first two are the ethical consciousness of other people as precious beings and the understanding that those beings are precious because they were created by a higher power. Self-control comes from consciousness of the self, others, and the organizations to which we all relate.

Then Peck introduces the third cornerstone, which is that each individual must submit to that higher power. We do so by behaving in a very individual way. What we must do, Peck argues, is become more completely conscious of our selves and our vocation—which is given to us by this higher power—and in so doing, we're consciously cooperating with the higher power in its designs for us. If we are successful in listening to the voice of the higher power in our lives and accepting our vocation, Peck believes, we will be more successful in integrating ourselves into the consciously motivated organizational behavior. This higher power in Peck's view turns out to be a Christian God. Peck says it doesn't *have* to be, but that's the only one to which Peck refers.

The law, by the way, is according to Peck an insufficient higher power, especially in America. He quotes Aleksandr Solzhenitsyn's view that Americans believe that, as long as an act is legal, it's acceptable.[20] Peck says that we too readily rely on the law and its mechanisms of dispute resolution such as litigation. The reason is that we don't like tension and conflict, and we want them resolved as quickly as possible. Thus we resort to what are ultimately, and ironically, expensive, time-consuming, and alienating methods such as litigation.

Thus, while Martin emphasizes respect for the other person, Peck finally urges respect for the vocation in ourselves, because it is a call from this higher power to which we must all submit. We must also allow others to respect their vocations, and, in fact, empower them to find those vocations without narcissistically forcing our own ideas on them. In behaving this way, the organization—a corporation, if you will—becomes a more civil place to be. In fact, the corporation becomes a community of people all seeking the same ends. If we do the hard work of finding ourselves and our vocations, allowing others to pursue their vocations, and working to create community, then presumably we will no longer have the conflict and tension that we now resolve through law and litigation.

Our third commentator, Stephen L. Carter, is a law professor at Yale. In his book, *Civility*,[21] he gives a brief definition of how he will treat it: "I do not think civility synonymous with manners (although I do think manners matter). I have in mind an attitude of respect, even love, for our fellow citizens, an attitude, as we shall see, that has important political and social implications. Moreover, civility is a moral issue, not just a matter of habit or convention: it is better to be civil than to be uncivil."[22] Civility, he says, "is the sum of the many sacrifices we are called to make for the sake of living together."[23]

Carter sees the lack of civility as having grown out of a loss of community. After 1965, he argues, we lost our sense of consensus of what it was to be living an American life. We lost our sense of community, and modern life makes it easy not to retrieve it. A world of competitive markets has made us selfish. Technology has enabled us to retrieve the information we need without recourse to contact with others; we can connect to the rest of the world by computer and thus not actually speak to another human. This loss of the neighborhood has isolated us. We have divided ourselves on the basis of our singular interests—the NRA, the AARP, and so on—which are the means by which we exercise our selfishness. Talk of rights of the individual overcomes our trust in institutions. Without the sense of community, we are unable to conduct useful public debate. Yet we are not, Carter argues, traveling alone, and we do ourselves and society a disservice by behaving as though we are.

He argues, finally, that the way back to civility is through religion—and Christian religion at that. We must, he insists, have unselfish, loving concern for our neighbors, the same love that God gives us. This love must be manifested in actions. We must be generous when there is a cost to us, and we must trust others when doing so puts us at risk. The foundation for establishing this mode of behavior, he believes, is investment and trust in the three institutions that mean the most to us: family, school, and, most importantly, church.[24]

We cannot rely on laws to enforce notions of civility, Carter argues. Laws are "in a sense ultimately uncivil, because they are, at their core, ultimately violent."[25] By that he seems to mean that when we enact a law, we must be certain that we can imbue it with a moral force, because we must be willing to enforce it, including, presumably, by committing an act of violence.

These three commentators have quite different views on how to achieve a more civil society. What they seem to agree on, at least essentially, is that civility must be motivated by something more like respect for the other person or persons whom we encounter. It can't be legislated. Carter believes that law is ultimately violent, because the bottom line is that one may have to use force to enforce it. He would prefer that mutual respect govern our undertakings. Martin thinks that etiquette is a better governess because it is a great leveler and ultimately provides more freedom than law. Peck thinks that law is insufficient because it doesn't preclude legal but uncivil acts.

In this book, one of our purposes is to take their contentions a step further. We consider the intersection of law and civility and explore more thoroughly the use of law as a tool to encourage civility in everyday interactions among people. We'll show that not only is American law perhaps not the best mode to enforce our notions of civility but, indeed, the sources and evolution of American law serve in many ways as countervailing forces to our behaving with civility.

We will also take their contentions a step back, as it were. Most of the cases in this book arose before the last quarter of the twentieth century, and a good number before that. More important, the law upon which the litigants sued is very old, and the implications that the development of those laws had for civility were present when the law was being made. Thus, while, as we saw before, seemingly new types of incivility are being visited upon us, there is an argument that the basic uncivil nature of our society was there all along.

Consider, for example, the law of nuisance, which we will see is an Anglo-Saxon tort of ancient origin. As neighbors, we are all bound to live together and respect each other's property rights. However, what happens when Jones is holding parties nightly featuring loud music such that his neighbor, Smith, is annoyed? Who wins? As it turns out, Smith's use and enjoyment of his property must be interfered with rather substantially before Jones will be held liable. Jones, then, may give rambunctious parties (up to a point) and meanwhile thumb his nose across the property line at Smith. This result is mandated at least in part by our ancient and staunch defense of our right to do what we wish with our property. That a person's home is his castle is an old cliché, but nonetheless true in American society. Not only does the law not discourage the possible incivility occasioned by one's using one's own property as one wishes, but Americans simply would have it no other way. Thus, our cultural heritage, as embodied in our common law, fails to discourage incivility.

Each chapter of this book will take up a different type of legal action and examine how it encourages or discourages civility, and, in some cases, how American cultural traditions have resulted in law that doesn't adequately address issues of civility. Most of the causes of action that we'll encounter come under the law of torts, which includes those causes of action for intentional wrongs done by one against another. A tort is difficult to define, but it is, generally, a civil wrong by one person against another that is not a breach of a contractual obligation.[26] A tort action is not a criminal action, though we will consider a few crimes here.[27] Further, the cases in tort that we will consider involve some form or another of intentional behavior, as we presume that unintentional behavior—purely negligent acts, for instance—may not be a matter of active incivility but more of inattention. Generally speaking, we have chosen to consider cases from the civil, rather than the criminal, law as crimes are an offense against society, rather than the individual, and we are limiting ourselves to matters involving ordinary lack of respect. As Carter might note, criminal matters are so important that society has already determined that it has the moral force to sanction individuals who would commit those acts.

All of the cases in the book concern lawsuits by individuals against individuals (though for technical reasons, sometimes a corporation is a nominal party). Such a collection might strike a lawyer as remarkable, because so much American litigation concerns corporate or governmental bodies, mainly because they can more easily afford the time, resources, and, most important, money necessary to wage courthouse war. However, obviously, issues of civility are more critical to individuals acting face-to-face than to faceless corporations (though, of course, the CEOs' egos may become involved). Nevertheless, we should keep in mind—and we'll examine this point more thoroughly in chapter 11—that litigation does strain resources of all sorts. The implication is that the individuals described in this book were mightily motivated to throw literally everything they had into their causes, even when, as we'll see, the cause may have involved very little in the way of a monetary recovery. When the people described in this book took offense, nothing short of a costly courthouse victory would vindicate them.

We will start with the simplest torts, the offenses against the individual's person: battery and assault. Next we'll examine torts concerning property rights: trespass and nuisance.

Matters become more dicey as we take up the tort of the intentional infliction of emotional distress. This action addresses the acts by which one person seems determined simply to bedevil another so outrageously that the victim suffers true and severe emotional distress.

We next consider an arena made more complicated by Americans' intense desire to say what they wish. We'll look at simple verbal abuse and how speech codes have attempted to moderate our speech. Then we'll look at the ways one person may badger or even stalk another: over the telephone, on the street, and by way of the computer. Further, we'll examine laws that attempt to regulate types of speech—obscenity, blasphemy, and swearing. (In these chapters we do veer off into the world of criminal law somewhat. Because speech is so personal, it does bear on matters of civility.)

Next we'll examine the law of defamation, which provides a remedy when one person makes a statement damaging to the reputation of another. Here again we will encounter issues relating to Americans' treasured rights of free speech and expression of opinion.

Next, and finally, we'll take up issues collateral to the causes of action themselves. Throughout the book we'll describe cases litigated in trial courts and most often appealed to state or federal appeals courts. We'll examine how the legal process can, in and of itself, be an uncivil process. In some cases, in fact, the winner in the litigation has been so wronged by it—that is, the litigation has been brought for some unlawful purpose—that she is entitled to bring an action for wrongful civil proceedings.

In conclusion, then, we'll look at a number of intentional acts of incivility and how they've been punished by our laws and litigated in our courts. We'll examine what effect the law has on enforcing our notions of civility. In some cases, we'll see that the law effectively *encourages* incivility. In other cases, while the law wants to encourage civility, to do so would be to crowd the courts with plaintiffs complaining of uncivil but not very injurious acts. In still others, we'll see that the law has priorities more important than enforcing civility, such as carefully protecting Americans' freedom of speech. In these cases, Carter and Miss Manners are obviously correct: The law is simply the wrong vehicle.

Then we'll conclude by examining the implications of the outcomes of these cases on how we might force ourselves to behave with a little more civility. Specifically, we'll question whether or in what circumstances the law is the best engine for enforcing our notions of civility. We'll also look at certain quasi-legal solutions that have been proposed as substitutes for the law. Finally, we'll propose other possible solutions for approaching incivility in American society not from the standpoint of working through the legal system, but by trying to avoid it altogether.

We shouldn't move on without a final word about Miss Nickerson's lawsuit. Upon her death, her heirs were substituted as the plaintiffs. At a trial of the action, judgment was for all of the defendants. Miss Nickerson's heirs appealed. The Louisiana Supreme Court recited the facts and concluded in a sad tone:

> The conspirators, no doubt, merely intended what they did as a practical joke, and had no willful intention of doing the lady any injury. However, the results were quite serious indeed, and the mental suffering and humiliation must have been quite unbearable, to say nothing of the disappointment and conviction, which she carried to her grave some two years later, that she had been robbed.[28]

The Louisiana Supreme Court reversed the trial court's judgment and awarded damages in the amount of only $500, rather than the $15,000 requested, given that the plaintiffs were no longer Miss Nickerson, but her heirs, who, after all, hadn't suffered the same humiliation at the bank's front doors that Monday morning. Furthermore, the judgment extended not to the whole gang named, but only to those who truly seemed part of the conspiracy: H. R. Hayes, "William or 'Bud' Baker," and Miss Minnie Smith. Despite the court's failing to lay out or even state any real legal theory, at least a kind of rough justice was done. The court said, in effect, it's not nice to treat someone with the sort of disrespect that the practical jokers displayed toward Miss Nickerson; someone ought to pay. Civility ought to be enforced. However, as we'll see in this book, including in our very first chapter on battery, sometimes the law doesn't allow things to work out that way. Also, as we will argue, it is true that in many contexts it's not the law's place to enforce civility.

Keep Your Hands to Yourself
Assault and Battery

> Every action done in Company,
> ought to be with Some Sign of
> Respect, to those that are present.
>
> GEORGE WASHINGTON'S
> 1ST RULE OF CIVILITY,
> *Rules of Civility*
> *for the 21st Century*
> *from Cub and Boy Scouts*
> *from across America*[1]

In John Updike's 1968 novel *Couples*, the husbands of the title are all playing basketball on an outside neighborhood court as some of the wives look on. The clumsy Freddy Thorne persistently bumped Piet Hanema, who passed the ball, and "in the same stride he hooked one foot around Thorne's ankle and by a backwards stab of his weight caused the bigger man to fall down." Thorne, a dentist, dislocated his finger in the fall. "Hanema, kneeling, blurted, 'Jesus, Freddy, I'm sorry. This is terrible. Sue me.'"

Later in the same scene, another husband, Harold Little-Smith, told Hanema, "'You didn't do it on purpose.'

"'But I did,' Piet said. 'I deliberately tripped the poor jerk. The way he bumps with his belly gets me mad.'"[2]

Hanema anticipated and invited the American response to his foul: a lawsuit, for battery. Battery is fairly simple. Under American common civil law, a battery occurs when one person acts intending to cause and does cause contact that is harmful or offensive to another person. That's it. The person committing the battery needn't have intended to cause physical injury or have any malicious intent at all. He merely needs to make a contact that would offend the ordinary person. The victim needn't even prove that he suffered any harm. In our example, though, Freddy Thorne certainly suffered an injury. Had he been unable to work, he could have recovered money for his lost wages, as well as for any medical expenses, of course. A defense to a claim of battery is that the injured party consented to the contact, but here, of course, Freddy Thorne did no such thing.

This scene is an everyday way in which a battery could occur in our otherwise civil society: a group of neighborhood men playing a friendly game of basketball.[3] For that reason the scene is an appropriate introduction to the tort of battery and how our sense of civility has been affected by it.

Judith Martin, also known as Miss Manners, has bemoaned the fact that law has taken over from etiquette in the matter of smoking.[4] In bygone days, if one wanted to light up, one asked one's companions if they minded. The question was not rhetorical. If one did mind, then the smoker graciously abstained or took it outside.[5] After dinner, the smoking gentlemen repaired to a room separate from the ladies, all of whom were presumed nonsmokers. Men wore smoking jackets that absorbed the smell and could be tossed aside when the fellows reckoned they'd return to polite society. Eventually, though, as women began to smoke openly, the etiquette was abandoned, and smokers asserted majority rule.

Nonsmokers finally began to object, and, citing health concerns, cities gradually enacted anti-smoking ordinances.[6] Now, even in tobacco-growing states, smokers are directed gently but firmly by signs on the walls to smoke outside or face a fine. (Which is worse? A fine or the stigma of skulking in a building's entrance, cigarette held surreptitiously down at one's side? As if others didn't know what one was up to.) So society as a whole has weighed in: Smoking is dangerous, secondhand smoke is dangerous as well as unpleasant, and smokers may not impose the dangers of their habit on nonsmokers.

Before the battle had been won—before society sent smokers packing—an agonized individual still encountered the person who, thanks either to rudeness or power or both, refused to obey the old but recently discarded etiquette. As Miss Manners suggests, with no rule of etiquette firmly in place, the law was asked to intervene. When a lawsuit found its way in 1979 before an apparently mystified North Carolina Court of Appeals (and in what an excellent state for the case to arise), it said that there was no other case law on the subject to which it could turn for guidance.[7] Courts generally rely on existing cases from their jurisdictions for an explanation of the law that they can and must follow, unless the new court makes a conscious decision to overturn the law and make a new law. Here, the North Carolina Court of Appeals didn't have any help from prior cases.

O. B. Sloan was the postal inspector in Charlotte, North Carolina. He smoked cigars in his office, even though he knew that the smoke was obnoxious to William McCracken, a postal employee. McCracken had complained and had handed out literature around the post office detailing the dangers of smoking, which must, of course, have annoyed Sloan to no end and reinforced his resolve to keep smoking. Twice, in April and May 1975, McCracken's allergy to smoke caused him to request sick leave, which was denied. At meetings held to discuss McCracken's request, Sloan puffed away on his cigars, maybe enjoying the irony of engaging in the very conduct that had caused McCracken to seek sick leave. Finally, McCracken sued, alleging that Sloan had committed a battery: When Sloan smoked a cigar, the smoke touched McCracken, a touching he found offensive as well as harmful in that it aggravated his allergies. That is, Sloan acted intending to cause and did cause contact that was offensive. Though he wasn't required to, under the tort of battery, McCracken could even show injury, that is, aggravation of his allergies.

Without any specific case authority, the North Carolina Court of Appeals simply applied the general law of battery. First, it recognized McCracken's interest in freedom from intentional and unpermitted touching. The contact needn't come from "a direct application of force," but merely meet the criterion that Sloan "set in force a motion which ultimately produces the result."[8] In accordance with the tort, McCracken didn't have to prove that Sloan's intent was hostile. McCracken only had to show that he hadn't consented to the contact. The court recognized that McCracken found the smoke offensive, and Sloan knew it because McCracken had certainly told him about it often enough.

Reading to this point, one might be excused for having hope for McCracken's case. That hope would be misplaced. The court went on to say that the world is a crowded place, and we must all accept the possibility that a certain amount of personal contact is going to occur and we have to put up with it. The world assumes our consent to those ordinary contacts, and—here's the part that reveals the age of the opinion—"smelling smoke from a cigar being smoked by a person in his own office would ordinarily be considered such an innocuous and generally permitted contact."[9]

The court quoted one of the leading lights in the world of torts, Dean William Prosser, for the proposition that a person can't expect to be allowed "to erect a glass cage around himself, and to announce that all physical contact with his person is at the expense of liability."[10] Stephen Carter might agree—civility comes in the making of small sacrifices.[11] One of those small sacrifices is accepting that we are going to have to expect to be bothered by some of the people some of the time.

There was evidence from McCracken's doctors that he was allergic to smoke, but no evidence that he suffered any injury. Maybe McCracken suffered some mental distress, but the court felt that wasn't enough to support a claim of battery. In the absence of some physical injury, the court felt that its hands were tied. It hastened to say that if there were evidence of a physical injury, the holding might be different. However, we should remember that under the law of battery, McCracken didn't have to show physical injury. Nevertheless, the court concluded that it couldn't say that a battery had occurred when a person was "subjected either to the apprehension of smelling cigar smoke or the actual inhaling of the smoke. This is an apprehension of a touching and a touching which must be endured in a crowded world."[12] The clear implication is that the court thought that no real touching had occurred.

One could argue, however, that being touched by microscopic smoke particles satisfies the law's requirement of a touching. That would constitute an offensive touching to which McCracken hadn't consented. As we noted, he wasn't required to show physical injury. Yet the court found no battery. So what was going on here? We can only guess that by referring to Prosser's glass cage theory, the court is struggling to get to the conclusion that it wants: As a society, we're not going to allow lawsuits in battery against smokers, even when people object to the smoking and make their objections clear, and the smoker chooses—out of bad manners, we might say—to ignore the victims' pleas.

This opinion introduces one of the important themes of this book: The law will force us to put up with a certain amount of incivility. McCracken would have to put up with Sloan's smoking, even though a battery had occurred under the law.

A good number of years later, in 1993, an Illinois state court had the occasion to confront the same issue, for the first time in Illinois.[13] An employee of Dyna-Pro, Pamela Pechan, sued DynaPro for, among other things, authorizing a battery by allowing its employees to smoke on the premises. DynaPro argued in response that the employees who smoked didn't intend for their smoke to touch Pechan. That is, Pechan's claim failed to meet the first requirement, that the smokers intended to act. Anyway, DynaPro argued that because the very act of smoking was a lawful one, it couldn't be a battery. If this court held that it was, DynaPro warned, lawsuits would start flying thick and fast.

The way the court framed its analysis demonstrated that the question would be easily decided; it stated, "We must decide whether the employees who smoked did so with the intent that the emitted smoke touch nonsmokers such as Pechan." Well, of course they didn't. Why waste smoke on someone else?

As there was no governing law in Illinois, both parties invited the court to review the *McCracken* case from North Carolina for guidance. Pechan had an advantage over McCracken in that she could prove physical injury, the serious exacerbation of her allergies. Yet the court felt that she still didn't have a viable case. Smoking was not a battery because, generally speaking, smokers don't intend to touch nonsmokers with their smoke. There was, therefore, no *intentional* touching, so there couldn't be a battery. So again, a court had found a way, a more graceful way than the *McCracken* court, to find no liability. The offensive touching had to be intentional. Here, there was no intent, so no battery. End of story, except that the court did hold out to *Pechan*-type plaintiffs a little hope: Someday, somehow, a plaintiff might make a case that touching him with secondhand smoke could be a battery.

The self-described "nationally known" antismoking advocate, Ahron Leichtman, had to hope that he was that plaintiff. He was invited to speak on a radio show broadcast by WLW in Cincinnati to discuss the harmful effects of smoking and secondhand smoke. The occasion was auspicious: the annual Great American Smoke-Out. Also speaking were two employees of the radio station, Bill Cunningham, who was hosting the show, and Andy Furman, another WLW host who had been asked to join them.

The show did not go as Leichtman might have expected. At Cunningham's urging, Furman lit up a cigar and puffed away. He even blew smoke in Leichtman's face despite his protests.

Such an insult would not go unpunished. Leichtman brought suit against the radio station, claiming that its employee Furman's blowing smoke on him constituted a battery. The judge dismissed the action because Leichtman's claim didn't meet the technical requirements of a battery. Leichtman appealed to the Ohio Court of Appeals.[14]

The court of appeals quoted from Roscoe Pound's *An Introduction to the Philosophy of Law*: "In civilized society, men must be able to assume that others will do them no intentional injury—that others will commit no intentional aggressions upon them."[15]

The court reasoned that the elements of the tort had been met: Furman undertook the intentional act of blowing tobacco smoke intending that it reach Leichtman's face. As tobacco smoke contained particulate matter, it therefore was physically capable of making an offensive contact, no matter how slight, with Leichtman's face. A battery, no matter how technical it may have seemed, did occur. The court was quick to say that it was not creating a smoker's liability where the plaintiff merely *smelled* smoke. The court also hastened to add that it wasn't creating the "glass cage" criticized by Prosser and the court in *McCracken*; here, Furman deliberately blew smoke in Leichtman's face and hit him with the particulate matter: Furman thus intentionally touched Leichtman offensively without his consent.

The court of appeals sent the case back to the trial court on that issue at least. But it closed its opinion with language that might be appended to a number of the cases in this book and that introduces another of our themes:

> Arguably, trivial cases are responsible for an avalanche of lawsuits in the courts. They delay cases that are important to individuals and corporations and that involve important social issues. The result is justice denied to litigants and their counsel who must wait for their day in court. However, absent circumstances that warrant sanctions for frivolous appeals . . . we refuse to limit one's right to sue. Section 16, Article I, Ohio Constitution states, "All courts shall be open, and every person, for an injury done him in his land, goods, person, or reputation, shall have remedy by due course of law, and shall have justice administered without denial or delay."
>
> This case emphasizes the need for some form of alternative dispute resolution operating totally outside the court system as a means to provide an attentive ear to the parties and a resolution of disputes in a nominal case. Some need a forum in which they can express corrosive contempt for another without dragging their antagonists through the expense inherent in a lawsuit. Until such an alternative forum is created, Leichtman's battery claim, previously knocked out by the trial judge in the first round, now survives round two to advance again through the courts into round three.[16]

According to counsel for one of the parties, the litigation was settled after that. One of the terms of the settlement was that Leichtman was given an hour of airtime during which he could speak on any subject he wished.[17] A reader could speculate that, while Leichtman's battery claim clearly had technical merit, the court of appeals' annoyance with Leichtman's claim may have contributed to the parties' decision to settle without further battle. One of the risks of litigation is that one will lose; better to settle, to compromise, on the best terms available.

In any event, the *Leichtman* case is the one in which the plaintiff was likeliest to prevail on a battery claim. Furman acted, brimming with intent, causing smoke to blow right in Leichtman's face, knowing that it was offensive to him, knowing that he didn't consent, and knowing that, in fact, he was on the premises to express his objections to acts just like that.[18] Even Mr. McCracken couldn't have claimed so great an offense to his dignity.

The attitude of the law, if not the law itself, evolves in these smoking cases, and it's no stretch to speculate that society's evolving views on smoking had some effect on the holdings. In *McCracken*, the case from the 1970s, the court is very hesitant to impose liability on someone's smoking in his office, even though he knew it was offensive to an employee. (We can imagine the appeals court justices arguing among themselves: Shouldn't this be a matter of simple good manners?) In *Pechan*, the court follows *McCracken*: There's no intent to touch, so there's nothing the court can do. Finally, in *Leichtman*, a court found that Furman acted with the intent that Pechan's coworkers did not when he blew smoke in Leichtman's face. Yet how much less intent did Sloan, the postal office manager, have than Furman? And neither McCracken nor Leichtman suffered any injury. So it's reasonable to conclude that the movement from *McCracken* to *Leichtman* is not so much a movement in the law as in the willingness of society to ask the law to enforce the etiquette.

Another way of looking at these smoking cases is to conclude that common civility ought to have precluded them. The defendants, having noticed that the plaintiffs-to-be were in distress, ought to have found some way to accommodate them. Maybe there's an argument that the plaintiffs could have worked equally hard to resolve their differences without having to resort to the court system. Certainly the court in *Leichtman* thought so. Instead, we are left with two unsuccessful plaintiffs and *Leichtman* with its vaguely villainous defendants. The *Leichtman* court is right; the defendants were behaving intentionally and mischievously uncivilly, but why clog up the courts with claims against them? The fears of the *McCracken* and *Pechan* courts came to pass in *Leichtman*: The courthouse doors were opened to litigate matters of simple civility. As Miss Manners complained, the law had taken over for etiquette. We should not assume that the law wanted to intrude there, as these courts tried very hard not to. But the people harmed by the failure of etiquette apparently had no other recourse.

Let's back up and take a look at a basic battery and its milder cousin, assault. One day in September 1991, Nurse Snyder was scheduled to assist Dr. Turk in a gall bladder operation. Another doctor, a medical student, and two other nurses were there, as well as the patient, of course. Dr. Turk intended to insert a telescope into a small incision in the patient. However, he first had trouble inserting the necessary tubes. Then the telescope produced only a hazy picture. This he blamed on Nurse Snyder. Finally, a frustrated Dr. Turk had had enough.

So he reached across the operating table, intending to grab, and grabbing, Nurse Snyder's left shoulder, and jerked her across the table and down ninety degrees till her face was within just twelve inches of the surgical wound, surely an offensive touching from her standpoint. He asked her, "Can't you see where I'm working? I'm working in a hole. I need long instruments."

When he let her go, she asked one of the other nurses to fetch the night supervisor and ask him to replace her. But there was no extra help available, and she had to finish the operation, another half hour's worth. Meanwhile, Dr. Turk continued berating her in front of the others: She was incompetent, she was there only to collect a paycheck, and she exhibited passive-aggressive behavior (Did Dr. Turk think that that was worse than his obviously aggressive behavior?). Nurse Snyder strenuously disagreed, which would indicate that she wasn't entirely passive-aggressive, anyway. Finally, the operation ended, and she was allowed to escape. That she stood up for herself during the operation did not, apparently, mitigate the embarrassment that she felt, for she sued Dr. Turk for, among other things, battery.[19]

After the trial, the judge directed a verdict in favor of Dr. Turk. A judge can enter a "directed verdict" when he believes that the plaintiff has failed to state sufficient facts to prove one or more of the elements of her claim. In such a case, the judge believes that the jury shouldn't even consider the claim. Obviously, a directed verdict is a pretty harsh statement from the court, and one seldom made. Judges generally much prefer that juries sort things out by themselves. Also, a directed verdict truly invites an appeal by the party against whom it was made. In this case, Dr. Turk had argued that Nurse Snyder had to show proof of his intent to *inflict injury* on her. The trial judge had agreed and found that she hadn't presented sufficient evidence on that point, and so had directed a verdict for Dr. Turk on the battery claim.

In this case, sure enough, the Ohio Court of Appeals found that the trial judge had been incorrect in directing a verdict on the battery claim. The court of appeals stated that she needed to show only that Dr. Turk had acted intending to cause a harmful or offensive contact with her and that an offensive contact had resulted. That was it. It didn't matter whether he had wanted to hurt her. The court of appeals sent the case back for trial.[20]

On the way, though, the parties settled for an undisclosed amount.[21] One can only speculate that Dr. Turk didn't want to take any chances by having Nurse Snyder's case heard by a jury of their peers. (On the other hand, he may have thought he didn't have any.)

As it turns out, there is a little more to this case than is evident from the opinion of the court. Prior to bringing suit, and even prior to contacting a lawyer, Nurse Snyder met with hospital officials over the incident. They agreed that the doctor's behavior was beyond the bounds of what was tolerable; however, he refused to apologize. The hospital, struggling with other recent adverse publicity, hoped that Nurse Snyder wouldn't make a fuss. Though she would apparently have been satisfied by an apology, she wasn't going to get one. So she contacted a lawyer, and the matter wouldn't be settled until the litigation was. She never did get her apology from Dr. Turk.[22] Thus, for lack of the simplest civil gesture, a lawsuit was launched, and Nurse Snyder, Dr. Turk, and everyone else had to spend their time and resources on it. One wonders whether Dr. Turk preferred paying the settlement amount rather than making the apology.

Dr. Turk didn't injure Nurse Snyder's shoulder or neck when he pulled her over the operating table, but she still objected to being touched in this offensive way. The law of battery holds that it was an uncivil act that she didn't have to tolerate. As Dean Prosser told us,

> The original purpose of the courts in providing the action for battery undoubtedly was to keep the peace by affording a substitute for private retribution. The element of personal indignity involved always has been given considerable weight. Consequently, the defendant is liable not only for contacts which do actual physical harm, but also for those relatively trivial ones which are merely offensive and insulting.[23]

In other words, the old English common law courts, from which we get much of our law, understood the nature of the people with whom they were dealing. All sorts of offensive contact are batteries: spitting in someone's face, knocking off another's hat, even playing some kinds of practical jokes. The person who misbehaved might not follow up quickly with an effective apology, and the courts feared the brutal tit following on and overwhelming the mildly offensive tat. The law, for instance, wants to afford Nurse Snyder a choice other than giving Dr. Turk several good kicks under the operating table.

Prosser cites an early case from Pennsylvania demonstrating that even the legendarily mild-mannered and well-behaved Quakers and Puritans who came to the New World needed the balm provided by a claim of battery. (Note that a court, like this one, may speak of assault and battery both in tandem and separately but incorrectly. We'll discuss assault below.)

> As to the assault, this is, perhaps, one of the kind in which the insult is more to be considered than the actual damage; for, though no great bodily pain is suffered by a blow on the palm of the hand, or the skirt of the coat, yet these are clearly within the legal definition of assault and battery, and among gentlemen too often induce dueling and terminate in murder.[24]

The very theory of the tort tells us something about the nature of our Anglo-American society—and from not such recent days. We treasure our personal space. So when some angry or mischievous character was engaged in some manner of uncivil behavior, it was naive to expect this or that religious pilgrim-victim to turn the other cheek and forget about it. Just as was the rule in the Old World, rather than force the one with injured dignity to go unsatisfied, the courts in the New World found a way to allow him a peaceful remedy. But the bottom line of such a scheme is that society (and the law) implicitly understood that people who behaved uncivilly would—like the more recent and still quite relevant Dr. Turk—refuse to apologize and that we needed a way to address that behavior. From the beginning, then, the rules of etiquette have not proved a sufficient restraint.

A quick clarification: Quite often one hears the term battery in connection with another tort, assault. They are similar enough to cause confusion, and the terms used in the civil law courtroom mean different things from the same terms used down the hall in criminal court. A civil assault occurs when one acts intentionally in such a way as to put another in imminent, reasonable fear of a touching that would be harmful or offensive. Note that the touching needn't occur.[25] Many batteries, but not all, are preceded by assaults. For instance, if Nurse Snyder had not seen Dr. Turk reaching across the table, and thus hadn't been in apprehension of the contact, no assault would have occurred. However, if she had seen him reaching to grab her shoulder, and she reasonably believed that he was about to grab her, and she objected to being grabbed, Dr. Turk would have committed an assault.

The torts have in common the concept that we should have protection against offensive behavior that threatens our bodily integrity. If anything, assault takes the theory a step further, because no contact at all is required. We instead have a remedy for having suffered an assumed and purely mental injury caused by anticipating an unwanted touching. Imagine that Dr. Turk had shaken his scalpel threateningly under Nurse Snyder's nose in front of everyone else. Rather than picking up the nearest sharp object and counterattacking, she could have made him pay for his impertinence by filing a lawsuit for the assault. The ensuing litigation—hiring a lawyer and attending to the paperwork, the depositions, the court appearances, and the trial—might well have been a lot more painful than the cuts and slashes she could have given him in return.

The torts of assault and battery seem a simple and effective recourse to invasions of our personal space. Unfortunately, humans, with their boundless energy for innovation, have found ways to complicate things. A couple of other cases provide examples.

One day in the mid-1980s, Jerry Hough was sitting in his backyard watching Leonard Mooningham, a contractor, preparing to create an electrical hookup in an easement owned by the local power company. Mooningham was digging with a shovel. Because children typically played in the area, Hough had called the power company and asked that a representative come out and check Mooningham's work. He told Mooningham that he'd done so. But Hough took things a step further, telling Mooningham that he'd heard that Mooningham cheated his buyers by building shoddy houses.

Eventually Mooningham had heard enough and turned around and hit Hough on the side of the head with the flat side of the shovel. The blow was strong enough to knock Hough to the ground, and when he tried to get up, Mooningham hit him again, this time on the right arm.

Hough had to be taken to the emergency room, for Mooningham had gotten in some good shots. Hough's face was swollen for four months, his arm was bruised and painful, and he lost a few teeth. His back was injured permanently, requiring physical therapy and, maybe ultimately, surgery. He couldn't attend to his car-cleaning business for a couple of weeks.

Meanwhile, the police arrested Mooningham. He volunteered staunchly (if foolishly) to them that he would do the same again under the same circumstances. He subsequently pleaded guilty to criminal charges of aggravated battery.

Hough sued Mooningham for battery. In doing so, he would have claimed that Mooningham had swung his shovel intending to cause, and certainly causing, contact that was harmful to Hough's arm and head. At trial Hough won a verdict of $30,000 for his injuries, and, for good measure, the judge awarded Hough another $30,000 in punitive damages. (Awarding punitive damages is a means of both punishing a defendant who has behaved very badly and deterring him, and others, we hope, from similar activity in the future. A grant of punitive damages often creates a windfall for the plaintiff, but who's to say he doesn't deserve one if he's been treated especially shabbily?)

Here's the next step in the complication of the tort. Mooningham appealed to the Illinois Court of Appeals. He argued that Hough had provoked him with his insults, so Hough had to bear equal responsibility for the thumping he'd received. But the Illinois Court of Appeals disagreed. Mere words, it held, no matter how abusive, were an insufficient justification for the use of force.[26] That is, insulting provocation was not a defense to a claim of battery.

The two hadn't had any particularly bad history between them, nothing that would have led Hough to believe that his insults would provoke Mooningham to pound on him with a shovel. And nothing indicated that Hough had purposely attempted to incite Mooningham. Most importantly, Hough's remarks hadn't accompanied any overt act or physical threat. For good measure, the court noted Mooningham's training and experience with weapons of combat, implying that he'd well known what he was doing. (A dissenting justice disagreed; if Mooningham had truly intended to use his combat skills, he wouldn't have used the flat side of the shovel, but the sharp edges.[27])

The court concluded that Mooningham's use of force had been completely unjustified. Revenge is not a defense against a meritorious claim of battery. The court went so far as to say that use of that kind of force was "anathema to civilized society."[28] End of story; the verdict for Hough was affirmed.

To complicate the situation further, a court in Louisiana might have given Mooningham partial satisfaction. In one case from that state, Hazel Phillips was in a drive-through teller line at the Guaranty Bank & Trust Co. in Alexandria; she was on a "community mission," the court tells us, though what that signified is never made clear. Jeanette Squyres drove up behind her. Squyres, twenty-five years old and pregnant, was distracted by her child in the backseat and accidentally bumped the back of Phillips's car. Both women got out of their cars and inspected the one's front and the other's back bumpers and agreed that there was no real damage. Nevertheless, Phillips followed Squyres back to her car, and, after Squyres had climbed in, Phillips pulled her out, beat her, then forced her against a brick wall, banging her head.

Squyres sued Phillips for the battery: Phillips had acted by dragging Squyres from the car and beating her intending to cause, and again, certainly causing, contact that was offensive and harmful. Phillips, though, argued that Squyres had provoked her into giving the beating. Squyres, Phillips claimed, had acted first. Phillips stated that as Squyres was returning to her car, she continued heaping abuse on Phillips and, in fact, actually struck Phillips first. (What, we might wonder, did Squyres have to complain about, considering that she was the one at fault and was lucky enough to have caused no damage? Wouldn't she have been better advised to keep her mouth shut and tiptoe back to her by now, no doubt, squawking baby in the backseat?)

In any event, the Louisiana Court of Appeals agreed with Phillips that a *physical* provocation by Squyres could completely preclude her recovery for Phillips's battery. That statement seems in accord with the rule in *Hough*. But the evidence would have to establish that Squyres's actions immediately before Phillips's battery were sufficient provocation to justify Phillips's conduct.[29]

However, the court went on, again agreeing with the *Hough* court, mere words are never sufficient provocation to excuse a battery in return. Holding otherwise, the court said, "runs contrary to our system of justice under law which commands the use of judicial process rather than force for the settling of disputes."[30] We can hear the English common law courts and Prosser; after a battery, don't take revenge into your own hands. The correct retaliation is not a beating but a lawsuit.

All right, Phillips argued further, if Squyres can't be precluded completely from recovery because she didn't physically provoke Phillips, can't we at least reduce the amount of Squyres's recovery? Perhaps we could, the court conceded, in a step that takes the *Hough* logic a step backward, or forward, depending on one's point of view. However, unfortunately for Phillips, there wasn't enough evidence that Squyres had provoked Phillips. In fact, Squyres's witnesses had testified that Phillips had raised the first fist.[31] The trial court's judgment for Squyres, including the award of $2,000 in damages, was affirmed.

These provocation cases add another layer to our understanding of how the law treats battery. The early English courts created the tort to allow a wronged person a nonviolent way to obtain a remedy, and, perhaps more important to the wronged person, save face. But we must also account for the possibility that the victim is not so innocent. One man insults another's work as a building contractor. One woman so annoys another over a non-fender-bender in the bank's drive-through line that the woman who is provoked holds the other up against the bank building wall and beats her.

Each of those two scrapes has embarrassingly trivial issues at stake, though the injuries ultimately suffered are substantial enough in at least the first case. Mooningham's and Phillips's defenses were that they were provoked into behaving the way they did by Hough and Squyres, respectively. What the first two are admitting is that they were so conquered by emotion, ego, or pride that they could not excuse the first incivility. In each case, there was some moment at which any one of the participants could have backed off, saying, "I don't want any trouble here," and defused the situation. But apparently none of them did.

The rule in Illinois, the majority rule among the states, that the plaintiff's mere words can never be used to preclude recovery or reduce his damages, encourages forgiving an insult or a harmless threat. Presumably, Hough could have perched outside all day long, commenting on Mooningham's shoveling technique, attitude, profit margins, and overalls, and Mooningham's only recourse would have been to ignore him, keep digging with a foolish grin on his face, or shout back at Hough that he must have no life if he had nothing better to do than sit outside and watch Mooningham work. (The court did refer to Hough's being known as the neighborhood busybody.) The law codifies the childhood rhyme that "sticks and stones may break my bones but words will never hurt me." At least, one isn't permitted to bring suit against the speaker.[32] Thus the law doesn't exactly discourage the uncivil diatribe. As the only revenge the law allows is verbal abuse, it doesn't discourage either the start or the continuation of verbal incivilities. The law's real priority is to preclude a violent response. In the meantime, of course, the insults can fly thick and fast with no recourse for anyone. So the cause of civility is hardly advanced.

Assault and battery are torts that provide remedies for both major whacks and minor smacks. They give the plaintiff the opportunity to take revenge peacefully. In that way, the law picks up where human civility leaves off. Simple rules of behaving civilly among other civil people would dictate that the battery would not occur in the first place; we shouldn't go around striking people. If, by temporary loss of judgment, we do intentionally commit an offensive or harmful touching, we should do the right thing by accepting responsibility and apologizing. If we don't, our victim can seek vindication of his injury or indignity in the courts, rather than in violent recourse. Thus, ultimately, the cause of civility is served.

Even so, the law may have other priorities. We saw in the earlier smoking cases that the law wouldn't allow people to erect a glass cage around themselves, forcing them to accept that there are too many of us to avoid bumping into each other on occasion. Nevertheless, as the Ohio court pointed out in *Leichtman*, battery law also encourages people to seek recompense in court, even for essentially trivial matters. It makes a sad sense; after all, the original point of battery law was to encourage citizens to behave with enough civility to bring a lawsuit instead of taking violent revenge. Having encouraged plaintiffs to come into court, we can't exactly go shoving them back out again, at least not without taking a good look at their claims.

We might close with a last look at the characters from *Couples*, Piet Hanema and Freddy Thorne. The case of *Thorne v. Hanema* doesn't occur in *Couples*, partly, a reader of the novel might recall, because a lawsuit would be too direct a response for Freddy. Anyway, Piet does something like the civil thing. Of course he trips Freddy, but he's man enough to admit that it was deliberate. He also offers, via the ironically indirect American way of litigation, to pay Thorne's damages. Whatever Hanema's motivations, he apologizes, and Thorne does not take revenge. Undoubtedly, this pattern of events occurs frequently in American life as well; initial uncivil behavior is resolved in a civil manner without recourse to the legal system. But as the cases in this and the following chapters demonstrate, the sense of community and the thoughtful resolution of disputes do not always win the day. Hence the legal system, whether or not those who administer it would prefer, becomes involved in the daily acts of incivility that we all experience.

CHAPTER 2

Keep Your Hands to Yourself II
Civility between the Sexes

> If there has been no incidental
> assault or battery, or perhaps trespass
> to land, recovery is generally denied,
> the view being, apparently, that
> there's no harm in asking.
>
> CHIEF JUDGE CALVERT MAGRUDER,
> *Mental and Emotional Disturbance*
> *in the Law of Torts*

It's a lovely warm spring night in Yellow Springs, Ohio, the home of Antioch College. The smell of blossoms promises that the seasons have changed for good, and the nights are growing longer and lighter. Jeff and Marie are sitting on the front step of Jeff's apartment building watching other students walk by. The two are holding hands; they have been dating for a few weeks. They are like most kids at Antioch—bright, articulate, and clever. Jeff is a music major, and Marie thrills to the boom of his voice. Marie is a physics major, and Jeff enjoys her beautifully logical mind. The feeling between them is comfortable but not necessarily relaxed; they are energetic nineteen-year-old kids utterly bursting with hormones. So bursting that Jeff isn't sure he trusts his feelings for Marie. They have shared a few lingering kisses on the doorstep of Marie's dorm. Maybe it's because of the hormones, but he feels that he needs to know her better before committing his emotions.

Even so, suddenly glowing with good feeling for her, Jeff says, "You're sweet."

Marie thinks a second and concedes that she feels the same for Jeff. "You're sweet, too." Emboldened by Jeff's having volunteered his feelings, Marie leans toward him. He doesn't pull back, so she decides to make her move and leans forward all the way to kiss him on the cheek.

Alarmed by the effrontery, Jeff pulls back. "Excuse me," he says, "but what do you think you're doing?"

Uneasy now, Marie answers, "Kissing you?"

"Define kiss," Jeff asks.

Marie thinks. "Putting my lips together and pressing them against some part of your body? In this case, your cheek?"

"Define cheek," Jeff demands. He takes his hand away. "Anyway, I don't think you asked if you could."

Marie is confused. "But we've kissed before."

"So what?" Jeff asks. He crosses his arms. Physics majors think they're so smart that they're always intuiting conclusions. "That doesn't matter according to the Sexual Offense Prevention Policy."

"But I leaned toward you and you didn't act offended."

"Silence doesn't constitute consent," he reminds her. "You have to ask me. Otherwise you don't have my consent."

"But it was just your cheek," she explodes. "A week ago we had our tongues in each other's mouths."

"How did I know that kissing my cheek was what you had in mind?" he answers, about having had it with her now. "You might have been about to put your tongue in my ear. I don't know for sure, but that could be increasing the level of sexual intimacy. You can't increase the level of sexual intimacy without my consent either."

"Never mind," she says, crossing her arms. "I don't think you're sweet anymore."

"Besides," he concludes, "I've had a beer. I think you may have been trying to take advantage of me. That's also an offense under the Policy. And the beer was making me drowsy. I think I was about to drop off. Also an offense—kissing a sleeping person."

Marie stands up. "Have a nice evening with the Policy." She walks off, waving at him over her shoulder.

The scene is far-fetched, of course, but, under Antioch College's Sexual Offense Prevention Policy (SOPP), enacted in 1991, it would appear entirely possible.[1] Such, in fact, were the criticisms: that feminism gone mad had created a thoroughly unrealistic scheme that simply couldn't work, requiring consent to sexual activity at every step along the way and thus creating countless, insane situations like the one between Jeff and Marie. Popular opinion was initially strongly opposed to the policy.[2] Those on the Christian right feared that the

SOPP would serve to promote sexuality. Others believed that it sent negative messages about sex and sexuality.[3]

Indeed, on the face of it, those criticisms seem to bear weight. Under the SOPP, when Jeff and Marie had first shared those kisses on Marie's doorstep, whoever had initiated the kiss, whether Jeff or Marie, first had to ask the other whether he or she consented to the kiss. The exception would be if the kiss had been "mutually and simultaneously initiated."[4] It's easy to imagine Jeff gazing longingly and lovingly into Marie's eyes, and Marie gazing back, and, overcome with those teenaged hormones, throwing themselves at each other in a truly simultaneous expression of affection and desire. But who's to say whether that was truly the case?

Let's change the facts a little to assume that, a week after the first kisses, when Jeff hadn't called even to say hi, Marie, incensed, decided that the kisses weren't mutually and simultaneously initiated after all. She would be entitled to exercise any number of options, including from having the Dean of Students speak with Jeff to filing a complaint with the SOPP board, or worse.

To return to our original scenario, it's also true under the SOPP that when Jeff and Marie were holding hands a week after their passionate kisses, Marie had no right to assume that she could pick up at the same level of sexual intimacy. On the other hand, it's actually not entirely clear under the SOPP that Marie wasn't entitled to peck Jeff on the cheek, assuming that doing so constituted engaging in sexual activity less than open-mouthed kissing.

All of this is only nit-picking at a document that Antioch College felt that it had to enact—a document of a quasi-legal nature to govern how and when kids can kiss. How have we gotten ourselves into such a sad situation? There is a hint in the SOPP itself:

> 6. If someone has initially consented but then stops consenting during a sexual interaction, she/he should communicate withdrawal of consent verbally (example: saying "no" or "stop") and/or through physical resistance (example: pushing away). The other individual(s) must stop immediately.[5]

(Note the "individual[s]." Isn't this complicated enough already? Or do they simply have the possibility of more and different kinds of fun at Antioch than at other places?) The fact that the statement of the rule had to be made should send us running from the room in despair. But somewhere along the line, too many Maries had behaved disrespectfully toward too many Jeffs, and vice versa, and the persons showing disrespect failed to understand that they had done so. As the results in this context are so important, they require serious disapprobation. The infliction of indignity that the SOPP is designed to prevent is in some ways more serious than the inflictions described in chapter 1, for respect for another's sexuality is of the utmost importance.

Because sex is of such importance, however, shouldn't etiquette, society's rules governing the mere showing of respect for the dignity of the other, have been enough control? Apparently not. As Miss Manners notes, the problem is that the old "rituals by which the society brought eligible people together, right along with the ones that tried to keep them from getting too comfortable together," are no more.[6] She posits "the old-fashioned young gentleman who froze and retreated when the young lady on whose chair back his arm had come to rest squirmed away, instead of leaning back into his embrace."[7] He, she says, no longer exists. The advent of the widely acknowledged upheaval in sexual mores over the last thirty years meant, too, that there was no going back. No one wanted to surrender those gains against inhibition.

Mark Caldwell, in his book *A Short History of Rudeness*, notes that manners are constantly evolving in every context, "worsening or disintegrating in one context, re-forming themselves in another."[8] What more wildly shifting context than sex?

The evolving relationship between the sexes has recently been reflected by what's on the bookshelves. Of all of the self-help books written, those that don't have to do with losing weight, getting a job, or improving one's general ability to find one's place in the world probably have to do instead with dealing with sexuality. They range from the blunt depictions of how actually to engage the opposite sex sexually (*The New Joy of Sex*[9]) to descriptions of why the other gender is difficult to deal with on a day-to-day basis and how to overcome the problem (*Men Are From Mars, Women Are From Venus*[10]). Maybe we shouldn't be all that surprised, then, that simple etiquette might be insufficient to govern relations.

Without the etiquette to control, what else was there? The SOPP was meant to provide some rules. As Miss Manners notes, the irony, of course, is that in some ways we're back where we started but worse off.[11] Now, rather than everyone's understanding the clear manners of courtship and following them—or not, to the disapproval of one's peers—Antioch has a sort of extralegal code that apparently puts much more stringent requirements on the participants. Rather than relying on the implicit consent that a truly enthusiastic sex partner's behavior provides, one must obtain explicit consent before moving toward greater intimacy. As Miss Manners says generally, etiquette can provide more freedom than actual regulation. Where a college enacts an extralegal code, any such freedom of choice has been lost.

But better an extralegal code than the cold application of the law. Society surely doesn't want Jeff to sue Marie for threatening to kiss him on the ear, any more than the Ohio Court of Appeals wanted Ahron Leichtman to sue WLW over cigar smoke's being blown in his face. The SOPP lists a number of options that Jeff could pursue, but civil litigation isn't one of them. (The SOPP's omission wouldn't preclude his suing, of course, but fortunately a violation of the SOPP itself doesn't appear all by itself to impose civil liability.) The SOPP suggests a number of options, from mediation to a meeting with the Dean of Students to more formal proceedings, such as filing a criminal complaint, though certainly this is intended for serious sex crimes like rape, rather than our innocent scenario. No doubt the courts appreciate the SOPP's offering an alternative to Jeff's suit against Marie, as the legal system doesn't want to entertain those suits. Historically, they didn't offer a chance at recovery in some contexts anyway. The SOPP brings us full circle to Chief Judge Magruder's comment, which headed this chapter. Not only is there no harm in asking, but, under the SOPP, you're supposed to.

But the story of the SOPP is a good one. The system works. Since the SOPP's inception and as of this writing, there have been only seven formal hearings before the SOPP board, all having to do with serious sexual misconduct, including rape.[12] Those hearings, which were certainly adversarial, and in which the accused generally took a defensive posture, were driven by the complainants' wanting to be heard and wanting their views, that the conduct was wrong, to be affirmed by a third party. The spirit of the SOPP is otherwise educational as well, and the students are enthusiastic about participating; an explanation of the SOPP at a recent fall orientation drew about thirty students who volunteered to help with the orientation. Each year, the student body is asked what revisions they would suggest to the SOPP, and the students generally have none.

The initial negative public uproar over the SOPP appears to have been ill founded as well. There were fears of campus kissing police and questions about whether students would be forced to sign contracts before engaging in any sexual activity. In fact, neither has occurred; in actuality, the scenarios laid out above are highly unlikely to take place. The SOPP forces students to think about sexuality, respect, and consent. However, according to the students, it's followed in spirit, not to the letter, and common sense rules.[13] Finally, the fears that the SOPP would be viewed as inculcating a negative view of sexual activity were also misplaced; instead, the SOPP is, after all, about *consent*, about arriving at a mutual "yes."[14] No doubt that is exactly as it should be.

It ought to be noted that Antioch is a small college and a close community. Students can't avoid seeing others with whom they've previously interacted, and, as in any small town, one can easily gain a reputation for unsavory conduct.

Thus there is serious peer enforcement of the behavioral norms as embodied in the SOPP. It's not clear how successful the SOPP would be at much larger universities, and there's little indication that any have adopted it.[15] That fact is the bad news, though hardly unexpected: If there's no real community, there are no real shared values, as we will see later in this book. As noted above, the students consistently refuse the invitation to revise the SOPP.

Let's now reconsider assault. Remember that one assaults another when one acts intentionally in such a way as to put the other in imminent fear of a harmful or offensive touching. For instance, Marie's leaning over to kiss Jeff's cheek may well have been an assault: Jeff had been put in apprehension of an imminent touching that he found offensive.[16] On the other hand, generally, you can't assault someone with mere words, according to Dean Prosser.[17] But he also says that courts typically placed too much emphasis on some overt physical acts accompanying the words. Sufficiently violent words in the right context—Prosser suggests a highwayman sitting perfectly still holding a gun and demanding money—don't need an overt act to amount to an assault.

Earlier in the last century, several courts struggled with facts such as these: A woman is either at home or otherwise minding her own business when a man solicits her to engage in sexual intercourse with him. Could that be an assault? In one case from 1903, *Reed v. Maley*, a man confronted a married woman on her front porch and suggested that she meet him alone, there being no question for what purpose.[18] The court struggled mightily to find some sort of liability. But it had to concede right away that the solicitation, mere words, could not constitute an assault. In the end, the woman, while certainly insulted, hadn't been put in fear of an imminent harmful or offensive touching. The court seemed to regret affirming the verdict for the ill-mannered defendant.

The Supreme Court of Georgia added its agreement in 1938, noting that a person had protection for her body, reputation, and property only.[19] "The law does not yet attempt to guard the peace of mind or the happiness of everyone by giving recovery of damages for mental anguish for a violation produced by a mere moral wrong."[20] This reasoning might remind us of the glass cage that the *McCracken* court wouldn't let the plaintiff erect around himself, no matter how noxious the cigar smoke.

An exception to the rule came when one court was presented with facts gruesome enough that something like the overt act required was committed—something like the stagecoach robber. In *Newell v. Whitcher*, a case from Vermont in 1880, a blind piano teacher taught her students their lessons and then was given a room in which to spend the night.[21] Her students' father came to her room and, leaning over her in bed, repeatedly solicited her sexual favors. The court held that his leaning closely over a blind woman and propositioning her constituted enough of a threat as to amount to an assault.[22] Perhaps the court was taking into account the woman's blindness; that is, her inability to perceive the threat visually made it more likely that she was in imminent, reasonable fear of an offensive touching by his intentional act.

So the efforts to enforce a civil tongue regarding sexual matters were limited to the rare *Newell*-type situations until, finally, courts began to recognize a person's right to be protected from outrageous behavior. As Prosser notes, by the 1930s, courts were creating a new way to find liability for one who repeatedly solicits a woman for sexual intercourse. The tort has come to be known as the intentional infliction of severe emotional distress.[23] As we will see in chapter 6, it is a remedy rather limited by strict requirements.

Further, we now have legal protection in the workplace against even more than assaults and batteries. A federal statute mandates a person's right to be free from purely verbal sexual assaults. That statute, Title VII of the Civil Rights Act of 1964, 42 U.S.C.S. § 2000e *et seq.* (1999), provides that sexual harassment that creates a hostile or abusive work environment gives rise to a claim of discrimination in employment based on sex.

The federal Fifth Circuit Court of Appeals described the proof required for protection by the statute in *Farpella-Crosby v. Horizon Health Care.*[24] There, Ms. Farpella-Crosby had gone to work as a nurse at a nursing home. Her supervisor, Mr. Blanco, often referred to her having seven children as evidence that he "knew what she liked to do." At a baby shower held at the nursing home, Blanco commented that she "doesn't know how to use condoms." On occasion he asked what she and a coworker, Ms. Vujevic, had done the night before, whether they had taken men home with them, and whether they "got any." Farpella-Crosby testified that he made those kinds of comments so frequently that she couldn't remember every instance. When Farpella-Crosby asked him to stop making those comments, he threatened to fire her. Also, Blanco and another employee blew in her ear and pretended that the air exited her other ear. Finally, Blanco asked her to make copies for him and get him fresh coffee, menial jobs that were outside her job description.

Farpella-Crosby eventually brought suit, and the jury found for her at trial. Horizon Health Care, the employer, appealed.[25]

The Fifth Circuit Court of Appeals stated that Farpella-Crosby could prevail if she proved facts constituting the following elements under the law of Title VII: she belonged to a protected group; she was subject to unwelcome sexual harassment; the harassment was based on sex; the harassment affected a term, condition, or privilege of employment (that is, the sexual harassment was so pervasive or severe as to alter her conditions of employment and create an abusive working environment); and Horizon Health Care knew or should have known of the harassment and failed to take prompt remedial action. The bottom line was that there had to have been sexually discriminatory verbal intimidation, ridicule, and insults that were so severe or pervasive as to create an abusive working environment. The question was whether a reasonable person would find those conditions to have existed for Farpella-Crosby at Horizon Health Care.

Farpella-Crosby testified that Blanco's comments made her feel "very embarrassed, very belittled," "very disgusted," "hopeless," "about two inches high," and "pretty stupid." She also said that she must have "done something wrong to deserve somebody to talk to me like that."[26]

The court found that the record was clear that the comments were severe and pervasive; Blanco made them two or three times a week, sometimes in front of coworkers. The court affirmed the verdict for Farpella-Crosby.

In this case, no battery occurred at all except, perhaps, for the blowing in the ear.[27] Yet we haven't strayed far from the original subject of common law assault or battery, as Farpella-Crosby's case is similar to that of the blind piano teacher's in the *Newell* case. But now, thanks to Title VII of the Civil Rights Act of 1964, Farpella-Crosby had a remedy based on a statute. And her chance for vindication, of course, is much greater than under a common law assault, where mere words probably wouldn't amount to a claim.

While Miss Manners would no doubt agree that it is a good thing that Farpella-Crosby has her remedy, she may not be happy that we have come to this pass. Here the law works, but again it's regrettable that we had to resort to it for enforcement. As we have noted, Miss Manners regrets generally the legislating of etiquette. The mistreatment of women on the job, she argues, arises out of unprofessional or ungentlemanly behavior that should properly be dealt with by the rules of etiquette. The presence of a woman on the job requires a gentleman to treat her as any other professional worker, all of whom should be "accorded tasks, salaries and deference by job, rank and performance."[28]

The rules of etiquette, then, ought to have been sufficient to resolve the question of what to do about inappropriate sexual behavior in the workplace. However, Miss Manners notes with good-natured chagrin that she "does not make the sentimental mistake of believing that disobeying the rules of etiquette is too interesting an idea to have occurred to our forebears."[29] In fact, the problem has been with us as long as women have been in the workforce. Finally, the impulse to behave in uncivil ways forced the legislature to do something, to help protect the rights of all workers to be free from discrimination. Etiquette just wasn't strong enough.

As serious as these cases and the situations that gave rise to them are, there are batteries with worse consequences, involving sex. In one case, Kathleen K. had sexual intercourse with Robert B. He didn't tell her that he was infected with the herpes virus, and the result of their intercourse was that Kathleen became infected too. Kathleen sued Robert, alleging, among other things, that Robert had committed a battery—Robert had intentionally acted and had caused contact that was harmful or offensive to Kathleen. The trial court found for Robert, and Kathleen appealed to the California Court of Appeals.[30]

Robert's most important argument on appeal was simply that this situation was not any of the court's business. By the time this case was heard, in 1984, the U.S. Supreme Court had long recognized the right of privacy in matters of marriage, family, and sex, and disfavored any unwarranted governmental intrusion into them.[31] This situation, Robert argued, concerned sexual relations between two consenting adults, so the court ought to leave it alone.

The court agreed that normally it wouldn't be proper to involve itself in such cases—but now, however, there were important public interests to protect. Kathleen had alleged that she had suffered a real physical injury because Robert infected her with a serious disease that was, at least at that time, not effectively treatable. Public health concerns, if nothing else, justified the court's intervening. The right to privacy was outweighed by concerns for public health and the injuries suffered by another.

The court also didn't buy Robert's assertion that the issues concerned *consenting* adults and so Kathleen's consent was a defense to his battery. Remember that ordinarily this is true under the law of battery; if one consents to the contact, one cannot complain that it was offensive or harmful. Kathleen had certainly consented to the sexual intercourse, but in other cases of this kind, the consent was nullified because the person committing the battery had misrepresented himself. In an earlier California case, *Barbara A. v. John G.*, Barbara suffered injuries resulting from an ectopic pregnancy.[32] She sued the man who had impregnated her, alleging that she had consented to intercourse only after he said that he was sterile. The court there held that she had a right to recover damages for a battery because John G.'s misrepresentation of his sterility nullified her consent. Kathleen, too, had consented to one act, sexual intercourse, and unwittingly engaged in a different act, sexual intercourse with a herpes-infected partner. Obviously Kathleen had not consented to this different, offensive touching.

Robert also attempted to distinguish his case from similar cases on the grounds that they had involved a husband and a wife. He and Kathleen weren't married. The law generally recognized that a relationship of trust and confidence existed between married people that did not exist between unmarried people. Robert argued that it was incorrect to find the same relationship between Kathleen and him.

The court wasn't having any. It held that trust and confidence existed in any intimate relationship,

> at least to the extent that one sexual partner represents to the other that he or she is free from venereal or other dangerous contagious disease. The basic premise underlying these old cases—consent to sexual intercourse vitiated by one partner's fraudulent concealment of the risk of infection with venereal disease—is equally applicable today, whether or not the partners involved are married to each other.[33]

Thus the court broke through to the heart of things. Simply because Robert and Kathleen weren't married didn't mean that they didn't have, to some degree, an intimate relationship. That relationship imposed on him a duty of trust and confidence. Failing to reveal his condition to her breached that duty. He had treated her with a lack of respect. Put another way, it is an understatement to conclude that Robert had behaved uncivilly.

In chapter 1 we saw that the average battery is more obvious: bashing someone with a shovel, slamming someone against the wall of a bank. We might not ordinarily say that an act of consensual sexual intercourse in any circumstance looks or acts like battery. However, it should come as no surprise that the law is well settled that one partner has a cause of action for battery against the other for this sort of behavior.[34] Courts didn't need to stretch the law of battery much at all to hold that it encompasses intentionally exposing another person to a disease without that person's knowledge. The act fits the law of battery: The defendant has intended to cause, and has caused, a touching that is harmful to the other person.

The shame, of course, is that the courts had to be inventive at all. The only possible explanations for this truly uncivil behavior are unpleasant at best: giving way to lust without regard for its consequences; a desire to wreak revenge on this person or all persons of that gender; or, perhaps, mere reckless disrespect for another human being. That the battery itself is a heinous act of incivility is one thing. It is quite another to find these shameless defendants disputing the issues so vigorously, having the nerve to raise defenses to their utterly disrespectful behavior, in the appellate courts. As the court in *Kathleen K. v. Robert B.* held, these people were in an intimate relationship with each other, and one had so little respect for the humanity of the other that he infected her with a contagious disease.

Respect for the other is what Antioch's Sexual Offense Prevention Policy is about. The preface states,

> Antioch College has made a strong commitment to the issue of respect, including respect for each individual's personal and sexual boundaries. Sexual offenses are dehumanizing. They are not just a violation of the individual, but of the Antioch community.[35]

Indeed, Stephen Carter believes that "a loss of respect for our fellow humans is at the heart of our incivility crisis,"[36] thus his rule that "we must come into the presence of our fellow human beings with a sense of awe and gratitude."[37] Peck might put it another way, believing that we must become more conscious of others, that the narcissism expressed by the individuals in the sexual assault cases is a principal root of incivility.[38] Carter might well wince at the SOPP, as he would prefer that, rather than rely on law alone, we lean on reason, religion, and education, all provided or inculcated by family.[39] His approach is in some ways similar to Miss Manners's, though she may more readily admit that it suffers from naive idealism. That such an individual-to-individual approach failed is why Antioch enacted the SOPP. Instead of being able to rely on each individual's acting out of respect for the other, a more formal mode of mediation and intervention had to be invented. In the employment context, matters were even worse, requiring a federal statute to legislate respect.

Finally, there is something about the nature of sexual relations that may defy nonlegal governance. As Miss Manners states, there have always been cads.[40] It's only now that, with the advances of sexual freedom over the last thirty years, what rules there were are failing to work altogether. We are left with legal or quasi-legal codes, which will always govern imperfectly.

In the next two chapters, we turn to the various incivilities that neighbors are capable of visiting upon each other with regard to the real estate that they own. Fortunately, the damages will be mainly to hedges and eardrums, but the nasty moods, obstinate attitudes, and refusals to compromise continue.

CHAPTER 3

Trespasses to Property
A Man's Home Is His Castle

> October 20, 1:30 P.M. A suspect was
> reported trespassing in a Winslow Way
> business. She was contacted, and said
> she didn't know she was forbidden
> from being on the grounds.
>
> "POLICE BLOTTER,"
> *Bainbridge Island (Washington) Review,*
> NOVEMBER 1, 2000

How can we credit the unnamed miscreant in the quotation above? Anyone who has ever cut across someone's yard without permission in hopes of arriving somewhere else more quickly has thought to himself, briefly and with little remorse, "Whoa! I don't own this yard. I'm trespassing. Hope old lady Simmons hasn't loaded her shotgun!" In truth the theory of trespass is not much more complicated than that. One commits a trespass when one intentionally enters land in the possession of another without respect to whether he causes harm to the property. So a trespass is merely the interference with someone else's rights of possession in real property.[1] The most important interest is the owner's right of exclusive use of the property.[2] All one needs to do to trespass is to enter upon property owned by someone else without the owner's permission.[3] The hypothetical stroller across old lady Simmons's place earlier in this paragraph is, technically, civilly liable for his trespass, even if in the process he causes no damage to the land, like trampling her prized tulips. As with the rules of battery, this rule is strict and simple.

Yet how furiously we Americans can litigate this rule—even when our courts try to make applying it easy. This chapter will discuss a few trespass cases involving a specific form of trespass: when neighbors disagree on how to deal with the plant life affecting both properties. In each case, the litigants insist obstinately on protecting their rights. At bottom, the insistence indicates something fundamental about the nature of our relationship to our property that makes it difficult for Americans to behave civilly toward each other regarding it.

Take, for instance, the case of *Hasapopoulos v. Murphy*.[4] The Hasapopouloses moved in next door to the Murphys in 1969. In the next few years, the Hasapopouloses noticed a couple of Chinese elm trees on the Murphys' property. They were growing so prosperously that some of the branches had begun to hang over the Hasapopouloses' property. Worse, the roots were growing under their driveway and cracking it. They appealed to the Murphys to do something to alleviate the problem, but the Murphys refused. So they sued the Murphys, arguing that the trees were, in essence, trespassing on their property—that is, the Murphys were intentionally allowing the trees to enter the Hasapopouloses' land and thus interfering with their exclusive right of possession and use. They claimed that it would cost $300 to have the branches cut and hauled away. This dispute actually went to trial, where the Hasapopouloses' expert witness testified that it would cost $2,920 to repair the damage to their driveway. (And what was his fee for preparing for and testifying at trial? We'll explore the costs of litigating civility as further useful examples appear.) The Hasapopouloses testified that their damages totaled $5,000.

The Murphys' argument in response relied on a rule followed in some states that held that if the trees were growing naturally, as these elm trees were, then the Murphys could not be liable. If the trees had been planted and maintained artificially, then it would be right to charge them for any damage. Here, the Murphys said, their neighbors had failed to say which sort these trees were, natural or artificial, so the court had no way to determine a fact necessary to giving a verdict to the Hasapopouloses. The trial judge bought this argument and found for the Murphys. The Hasapopouloses, still anxious for relief from these roots, appealed the judge's ruling to the Missouri Court of Appeals.

The court of appeals disagreed with the Murphys, finding many faults with the rule itself and noting both that Missouri hadn't explicitly adopted it and that it had not been followed in the majority of the states. What, the court wondered, *was* the origin of the tree? Wasn't it always going to be difficult to figure out what was natural and what was artificial? So the rule was skewed to finding someone who planted trees liable—yet don't we *like* trees? Also, wouldn't the Murphys' rule impose too much trouble on someone in a rural area, where there's little potential for harm, as opposed to someone living in a close-set urban neighborhood, where a falling branch from one of his trees might brain a passing pedestrian? The court embarked on a careful, lengthy examination of cases from a number of states and concluded that

> imposition of liability upon the tree owner under such circumstances would create the potential for continuous controversy between neighbors and could promote harassment and vexatious litigation, disruptive of neighborhood serenity. Possible exposure to liability would warrant the uprooting of trees and shrubbery in proximity to boundary lines resulting in non-aesthetic barrenness.[5]

With this adverse reaction to neighbor suing neighbor over these matters, the court laid out the policy behind the rule it finally adopted, referred to as the "Massachusetts rule" for the home of the case and the court in which the rule originated.[6] Under the rule, the Murphys had no liability for damages caused by the encroachment of the roots or branches of healthy trees on the Hasapopouloses' property. However, the Hasapopouloses had the right to exercise self-help—that is, they were free to cut the trees back at the property line, at their own expense, of course. And so this hard-fought litigation came to an end, but not without praise from the court:

> Although the monetary amount involved is small, this case is important to the litigants. Counsel for both parties, despite the relatively small amount involved, have briefed and argued this appeal with commendable zeal, thoroughness and ability. Their efforts represent the highest standards of the legal profession and are to be commended.[7]

That's one way to look at it. Another is to wonder what there was about the dispute that so compelled the parties to fight into their state's court of appeals. Each party would incur expenses probably at least ten times the amount of damages at issue. Ms. Murphy's husband was deceased by the time the opinion was written. Nothing prevented these people from thinking about who they were— neighbors sharing a property line—and compromising, like other neighbors do. But instead they felt compelled to fight.

At least the Missouri Court of Appeals tried to put an end to such lawsuits in Missouri. Potential plaintiffs needn't file suit, and in fact, the court implied, shouldn't; instead, they were free to hack away at offending vegetation all they wanted, at least up to the property line. The rule makes sense, especially within the strangely strict context of trespass, which holds, as we recall, that one is liable when one intentionally enters onto the land of another, even if the trespass causes no damage.

A later case from Maryland provides a little more history and discusses some alternative rules that demonstrate courts' struggling to reconcile neighbors' competing interests. In *Melnick v. CSX*,[8] the court said that Maryland had already implicitly adopted the Massachusetts self-help rule, and now this court would do so formally.

Mr. Melnick had been troubled by heavy vegetation growing onto his property from off of the railroad's easement. The heavy growth clogged drains, left standing water, and damaged his roof. He tried to get the Baltimore and Ohio Railroad to keep the growth under control, but it refused. (Though CSX was the party named, it was the B&O's property.) He sued, seeking compensation for the damage done to his property. He lost in the trial court, and the court of appeals affirmed the decision. Those courts held that Mr. Melnick was limited to his Massachusetts rule self-help remedy. Not satisfied, Mr. Melnick appealed to the Maryland Supreme Court.

The court first surveyed other states' responses to the issue. One was the "Virginia rule," which held that a landowner was limited to the Massachusetts rule self-help remedy unless his defendant's plant was "noxious."[9] Under that theory, the owner had a duty to prevent his greenery from causing damage to property. The Maryland court wondered how one could decide exactly what was "noxious." (Perhaps this theory informs Ronald Reagan's assertion that trees caused pollution and were thus "killer trees," a position that even his press secretary, James Brady, derided.[10]) So the *Melnick* court was left without a very clear idea of what was and wasn't noxious. Exit the Virginia rule. In a footnote, the court quoted another case that expressly questioned the term: "There is some confusion . . . as to whether a tree or plant is 'noxious' merely because it does injury or whether it must be inherently injurious or poisonous."[11] This rule calls for such a complicated analysis and such arbitrary judgments that the *Melnick* court was right to walk away from it.

There was also a "Hawaii rule," set down by the Hawaii Court of Appeals in *Whitesell v. Houlton*.[12] The tree at issue was a banyan tree, eighty to ninety feet high with foliage extending over one hundred feet. The court would impose liability if the landowner's trees, plants, roots, or vines caused "harm . . . in ways other than by casting shade or dropping leaves, flowers, or fruit."[13] That is, if the branches or roots actually cause, or if there was an *imminent danger* of their causing, harm to property other than plant life, the neighbor may require the owner of the tree himself to cut back the branches and roots. Of course, the victimized landowner could also do the cutting himself. If these courts were concerned that property line disputes would create litigation over apparently minor matters, then the Hawaii court would seem to be on the right track in putting the onus back on the landowner to trim his greenery, given its state's tropical environment.[14] Yet the Hawaii rule made the Maryland court nervous. Like the Virginia rule, the Hawaii rule depended on vague and maybe arbitrary distinctions—when, for instance, is the danger imminent? Finally, after much wringing of hands and furrowing of brows, the Maryland court concluded,

> to grant a landowner a cause of action every time tree branches, leaves, vines, shrubs, etc., encroach upon or fall on his property from his neighbor's property, might well spawn innumerable and vexatious lawsuits. We have gotten along very well in Maryland, for over 350 years, without authorizing legal actions of this type by neighbor against neighbor.[15]

Instead, the court said, adopting the Massachusetts rule,

> [Mr. Melnick's] remedy is in his own hands. The common sense of the common law has recognized that it is wiser to leave the individual to protect himself, if harm results to him from this exercise of another's right to use his property in a reasonable way, than to subject that other to the annoyance, and the public to the burden, of actions at law, which would be likely to be innumerable and, in many instances, purely vexatious.[16]

Thus the holding of the lower courts, limiting Mr. Melnick's remedy to the Massachusetts self-help rights, was affirmed, and the rule was explicitly adopted for Maryland. These holdings from the Massachusetts and Maryland courts should put to rest the question of whether and when you may sue your neighbor because either her trees and plants cast too much shade on your property or her trees' roots are insidiously slithering their way to infiltrating your sewer pipes. Each court states that it wants to adopt a rule that will keep swarms of plaintiffs from buzzing at the courthouse doors—the courts prefer that good neighbors be good neighbors and keep a courteous eye out for the damage their plants might be causing others. Unless neighbors have serious disputes about where the property line is, and thus where self-help begins, no lawsuit should be filed in the face of the Massachusetts rule. The cheap, easy, and legally irreproachable remedy is to chop off those branches or roots at the property line and then saunter off, brushing hands together in a job-well-done gesture.

The fellow on the other side can have no complaint, and neighbor is free to treat neighbor civilly and without dispute. The community of common interest is maintained. Thus, the law not only encourages but mandates civility. It is true that trespass, like battery, we recall, encourages litigation by not requiring a showing of actual injury; in trespass, one only has to enter someone else's property intentionally. But, unlike in battery, the Massachusetts trespass rule makes it easy to gain a remedy short of forcing access to the courthouse. Thus the law of trespass appears to have evolved in such a way as both to encourage real civility and to discourage litigation.

Unfortunately, but inevitably, neighbors will create complications. What happens when a line of bushes sits directly *on* the property line? The Pattersons and the Oyes lived next door to each other in Omaha, Nebraska, and shared a 132-foot property line. The owners before the Oyes had planted a long set of bushes along the line. After living for a while on the property, the Oyes decided that the bushes were ugly. What they wanted instead was a good solid stone wall. They ripped out about forty-eight feet of the bushes before the Pattersons objected. Efforts to compromise failed, and the Pattersons sued in trespass: The Oyes had entered onto the Pattersons' property intentionally, and, in this case, had caused damage to the Pattersons' property. They asked both for money in an amount to replace the bushes and for an injunction. An injunction is an order from the court preventing a certain act or restraining someone from continuing in an act, in this case, preventing the Oyes from hacking at the bushes any farther along the line. Often, the point of an injunction, particularly apt in this case, is that, if the defendant continues to act as he has, the plaintiff will be harmed in a way that can't be fixed by an award of money. Here, if the Oyes kept ripping out bushes, it would take years to grow them back, and mere money damages couldn't help.

The trial court agreed with the Pattersons that the Oyes had indeed trespassed, and found damages of $400. The court also enjoined the Oyes from ripping out any more of the plants. The Oyes, apparently still fancying their stone wall, appealed, and the case was finally heard by the Nebraska Supreme Court.[17]

There, the Oyes argued that the previous owner had planted the bushes, so the Oyes owned them; further, the Oyes had taken charge of most of the care and maintenance. The bushes were, the Oyes reiterated, ugly. The Pattersons, on the other hand, liked the privacy that the bushes provided (and which, by this point, they no doubt wanted with respect to the Oyes) and felt they added aesthetic value to the property.

The supreme court agreed with the trial court and the Pattersons. The law was that if bushes stand directly on the property line between the adjoining owners, then the bushes are the common property of both of the parties. If one destroyed the bushes without the consent of the other, then there had been a trespass.

The Oyes had another point they wanted addressed. They didn't like the sound of this injunction business, in which the trial court had restrained them from damaging or destroying the hedge currently existing . . . or any hedges subsequently planted thereon, or taking any actions whatsoever which are unreasonably dangerous to the continued good health and existence of such hedges or taking any actions whatsoever in violation of [the Pattersons'] joint ownership interest.[18]

One can see the Oyes' point; those "whatsoevers" sound pretty loose. Relations with the Pattersons were already a little strained, and now a court was proposing with vague phrases like "unreasonably dangerous" to put the Oyes under the Pattersons' command and dominion for who knows how long. That was tough luck, the court said. The Oyes could always petition the court if circumstances changed.

What the court might have suggested was that nothing prevented the Oyes from building a ten-foot-high stone wall on their own property. That way the Pattersons could gaze on their hedges, and the Oyes could enjoy their stone wall, which would block any view of the hedges. Instead, now the court was inviting the Oyes to come back to court any time they thought that "circumstances had changed"—whatever that meant—to launch into further litigious exploration. But that would be for another day and another court.

A last case to note in the plants-and-boundaries arena is *Beals v. Griswold.*[19] The Griswolds had become apprehensive about a 130-year-old oak growing on Ms. Beals's property. Its huge branches menaced their own land; what if one of those branches came down on the Griswolds' house in a thunderstorm? They hired a tree surgeon, Mr. Juttner, to exercise their Massachusetts-rule self-help right to cut the branches down. They suggested, though, that Juttner get Beals's consent before doing so, as he and his employees were going to have to enter her property to climb the tree to get at the offending branches. Merely entering onto her property intentionally, of course, would be a trespass, unless they obtained her permission first.

According to Juttner, he did ask Beals for her consent. According to her, she gave no such permission, and, when the cutting had been under way for some time, she interrupted Juttner's work and ordered him to stop. Then she sued the whole gang in trespass and conversion. (She had also sued them in negligence, but, because, as we have noted, negligent acts are unintentional and may have little to do with civility and thus are beyond the scope of this book, we won't take it up here. Suffice it to say that Beals lost on the negligence claim.)

The conversion, she said, occurred when they disposed of the $800 worth of tree limbs rather than giving them to her. We'll deal briefly with the conversion claim after we deal with the trespass claim.

The Griswolds and Juttner disputed Beals's view of the facts regarding trespass. Juttner testified that he had asked her permission to enter her property and cut the branches, and she had granted it. With that permission, of course, there would be no trespass. The Griswolds corroborated his statements, saying that he had walked over, spoken to Beals, and returned immediately to report that he had gained her permission to enter her property. It was, then, Beals's word against Juttner's, as confirmed by the Griswolds. At trial, the jury found for the Griswolds and Juttner, and the court of appeals said that it had no reason to disturb that finding. The dispute was simply over who was telling the truth, and that question is just about always one for the jury to decide. Generally, the judge decides what the law is and describes it for the jury, and the jury decides what the facts of the case are. Then the jury applies the facts to the law that the judge has described to determine whether the plaintiff has proved that, more likely than not, her version is true. Here, the jury believed that Beals hadn't proved that Juttner and his men had entered her property without her permission. The court of appeals wouldn't overturn their finding unless it was clear to them that the jury had gotten it flat wrong.

The jury also found for the Griswolds and Juttner on the conversion claim. Conversion is essentially the civil law version of theft. Conversion occurs when one intentionally exercises dominion and control over personal property that so seriously interferes with the owner's rights that the actor should rightfully pay the property's value. Juttner had testified that Beals had asked for the branches for firewood only after the cutting had begun. At that point, he said, she had become "irate and irrational," and, presumably, he was in no mood to expend the time and effort to cut and drag the long, heavy branches to her property. None of Juttner's employees kept her from taking the wood herself. Also, she had earlier given permission to cut the branches *without* saying, "Oh, and by the way, you can do so only if you cut the branches up nice and short and bring them over to me so I can use them for firewood." As there was insufficient evidence that Beals's rights to the wood were interfered with, the verdict for the Griswolds and Juttner on the conversion claim was affirmed.

Part of the evidence at the "protracted trial," as the court described it, consisted of the jury's trooping out to the property to have a look at the tree themselves. Add the expert evidence, "as well as the combative atmosphere surrounding the entire incident," and, the court of appeals concluded, it couldn't say that the jury had been incorrect.

We read some telling language in this case. Seldom does a court of appeals comment on either the length of the trial or the attitudes of the litigants. From the note here, we can assume that the case was bitterly fought up through Louisiana's court of appeals over, essentially, the loss of $800 worth of firewood. The case was worth even less than the *Hasapopoulos* litigation.

No one was generous in any of these cases, and no one seems to have trusted anyone else, either. The community was sundered, and not even for any legal matter of much consequence. You're allowed to cut off branches and roots that come onto your property. If a plant sits on a property line, it's owned jointly. That's about it. These cases are not about legal principle, then, certainly. The sad thing is, they don't appear to be about any principle at all.

Trespass is a very old legal theory, handed to us from our Anglo-Saxon ancestors.[20] It derives from our common law tradition regarding real property rights. Angelo Codevilla has noted that the concept is not universal by any means. A large number of cultures, including those of ancient Egypt and the other empires of the Near East, treated possessors of the land as mere tenants, suffered to live there by the sovereign. Russians had no property rights until the nineteenth century.[21]

In contrast, Western Europe was imbued with a strong sense of private property ownership, due to "the reverential attitude toward property . . . [which] is a mixture of sacred right (often because ancestors were buried on the family farm) and the sacred obligation to develop and defend it, both singly and along with one's countrymen."[22] Because of the strength of the respect for and acknowledgment of the right to own real property, the English common law couldn't help developing, because disputes regarding real property required continual adjudication.[23] Because we come by this fierce tradition of protecting our property honestly, the tradition is so embedded in our law and our culture that some of us can't help fighting issues of property ownership all the way through a trial and into the court of appeals.

Assault, battery, and trespass are quite similar, then, in that they attempt to enforce respect for the rights of others to be free from fear of harmful or offensive contact and invasions of property. None of the torts requires a showing of any actual damage or injury. It's as though the early courts understood all too well both how important these rights were and how easy it was to violate them (or how much someone might want to) so that the courts made vindication under the law relatively simple to obtain. Again, society would rather entertain the courtroom battle than suffer someone's taking physical revenge. At that, we saw the Massachusetts self-help rule try to discourage even the litigation itself and force neighbors to work things out among themselves.

In the next chapter, we'll see matters become more complicated. The issue will still be whether a violation of one's property rights has occurred; the complication will be that each side has competing rights in property to be considered, and the courts have to figure out how to accommodate them all. One thing will still hold true: What's missing is respect for the neighbors.

CHAPTER 4

Nuisance
Trespass's Messier Companion

> November 29 . . . 2:20 P.M. An Alder Avenue
> resident reported that her family has
> been the target of ongoing harassment.
> "POLICE BLOTTER,"
> *Bainbridge Island (Washington) Review,*
> DECEMBER 9, 2000

The simple notation from the newspaper quoted above is painfully tantalizing in its vagueness. There are so many ways in which one family can harass its neighbors, sometimes to the point that the harassment rises to the level of a tort. This chapter will examine some of many ways. In some of them, the activity may annoy the owner and interfere with her use or enjoyment of her property, but it may not be one that involves an actual physical entry onto the land. In that case, the activity doesn't actually *dispossess* the owner of her exclusive rights of use and ownership and thus doesn't meet the strict requirements of trespass.[1] When one engages in an activity that only *interferes* with a neighbor's right to use or enjoy her property, but doesn't actually commit a physical trespass, one literally becomes a nuisance. The elements of nuisance are an unreasonable interference with the use or enjoyment of a property interest held by an owner or possessor of land.

Nuisance, like trespass and battery, is a very old tort, having been fixed in the English common law as early as the thirteenth century.[2] A nuisance can take many forms, and in some cases can look an awful lot like a trespass: blasts that damage a house, floods, pollution of a stream, smoke, gas, unpleasant odors, excessive light, and high temperatures.³ As we will see, it can also be loud music or even a fence.

We should take quick note of the difference between a public nuisance and a private nuisance. Jones is annoyed because Smith is running a pig farm next door, and the smelly, untreated waste from it is insinuating its way into the back of Jones's property and into the neighbors' yards as well. Jones can bring a private nuisance suit just like our plaintiffs in the trespass cases. He is suing to protect his own interest in the enjoyment of his property. On the other hand, Smith's conduct—allowing animal waste to flow through the neighborhood—interferes with the public health. Thus he would also be subject to the maintenance of a public nuisance suit. Of course, that conduct is also a private nuisance as it interferes with a private person's, Jones's, interest in his property as well.⁴

Let's take another specific instance, loud music. We've probably all been annoyed by its emanating from next door or down the block. But even if the music doesn't stop reasonably early, then at least the party's eventually over, someone punches the off button on the CD player, and that one special night ends. The occasional teenager left alone may make a weekend of it with his boom box, but the neighbors indulge him, knowing that their own kids are every bit as likely to misbehave similarly, and someday soon at that. If we live in a college town, and the kids take it too far, too long, for too many nights, and, if gentle remonstrances the next morning fail to rouse their beer-soaked consciences, we ask the police to make a point of enforcing the noise ordinance. No one likes to have to call the police, but finally the music has become an actual nuisance, and a public nuisance justifying the police department's intervention.

Mr. Jacobs may have had exactly that course in mind when he managed to convince the district attorney's office to bring a criminal action for public nuisance against Mr. Cifarelli.⁵ Jacobs lived in Queens, New York, next door to Cifarelli, a percussionist who practiced his drum playing for two hours every day after he came home at 5:30 P.M. from his day job. Apparently, Jacobs asked him to cease the thumping, and, as Cifarelli needed to practice, he refused. Cifarelli was no kid, the court noted; he was a professional who had participated in recording several record albums and played in live performances. But Jacobs wanted him to stop.

The criminal statute under which Cifarelli was called to account by the state was § 240.25 of the Penal Law, Harassment:

> A person is guilty of harassment when, with intent to harass, annoy or alarm another person . . . he engages in a course of conduct or repeatedly commits acts which alarm or seriously annoy such other person and which serve no legitimate purpose.⁶

Here, New York embodied the criminal law of nuisance in a statute that it labeled "harassment." The judge wouldn't buy the argument. Cifarelli was only trying to practice his drums, not to annoy Jacobs purposely. Cifarelli certainly *knew* that Jacobs was troubled, as Jacobs let him know (this was Queens, after all), but that didn't matter to the judge. To prosecute a criminal action under the Penal Law required that Cifarelli have the specific intent to harass or intimidate Jacobs. There was simply no proof of that. Further, the drum-playing served a legitimate purpose; Cifarelli was practicing to advance his career, just as a writer might come home to tap at her computer or a potter might fire up his kiln.

In support of its view, the court cited *People v. Markovitz*, brought under the same statute but involving an auto repair shop that "created loud and unnecessary noise by loud banging, dropping tools, sanding, screeching . . . and a variety of esoteric annoyances geared to making life intolerable for residents of the block."[7] But that court had found that the normal operation of a legal business couldn't give rise to criminal sanctions, so the statute didn't apply in that case either.

Furthermore, this judge went on, the district attorney had no business bringing this action. What Mr. Jacobs was actually trying to do was turn his civil *private* nuisance claim into a *public* nuisance for which criminal charges could be brought.[8] In fact, the court said,

> The District Attorney's office should have known that this was an improper forum for resolution of this private dispute and should have, in their discretion, refused to prosecute this case. Their insistence on prosecuting this case was an unwarranted waste of judicial time and efficiency.[9]

Ouch. The district attorney would think twice before doing that again.

Though the case was essentially over, the court couldn't help itself and went on to decide a question not before it. (In usual practice, courts are careful never to address a question not raised by the parties. Occasionally a court may pose a hypothetical situation close to the actual facts of the case and speculate on its outcome, but this court goes much further.) The court said that even if the case had been brought as a civil action for private nuisance—*Jacobs v. Cifarelli*—the facts didn't amount to one. In a private nuisance suit—that is, a civil instead of a criminal action—Jacobs wouldn't have to prove either that Cifarelli had the specific intent to harass or that Cifarelli's actions served no legitimate purpose. The court would only have to balance the conflicting interests of the parties: Is the harm to Jacobs greater than the usefulness of Cifarelli's conduct?

Weighing the interests, the judge came out for Cifarelli (or would have, if he were actually trying *Jacobs v. Cifarelli*). It's useful for society that someone practice and develop his musical abilities. The practice wasn't unreasonable, seldom lasting past 8:00 P.M. and never past 10:00 P.M. In light of those facts, no private nuisance existed. The court quoted *People v. Markovitz* a second time: "It is also obvious that the only resolution of this dispute will come when the parties realize . . . that they must learn to live with each other."[10] The *Cifarelli* court may have felt that it couldn't say it better itself. Enduring someone's practicing a musical instrument is one of those inconveniences that people living in urban areas like Queens have to accept. Perhaps imagining Jacobs's headache, the court went on to say that the drums were no less a legitimate musical instrument than a piano. Case dismissed—that is, the criminal action, anyway. But don't bother trying to bring your civil suit, Jacobs. Instead, Jacobs would have to put up with the annoyance. Whether we think that Cifarelli was behaving in an uncivil manner or not—did he have any choice about when or where he practiced?—the court raises a theme we've already seen and will see again. The strictures of urban society force us to understand that we are going to have to accept being bothered by our neighbors at least some of the time.

But there must be a point at which one can refuse to continue being bothered. What level of noise, specifically, would be sufficient to constitute a private nuisance to satisfy this New York judge? We have an example in the case of *Gorman v. Sabo*.[11]

There was little dispute about the facts of the alleged nuisance itself, but the opinion of the Maryland Court of Appeals is virtually silent on the history behind the dispute. The Sabos and the Gormans were next-door neighbors in Quincy Manor, Prince George's County, Maryland—very next-door, in that the houses were separated only by a narrow open space. It was in August 1952 that the Gormans put a radio in an open window facing the Sabos' house, turned it up loud, and kept it blasting. Why? All the court said was that the Sabos and their four children had moved in next door, and "trouble arose between the children which led to ill feeling on the part of Mrs. Gorman against the Sabo children, Mrs. Sabo, and, eventually, Mr. Sabo."[12] That's it.

Whatever the Sabos or their kids had done, the Gormans certainly took the affront seriously. The music went on for hours every day for *several years*. It's truly amazing that the Sabos put up with it for as long as they did. Still, the Sabos were desolate. In order for their children to take an afternoon nap, the Sabos had to move the kids from their room on the side of the house facing the Gormans. Mrs. Gorman also instructed her children to bang sticks and stones on metal objects to annoy the Sabos further. The Gormans closed the door to the room with the radio to lessen the effect on themselves and the other neighbors, but kept the window open even in cold weather.

For their part, the Gormans didn't mind the neighbors' knowing about their vendetta; Mrs. Gorman told neighbors that the point of the campaign was to make the Sabos so miserable that they'd move. As alternatives, Mrs. Gorman would happily accept that "Mr. Sabo would be struck down and never speak, and [she] prayed that she would see Mrs. Sabo lie bleeding on the floor, . . . and on several occasions, with Mr. Gorman present, she said that she intended to see that Mrs. Sabo was carried out of the house either in a strait jacket or in a coffin."[13] What, we have to ask again, was it that the Sabo kids did in the first place?

Finally, of course, the Sabos sued in nuisance, claiming that the constant noise amounted to an unreasonable interference with the enjoyment of their own residence. They weren't claiming that there had been any diminution in the value of their property, or even that they had suffered any physical injury, though there was evidence that Mrs. Sabo's nerves were rattled by the onslaught. After the testimony, the judge instructed the jury that it had to find whether the Gormans' actions had resulted in "a serious interference with the ordinary comfort, use and enjoyment of the [Sabos] of their property."[14] Note the important qualifier: The jury had to consider whether the Gormans' actions would bother someone in the "*ordinary* comfort, use and enjoyment." The court's goal was to have the jury focus not on the Sabos' subjective complaint, but whether an average, ordinary person would be annoyed. The *Sabo* court's particularity was correct but unnecessary. One would think that it would take an extraordinary person *not* to be bothered by music played so continuously and loudly. It should come as no surprise that the jury returned a verdict for the Sabos, and the court of appeals affirmed the verdict.

Note, though, that this "interference with the ordinary comfort" test is not the test that the New York judge used in *People v. Cifarelli.* A plaintiff in a nuisance case is permitted to ask not just for money damages but for the activity that he claims is a nuisance to be stopped. That makes sense; if the activity is currently proving so bothersome, why not simply ask that a court order it enjoined? In leaping ahead of himself to try a civil action not before him, the judge in *Cifarelli* seemed to have been using one of the tests in deciding whether to grant an injunction in a nuisance action: Does the utility of the defendant's actions outweigh the harm to the plaintiff? So the New York judge didn't pose the usual test, the test that the *Sabo* court used, about whether a nuisance existed. Instead, on the way to deciding whether to order the activity stopped, he seems to have conceded that there was a nuisance. Yet recall that he had been saying all along that no nuisance existed. Oh well. Perhaps he should have stopped talking after he dismissed the criminal case.

A few other interesting facts from the *Sabo* opinion speak to issues of civility. On appeal, the Gormans actually tried to argue that any verdict shouldn't apply to Mr. Gorman because he wasn't involved in the ongoing activity. The court disagreed, pointing out that Mr. Gorman had admitted that the radio belonged to him. Once, when Mr. Sabo complained, Mr. Gorman's response was to tell his wife to turn the radio up because it wasn't loud enough. So the court didn't buy his incredible protests. He was truly and fully aware of what his wife was doing, and the court would hold him as well as Mrs. Gorman liable. It is amazing that Mr. Gorman tried to exempt himself from responsibility for this awful hazing.

Another ground for the Gormans' appeal was that the trial judge had refused their request to postpone the trial proceedings because Mrs. Gorman had become ill and was unable to attend the trial. The court didn't buy that either. First, there was some evidence from the Sabo side that Mrs. Gorman was faking it. Second, the Gormans' counsel didn't show that their case would actually be damaged by her inability to be there. For instance, she could still be cross-examined later to counter any adverse evidence put on during her absence. The astounding part is that Mrs. Gorman had the nerve to claim that she had taken ill because of the strain of the trial. Just what, pray, did she think she'd put the Sabos through all of those years? The least Mrs. Gorman could have done would have been to accept the reasonableness of the dispute and seek to have it resolved expeditiously. But no: Even that much of a concession to civility was too great.

The *Sabo* court doesn't report any subsequent contact between the neighbors, and there probably wasn't much after the lawsuit was filed. One can't help but wonder about the state of the neighborhood in general while all of this was going on. Some neighbors testified about the Gormans' statements; other neighbors testified that when they were in the Sabos' house they couldn't have a conversation for the noise. But what were the neighbors doing all of this time? Didn't any of them try to persuade the Gormans to end the concert? It's interesting, too, that there's no testimony reported that any of the other neighbors were bothered by the noise.

That their reaction was so little discussed raises an issue about community. The events described in the case occurred in the early 1950s, the music commencing in August 1952. Stephen Carter, in *Civility*, posits that the years before 1965 were a period of a shared experience of what it was to be an American. One grounding point for Carter was the New York Yankees, whose dynasty had ruled baseball for the previous fifteen years:

> Throughout the fifties and into the early sixties, the Yankees were solid, predictable, as thoroughly a part of the known and shared experience of being America as Ed

Sullivan, the automobile, the Pledge of Allegiance, and the two-party system. America was like that, a singular experience, utterly known.[15]

Part of that singular, and shared, experience was the communities in which Americans lived:

> Everybody wanted the same things, and the market produced them. All over the country, real estate developers were aping the Levittown model: a planned community with shops and schools and churches in the middle and houses, row upon row of identical houses, spreading in broad circles like ripples from that central commercial stone. The typical monthly mortgage payment was about sixty dollars. As the developer William Levitt explained, there was a simple ideology behind the Levittown idea: "No man who owns his own house and lot can be a Communist."[16]

The effect of this "singular experience," Carter goes on, is that "there were duties and obligations and roles, and all of society's institutions worked together to enforce them."[17] Other commentators would dispute that view, at least to some extent. David Halberstam, in *The Fifties*,[18] cites numerous examples of events that Americans disputed hotly: whether and when to use atomic weapons; Joseph McCarthy and his hearings; the conduct of the Korean War; and General Douglas MacArthur's firing by President Truman, which Halberstam calls "as divisive an act as anyone can remember."[19] So American society was far from having reached consensus on all subjects.

Assuming, however, that there was an accepted, shared view of a neighbor's duties and obligations, who was enforcing them in Quincy Manor? The Sabos put up with the music for several years with minimal reaction before they felt compelled to sue. Because the Sabos were long-suffering, did that give the other neighbors a bye, a reason to avoid confronting the Gormans over their definitely uncivil behavior? Or were they frightened of getting the Gorman treatment themselves? If the neighbors in Quincy Manor had a sense of a "shared experience," then why didn't someone tell the Gormans about it? The facts of this case are extreme and thus far from commonplace. Nevertheless, the Sabos had to sue and defend their victory against an appeal. After reading this case, Carter's view of neighbors and neighborhoods seems hopelessly simpleminded and naive.

Further, the appeal appears to have been based on pretty weak grounds. So we're having to contemplate another uncivil act, one that will recur in this book: litigating for the sake of litigating. Perhaps the Gormans were simply trying to stall the inevitable. Perhaps, though, they were just mean and deluded enough to think that the jury verdict was incorrect and their behavior was defensible. Nevertheless, under the circumstances, there was no gracious acceptance of defeat. The Sabos won, but one doubts the Gormans ever conceded the point. So perhaps, at least in this case, the "duties and obligations" were not felt so universally, and there was less community than met the eye.

In fact, the place seems in need of a good dose of community building à la Dr. Peck. Certainly the Gormans were refusing to see the Sabos as members of their community. Peck does concede that if neighbors really have nothing much in common, they needn't kid each other into thinking that they can form a meaningful group.[20] But one doubts that he would condone this sort of adversarial relationship with no intervention from the neighbors.

There is something in the law that encourages behavior such as that exhibited by the Gormans, but, before examining that facet, let's look at a couple more cases of nuisance—for one neighbor can become a nuisance to another in a happy variety of ways.

The Slairds had lived in their home in Silver Spring, Maryland, for twenty-one years. They were avid gardeners, devoting much money and time to their bosky dell. (No, this is not a self-help case; here the shrubs and plants are the alleged victims, not the perpetrators.) Then the Klewers moved in next door, and, after about a year, they installed a swimming pool with a diving board. The Slairds objected, for the excavation had changed the slope and elevation of the Klewers' property. The splashing and draining of the chlorinated water damaged the Slairds' plants and left a disagreeable odor. The Klewers hung floodlights around the pool, and, of course, where there's a pool, there's a party.

The Slairds sued the Klewers, claiming that the splashing water and noise and lights all combined to interfere unreasonably with the Slairds' enjoyment of their property. They asked that the court enjoin the Klewers from using the pool and force the Klewers to restore the elevation of the land so that water wouldn't drain into the Slairds' property. The Slairds also wanted $10,000 in damages for the depreciated value of their property and their inability to enjoy their garden.

The Klewers disagreed. The contractor they hired had constructed the pool in accordance with Montgomery County regulations. In fact, after the Slairds complained, a county inspector visited the site and pronounced it compliant. Nevertheless, the Klewers had dug a dry well and put in a drainage swale to collect any extra water flowing away from their property. They had curtailed their activities, making sure that they ended the parties and turned off the floodlights by what they thought was a reasonable hour. They built a six-foot fence to block out the noise and protect the Slairds' privacy.

Ms. Slaird testified (her husband was deceased by the time of the trial) that such efforts hadn't mattered. She had once counted fifty-three visitors using the pool in a single day. She and her husband had been forced off of their patio and away from their garden, and they had even had to shut the windows in an unsuccessful attempt to block out the noise. They had built an extra wall to stem the flow of water and planted a tree to screen the noise. These efforts were unavailing; water still flowed over, carrying pebbles and dirt, killing some of the plants and leaving behind a foul odor. Finally Ms. Slaird had complained to the Montgomery County officials, prompting that visit to the pool during which the officials found nothing amiss.

Ms. Slaird testified that she had dedicated considerable time to watching the pool from her upstairs bedroom in order to witness the Klewers' misdeeds. She stated, for instance, that she had seen naked people in the pool. On cross-examination, however, she clarified that actually she had only seen people in bathing suits. She was able to supply the license numbers of persons visiting the Klewers and had taken copious notes illustrated with more than one thousand pictures of the pool and the Klewers' property.

The case was tried before a judge, who, with the lawyers in tow, inspected the properties himself. A hard rain had just ceased, but the judge didn't see any drainage problem on the Slaird property. After the visit and after hearing all of the evidence, the trial judge found for the Klewers. Ms. Slaird appealed.

The court of appeals asked the right questions.[21] Was the swimming pool a condition that reasonable persons would find could produce actual discomfort to persons of ordinary sensibilities, tastes, and habits, so that the condition was unreasonable and in derogation of the Slairds' rights? Not every inconvenience would qualify; it had to interfere seriously with the Slairds' ordinary comfort and enjoyment.[22]

The role of a court of appeals with respect to its review of a trial judge is that the appeals court is bound to accept his findings as long as they weren't clearly erroneous or he hadn't misapplied the law. In short, the court couldn't say that the trial judge was flat wrong. The court also noted that "testimony indicated that the Slairds from time to time had difficulty with nearly all their neighbors."[23] Given that, the trial judge could well have concluded that the Slairds were not persons of "ordinary sensibilities, tastes, and habits." Judgment for the Klewers affirmed.

This is our first encounter with a plaintiff whose apparently easy susceptibility to annoying situations does her in. Underlying the courts' decisions in the *Cifarelli* and *Sabo* cases is the assumption that we're all living close together—as neighbors—and we all have to put up with a little inconvenience. Not too much inconvenience, not unreasonable inconvenience, just some. The court's reciting Ms. Slaird's testimony hints at its determination that she was not a plaintiff of "ordinary sensibilities, tastes, and habits." In fact, the court said, the Slairds were "supersensitive, difficult, and troublesome." Taking more than a thousand pictures of the neighbors certainly seems an extraordinary thing to do; how could she hear the splashing over all that snap snap snapping?

Part of being a member of the community is trying to avoid annoying your neighbors. Another part is understanding that, on occasion, you are going to be annoyed. Civil behavior encompasses both appropriate action and reaction. We can't help looking back to the first cases of this book—the cigarette cases—and Prosser's caution, adopted by the courts, that we aren't allowed to build a glass cage around ourselves. Society is simply too crowded. The law of nuisance takes that view into consideration. As a result, the law forces us to put up with a certain amount of what we might, at least subjectively, consider uncivil behavior—loud music and late pool parties.

Our overview of the ways by which we can make a literal and legal nuisance of ourselves to our neighbors would not be complete without including a case involving a grand old Anglo-Saxon tradition, the spite fence. One good example comes to us from Georgia in a case decided by the Georgia Supreme Court in 1941.[24]

Ms. Smith sued Ms. Hornsby alleging that the latter built a high fence along the property line separating the two. It was a solid structure of thick planks, about eight feet high, and it completely blocked Smith's southern exposure. Smith claimed that Hornsby derived absolutely no benefit whatsoever from the fence except that it bothered Smith. The fence obscured not only Smith's view but shut out the sunlight so that her electric lighting bills shot up. It also cut off any breeze from that direction. Smith imagined that due to the fence the value of her house had declined by at least $1,250, a good sum in those days.

The court's decision was based on several questions: First, was Hornsby free to make whatever use she wanted of her property? Did Smith have a right to the free passage of air and light over Hornsby's land? And, finally, did Hornsby's motives affect her right to the use of her own property?

At English common law, we valued, to the exclusion of other rights, the right of the landowner to do whatever she wanted with her land, without respect to either its effect on her neighbor or her own motives. That right follows from the exclusive right to possession of property, any violation of which, we have seen, constitutes a trespass. Under such an absolute rule, to inquire into the landowner's motive would be to try to control moral conduct. Morality was not seen as being within a court's jurisdiction; it only administered the law as enacted by the legislature. The lawmakers, of course, are free to legislate morality as much as they think they can.

Though the absolute rights had been the English common law and the early law of this country, some state courts had begun to make exceptions. Those courts didn't think it made any sense to allow a person to use his property to effect no good for himself but simply to injure his neighbor. Those courts, including one from Nebraska, were now saying something of the opposite:

> Courts of equity would fail in the service that history shows they were intended to render to society if they are unable to protect those common rights which more clearly appear, and become more valuable, as civilization advances, and the relations of social life become more intricate and more enjoyable. As was said by Mr. Justice Hoke in his dissenting opinion in Barger v. Barringer, supra, we can not "allow causes of action to be based upon motive alone. For here we enter upon the domain of taste and temperament, involving questions entirely too complex, varied, and at times fanciful for satisfactory inquiry and determination by municipal courts." But when it appears that not only was the motive wholly malicious, but the intention and result were to seriously injure another, without benefit to anyone, courts of equity are not so impotent in these modern times that they are unable to prevent such a wrong.[25]

Such strong talk could easily have turned the Georgia Supreme Court's head. But one of its problems was that in 1784 the Georgia constitution had incorporated the English common law as the law of Georgia. The English common law allowed Hornsby to make any lawful use of the land that she wanted. To find for Smith, the court somehow had to find a way around that rule.

We see the court wrestling with several problems. It wants to find a way to allow Smith to maintain her suit against the allegedly malicious Hornsby, who erects fences for no reason other than to annoy people. But the court has to try to come out that way in the face of controlling English common law, under which one can do whatever one wants of a lawful nature on one's land without regard for one's neighbor. There need be no consideration of questions of community, civility, or reasonableness.

Now, the court says, this is bustling mid-twentieth-century Atlanta (The City Too Busy to Hate), and we are alarmed by such a rule. We are more civilized than our forebears, and we have a duty to "protect those common rights which more clearly appear . . . as civilization advances, and the relations of social life become more intricate and more enjoyable," as the Nebraska court had said. One of those common rights appearing more clearly is that we should all expect to be treated civilly. Never mind the theory that one's home is one's castle and that one has the right to do whatever one wants with one's property. That's a bit old-fashioned and ill-suited to modern life. What the court wanted to do was find a better formula: One can't do something injurious, but otherwise lawful, for the wrong reasons.

So the court began a separate inquiry. The salient question, the court said, was, what constitutes a lawful use? There was no law that allowed someone the right to injure another, whatever the justification. Instead, everyone was entitled to have the law protect her against someone else's invasion of her rights. Further, "the use of one's own property for the sole purpose of injuring another is not a right that a good citizen would desire nor one that a bad citizen should have."[26]

So now the court had to find an injury—that is, that Smith had a right that Hornsby had infringed. The court plowed right through this hurdle, holding that "air and light no matter from which direction they come are God-given, and are essential to the life, comfort and happiness of every one."[27] No one can interfere with that right without justification, and Smith had claimed that Hornsby not only had no justification, but was acting solely from malice.

After a little more harrumphing over the power of the courts versus the power of the legislature, the court concluded that it was within its rights to make this law. Therefore, Smith had a good cause of action against Hornsby, and, though the court doesn't state it so formally, she would be entitled to show at a trial whether Hornsby's fence was a lawful use of her property or whether it interfered unreasonably with Smith's use and enjoyment of her own property. Though there is no subsequent history to this case, we can guess how that trial would have come out—if Hornsby, having felt the wind change direction, as it were, even bothered to continue to defend her fence.

Looking at this case, then, the Georgia Supreme Court set upon an uncivil practice and attempted to eradicate it, finding that "civilization advances." That phrase, though, sounds suspiciously Victorian, smacking of the inevitable perfectibility of man, an idea discredited by the insanely avoidable slaughter of World War I. Instead, perhaps the court here is using such talk to sneak around the issue. Perhaps the court is only trying to make the law catch up with civility: You mean we've allowed people to build spite fences for no good reason? We *must* find a way around this one. Thus, in 1941, the court leaps upon an uncivil practice long secured by the rule of law in order to weasel a way to outlaw it. This court doesn't shrink from legislating civility, but, in fact, seems to believe that it has a duty to do so.

We see a number of litigants in this chapter fighting fiercely to maintain shaky positions. Mr. Jacobs seeks to have criminal charges brought against the drummer next door, who has refused to moderate his practice routine. The Gormans steadfastly refuse to cease playing loud music, hoping to drive the Sabos crazy or at least out of the neighborhood. Ms. Slaird defends her perceived right not to have a next-door swimming pool ruining her garden. And, finally, Ms. Hornsby builds a fence, the only purpose of which is, allegedly, to block out Ms. Smith's air and light.

The nature of the law of nuisance, unfortunately, but necessarily, encourages these obstinate stands. The rules are not so clear and strict as are the rules in trespass, in part because the courts have to deal with not one piece of property but two. The court's inquiry is whether the activity results in a serious interference with the ordinary comfort, use, and enjoyment of the plaintiff's property. That "ordinary" means that the plaintiff has to be reasonable in his expectations of what he may have to put up with.

Saddled with a more subjective test than that under trespass law, there's more room to argue. What is a reasonable activity? Whose sensibilities are those of an ordinary and reasonable person? No one easy question could address all of the issues involved in the law of nuisance, and courts would not try to make one for fear of making too narrow a rule and thereby cutting off a worthy plaintiff or encouraging a malicious defendant. But that means that it's not necessarily certain with which neighbor a court will side. We probably agree with the judge in *Cifarelli*, that the drumming didn't constitute a nuisance; but tweak the facts—the booming going on longer, into later hours—and we can see that case coming out differently (assuming again that there had been a private nuisance case to try).

Our plaintiffs and defendants, thus tacitly encouraged to litigate, take up the challenge eagerly. After all, the defense of our property rights is a cherished Anglo-Saxon tradition. Remember that under common law Hornsby could do whatever she wanted with her property, and Smith could not complain. With rights like those, we become obstinate to the point of arrogance in our defense of them and unwilling to give them up. Thus, it may be unrealistic to expect Americans to behave any differently than they do. Property rights have always been sacrosanct, and the law of nuisance is inexact. An unintended consequence of the well-intended law of nuisance is that it allows for some uncivil behavior. But, perhaps, given our devotion to property ownership rights, that's the way we want it. Our common law property rights dictate no other way.

What suffers, of course, is our sense of community. We might think back to what Stephen Carter reports that Mr. Levitt said: "No man who owns his own house and lot can be a Communist."[28] Within Mr. Levitt's very words is the hint of the problem: Ownership of private property may (or may not) prevent a person from becoming a Communist, but it certainly encourages a we-versus-them mindset. We think first, this is my house; next we think, this is my neighborhood. Thus the community is a secondary priority. We should remember that the laws of nuisance and trespass—and their emphasis on individual property rights—have roots older than our country. The incivility from which the law of nuisance arises is very old indeed, and it shouldn't surprise us that it continues unabated right now, just down the block or over the back fence.

CHAPTER 5

Stevens v. Hay, etc.
How Bad Things Can Get

> Good fences make good neighbors.
> ROBERT FROST,
> "MENDING WALL"

At this point, we'll pause in our march through the intentional torts to look briefly at a few cases—most of which are nuisance, but with a little trespass tossed in—that involve the very same parties. The cases are a good example of the persistence, bullheadedness, and refusal to give in, no matter the cost, that Americans bring to their disputes. These cases also introduce another theme that will contribute to our ultimate conclusion regarding the interplay of law and civility: In the wrong circumstances, litigation is useless as a means of resolving a community's disputes.

The Stevenses and the Hays owned adjoining properties at Cannon Beach, Oregon, a popular tourist resort. The Stevenses owned a home and ran a motel and restaurant to the south of the Hays. The Stevenses also owned property between the Hays' property and the beach. Imagine the Stevenses' property forming a block capital "L," with the vertical line of the "L" running along the beach, and the Hays' property cradled inside the "L." The Hays ran a motel and had a summer home on their property. There were five paths that ran across and over a cliff and down a steep incline from the Hays' property across the

63

Stevenses' to the beach. Going back many years, the owners before the Hays used the paths only during the summer tourist season and on weekends. Suddenly, one year the Stevenses put wire mesh and wood fences across the paths.

The Hays weren't happy about this, of course. The Stevenses had just blocked off the Hays' motel guests' path to the beach. Besides, according to the Hays, even though it was the Stevenses' property, people had used those paths for so long that using them amounted to a right—an easement—that the Stevenses shouldn't be allowed to withdraw willy-nilly.

In May of 1969, the Hays sued the Stevenses to win back the right to use the paths. The Stevenses argued that the Hays hadn't obtained any easement. An easement was created only when the use of the path was continuous. On the contrary, here whole months went by without anyone's scrambling down the hill to the beach. Furthermore, the Hays had failed to demonstrate that their use of the property was "adverse"—that is, essentially, a wrongful use that was open and notorious and not in subordination to the Stevenses.

This odd point of law has implications for civility. The law favors the person who goes tramping around on his neighbor's property in full view of everyone. If he has enough nerve about it, and if he does it for a long enough time, then he obtains a right to use the property—that is, he obtains a sort of ownership through an easement. Yet if he behaves with respect for the other person's own-ership rights and asks permission to use that path, he doesn't stand a chance of obtaining any rights at all. Thus, showing respect for another's property rights, a form of civil behavior, is a bad strategy under the law if one wants to establish any rights for oneself.

The trial court disagreed with the Stevenses' argument about continuous use; it didn't have to equate to *constant* use. The motel guests had used the paths continuously during the summer months going back about thirty years. Further, it didn't matter that the Hays knew that the Stevenses had the legal authority to prevent use of the paths. A use could be "adverse" even though the Hays recog-nized that the Stevenses owned the land and could forbid the Hays from using the paths.

A use was adverse as long as it was "not made in subordination" to the Ste-venses. So, presumably, tramping around on land you don't own and know you can be kept off of is a use "not made in subordination" to the owner's rights. The evidence, the court concluded (without reciting any of it), was that the Hays' use was not made in subordination. Though the court doesn't say so explicitly, the fact that people had used the paths routinely over the years meant that the Hays had established an equal right to use them.

Anyway, the court concluded, the paths were on property that was so steep and narrow that the Stevenses couldn't make any other real use of it. If someday they managed to find a new use for that property, they had the right to come back to court and try to prove that the easements put an unreasonable burden on this new use.

So, about a year after the suit was filed, the trial court found for the Hays, holding that they had indeed obtained an easement across the paths. The court's decree gave the Stevenses until June 6, 1971, to remove the fences. There apparently was some discussion between the attorneys for the parties about removing the fences by that date, though the Stevenses had appealed the verdict. In any event, June 6, 1971, came and went, and the fences remained.

The Hays took it upon themselves to recruit some friends and go out to the hated fences. They cut the lumber posts down at the base and separated the lumber from the mesh. Then they carefully rolled up the wire mesh and deposited all of the materials on the Stevenses' property.

Not to be outdone, the Stevenses rebuilt the fences but left openings in three of the five fences, effectively allowing the paths to be used in accordance with the trial court's decree. They didn't open up the other two because the decree had described the location of those paths inaccurately, creating some confusion of which the Stevenses took advantage.

Then, in June 1972, the Oregon Supreme Court affirmed the trial court's ruling: The fences must come down.[1] Still, the Stevenses didn't do anything about removing the last two fences, so the Hays again relied on self-help, taking down the two fences that didn't have openings. The Hays were apparently still annoyed about the three fences that did have openings, however, so they sued the Stevenses again. They claimed that the three fences were an unreasonable interference with the use of their property and thus constituted a nuisance. They asked the court to force the Stevenses to take the fences down. The Stevenses counterclaimed that the Hays had committed a trespass by coming onto the property to cut down the other two fences.

As if all of this combat weren't enough, now we must pause and back up a bit. As in any good Shakespearean comedy, a subplot had been unfolding.

The Hays, whose motel was a larger operation than the Stevenses', had a central vacuum system that collected dust, animal hairs, and fibers from the motel and blew it all out into the open air. The Stevenses, including their children, aged eight and ten at the time, suffered from allergies and bronchial asthma. And, the Stevenses claimed, the Hays also operated a laundry on the premises, whose chemicals might also be contributing to the pollution. As a consequence, the Stevenses sued the Hays, asking the court to enjoin them from exhaling that junk from their motel, whence, they claimed, it made its way south to the Stevenses.[2]

The judge issued a preliminary injunction against the Hays' venting their vacuum system into the open air pending a full trial on the merits. To obey the preliminary order, the Hays funneled the vacuum system into a closed room.

At trial, the Stevenses produced expert witnesses to boost their case: an allergist, a toxicologist, and a pollution engineer. The allergist and toxicologist testified as to the Stevenses' allergies. The pollution engineer spoke about the airborne particulates floating to the Stevenses' property. The judge himself trooped out to the property to have a look.

The judge determined that, whether or not the central vacuum system had caused any problems, the evidence didn't show any significant particulates in the air now. Further, the Stevenses seemed to be allergic to a lot of household items, and there wasn't much the Hays could do about that. Finally, the Stevenses hadn't really proved that their bronchial asthma had been caused by anything the Hays had done. Nevertheless, the judge continued his limited injunction, simply to enforce what the Hays had already done—to vent the vacuum system into a closed room, not into the open air.

The Stevenses appealed, complaining that the judge had erred and that they had indeed proved their case. The testimony of their expert witnesses, for instance, was uncontradicted by any witness from the Hays' side.

Nevertheless, in February 1974 the Oregon Supreme Court issued its opinion affirming the trial judge.[3] He was in a better position than the supreme court to judge the credibility of the witnesses. That is what any trier of fact, whether a judge or a jury, is entitled to do. Unless the supreme court could find a really important mistake, they had no reason to disturb the trial judge's finding. End of story. It's interesting to note that the court of appeals didn't say that the Stevenses were suing under a writ at common law such as trespass or nuisance, but stated only that the case had been brought in equity, for an injunction. Traditionally in the old English common law, one brought an action in equity when one didn't have an action at law, such as nuisance or trespass. Here, it seems that the Stevenses could claim that the particulates blowing onto the property constituted an unreasonable interference with the use or enjoyment of their property (that is, a nuisance). The Stevenses may very well have brought that action, but the court doesn't say so, focusing instead on the equitable remedy of an injunction.

In the meantime, of course, the parties had gone at it again over those fences, and the trial court had found for the Stevenses—the fences did not constitute a nuisance. The Hays were adamant that they did, and appealed. The parties heard from the Oregon Supreme Court again in January 1975.[4]

The Hays had argued that the fences unreasonably interfered with their right to enjoyment of their property. That interference certainly outweighed any utility that the Stevenses could claim that the fences had. What good did three fences with openings have in them anyway? The fences certainly couldn't keep anyone out. They were useless except to constitute a nuisance to the Hays. The Hays had even suffered economic damages; people didn't want to rent rooms that looked out on those hideous fences. (Their argument sounds like Smith's against Hornsby over the spite fence in the last chapter—the Stevenses had no right to put up fences that benefited the Stevenses not a whit while damaging the Hays.)

The Stevenses disagreed. The fences did have utility. Without them, the Stevenses couldn't get liability insurance. Their insurance agent testified that the steep bank amounted to a severe hazard to children—without some sort of obstacle, there was nothing to prevent kids from wandering onto the Stevenses' property and then toppling over the edge. Without some barrier, he wouldn't sell them comprehensive general liability insurance.

This testimony proved the trump ace. Everyone knows that without insurance to protect yourself from lawsuits by people injured on your property, you're out of business. Talk about utility—the trial court found, and the supreme court agreed, that the utility of getting liability insurance outweighed any inconvenience to the Hays.

As to the level of inconvenience, the Oregon Supreme Court, quoting Prosser, stated that where an interference to property rights

> involves mere personal discomfort or annoyance, some other standard must obviously be adopted than the personal tastes, susceptibilities and idiosyncrasies of the particular plaintiff. . . . The standard must necessarily be that of definite offensiveness, inconvenience or annoyance to the normal person in the community—the nuisance must affect "the ordinary comfort of human existence as understood by the American people in their present state of enlightenment."[5]

Unfortunately for the Hays, the supreme court didn't think that the fences were so ugly. The record contained photographs of them, and they looked normal enough. The verdict for the Stevenses was affirmed.

Thus, finally, ended the war between the Hays and the Stevenses. The tally: one win for each and one that wasn't a clear win for either. From the filing of the first suit in May 1969 until the last opinion was issued in January 1975—five and a half years—the parties spent who knows how much money and devoted untold waking (and probably nightmaring) hours to the disputes. What was the result? People approaching the beach from the Hays' property could continue to use the same paths that people had used for thirty years. Nothing of importance had changed, except that the Hays now vented their central vacuum system into a closed room instead of the open air, and the Stevenses had some fences on their property.

The cases are a story of obstinacy, a refusal to compromise, and ultimately a refusal to accept the judgments of the parties' state trial courts. What could have driven these people? Looking at Prosser's test above, as recited by the court, we can't help shaking our heads. How offensive could the fences have been? And, on the other hand, exactly how important were the fences to the Stevenses? Presumably an insurance agent had been selling liability insurance to them for a good number of years before the fences were erected. What, finally, was at stake?

Yet both parties were as dedicated to their causes as the Gormans were to theirs and Ms. Slaird was to hers. One of the factors contributing to this mess is the fact that there was no informal mechanism—a local presence that had the respect of both parties—that could grab these folks by the scruffs of their necks and say: Enough is enough; you've wasted enough time and money of your own, not to mention that of the courts whose resources you've appropriated. So let's all think sensibly for a minute and discuss a workable means by which you can manage to live side by side. While these cases aren't the first examples we've seen of such a need, and they won't be the last, they are perhaps the most extreme.

Next we'll look at the worst sorts of behavior we can imagine and then examine a series of cases devoted to freedom of speech, the other subject that arouses Americans to such uncompromising positions. In the meantime, we can keep the Stevenses and Hays in the backs of our minds, imagining them still seething, still annoyed.

CHAPTER 6

Outrageous!
The Intentional Infliction of Severe Emotional Distress

> Adoption of the suggested principle
> [that mental distress purposely caused is
> actionable] would open up a wide vista
> of litigation in the field of bad manners,
> where the relatively minor annoyances
> had better be dealt with by instruments
> of social control other than the law.
>
> CHIEF JUDGE CALVERT MAGRUDER,
> *Mental and Emotional Disturbance
> in the Law of Torts*

But sometimes the annoyances aren't relatively minor. And sometimes the law will sanction annoyances that it finds to be truly outrageous. For instance:

Andrew and Margaret Wilson moved into their home in Durham, North Carolina, in 1955. In 1957, they built a fence to enclose their backyard. Unfortunately, they goofed, so the fence rested on an adjoining lot and also crossed another one. We know from the chapter on trespass that the Wilsons committed one by building their fence on someone else's property. However, the fence stood unchallenged for twenty-three years.

Then, in 1980, Carl and Wanda Pearce purchased that adjoining lot, and, in 1982, two more adjoining lots. At the time of the purchase, the seller told the Wilsons that their fence encroached on the property that he had just sold to the Pearces. In all likelihood, the encroachment turned up when the property was surveyed for the closing of the sale. He advised the Wilsons that they had better move the fence, but they didn't. We can guess and dread what's going to happen next, and, at this point, we wonder why the Wilsons didn't simply do the right thing and move their fence.

Mr. Pearce began to harass the Wilsons about the fence in 1980. If the Wilsons were out in their yard, Mr. Pearce would stand outside, raise his fists, and make obscene gestures. He cursed the Wilsons loudly enough for the neighbors to hear. Pearce even stood in his window where Mrs. Wilson could see him and made gestures at his private parts. More than once he told both of them, while rubbing his groin, to "suck my dick."

Once, in January 1987, Pearce accused Mr. Wilson of knocking over some wood in his yard. He began cursing and told his wife to "go get my gun." She went into the house and returned with what appeared to be a gun covered by a towel. Another time, Pearce did fire a pistol into the Wilsons' yard when Mr. Wilson was there; Pearce claimed that he was shooting at a stray dog, as though that were any excuse. Wilson also saw Pearce throwing broken glass into the Wilsons' yard. Another time, when Mrs. Pearce reported that Mr. Wilson was working in his garden, Mr. Pearce yelled, for Mr. Wilson's benefit, that he would "get me some god damn rocks and knock his god damned brains out." Just like Mrs. Slaird in the swimming pool case, Mrs. Pearce photographed the Wilsons in their yard and kept a file on them.

Mr. Pearce also kept a large stack of wood piled against the fence, though he didn't have a fireplace. The stack was taller than the fence, which, as a consequence of the weight, bowed into the Wilsons' yard. Rats, it was speculated, lived in the woodpile.

Mr. Pearce also invited outsiders in on the fun. He complained to the city housing inspector about the Wilsons' yard, but, when the official had his look around, he found no violations for which to cite the Wilsons. In June 1988 Mr. Pearce called the police about a "juvenile disturbance" at the Wilsons. It developed that the only juvenile there was the Wilsons' eleven-day-old grandchild. The Wilsons' three grown children (one of whom lived at home) weren't exempt, either; Mr. Pearce cursed them in their parents' presence.

Finally, the Wilsons had had enough, and filed a complaint in July 1989. (Their gritted-teeth forbearance rivals that of the Sabos' tolerance of the five-year music concert.) Pearce was duly served with a temporary restraining order on July 3 to stop his alleged harassment of the Wilsons. The order either encouraged Pearce or perhaps enraged him further, for in August he threatened to kill Mr. Wilson. Pearce also mowed his lawn nine times in two weeks that August, parking his lawn mower as close as he could to the Wilsons' bedroom window.

On August 14, he asked a court to issue an arrest warrant for the Wilsons' daughter Andrea, but the court refused. Then he filed a civil action against Andrea, though we aren't told what he was alleging. On August 31, the Pearces were found in contempt of court for violating the terms of the preliminary injunction against harassing the Wilsons, and Mr. Pearce was ordered to serve two days in the county jail.

The suit filed by the Wilsons contained claims for adverse possession of the property on which their fence encroached and the intentional infliction of severe emotional distress. (A third count, malicious prosecution, is a fairly complex sort of claim, and we'll discuss its civil law cousin separately in chapter 12.) The verdict was for the Wilsons, though in favor of Mr. Wilson only on the intentional infliction count. Each party appealed, and the North Carolina Court of Appeals heard the case.[1]

Before examining the claim that is the focus of this chapter, let's dispose of the adverse possession claim briefly, as it echoes the Hays' claim to the paths leading from their property to the beach in the Hay-Stevens litigation. The Wilsons were claiming that they had acquired title to the property on which their fence encroached because it had been there for twenty-three years before the Pearces moved in. No one complained until the Pearces raised the issue in their answer to the Wilsons' complaint in July 1989. Thus, the Wilsons' use of the property had continued for thirty-two years and, the jury found, their use was actual, open, hostile, exclusive, and continuous—all terms of art that boil down to the Wilsons' having their fence all over that property, and everyone knowing it, and no one doing anything about it. The court of appeals affirmed the jury's finding that the Wilsons had acquired title to the property on which their fence sat. Thus, any annoyance that we might have felt for the Wilsons' stubbornness about their fence should dissipate; they were right to insist on its sitting where it sat.

The court took longer to explore the claim for intentional infliction of emotional distress. In contrast to battery, trespass, and nuisance, the tort of intentional infliction of severe emotional distress is a fairly new one. While it's easy to tell when a trespass occurs, and a battery happens upon there merely being unwanted contact, mental suffering was long thought too subtle and uncertain to measure. The courts didn't want to encourage inventive plaintiffs to recover damages simply because this or that event made them anxious or sad. Furthermore, the courts dreaded opening their doors to claims over mere insults or bad manners. Life's tough, said the courts, and people should be encouraged not to sue but to develop a thicker skin against the trivial insults to which we're all ordinarily subjected. The law evolved so that one can't recover damages in a civil suit for "mere profanity, obscenity, or abuse, without circumstances of aggravation, or for insults, indignities or threats which are considered to amount to nothing more than mere annoyances."[2] Again, as in the law of nuisance, for instance, we see the courts asking us to put up with a certain amount of incivility.

According to Dean Prosser, the first, leading case allowing recovery for emotional distress occurred in England in 1897.[3] In *Wilkinson v. Downton*, a man played a practical joke on a woman, telling her that her husband had had an accident and broken both of his legs, and she should find a cab and take him home. The resulting permanent shock to her nervous system brought on weeks of suffering. There was no assault or battery, but, the court found, the woman had suffered damage, and the man had behaved outrageously. The woman was permitted to recover for her suffering.

Other cases occurred sporadically in which courts allowed recovery until, around 1930, the tort became recognized as a separate cause of action in the United States. The elements generally are that the defendant, by extreme and outrageous conduct, intentionally and recklessly causes severe emotional distress. It's a difficult case to make, for the behavior complained of must either be intended to cause suffering or be very reckless, and it must be truly outrageous. The plaintiff must demonstrate that she has suffered severe emotional distress, though there need not be physical injury.[4] As we shall see, the difficulties presented in proving the necessary elements lead to varying verdicts. Nevertheless, the cases, even those that the plaintiff loses, stand as glowing examples of Americans' ability to behave more uncivilly toward each other than one could imagine.

Back to the Wilsons and their claim for damages under the intentional infliction of severe emotional distress. The court of appeals recited the law of North Carolina (and the law generally) that the Wilsons would have to show that Pearce's conduct "exceed[ed] all bounds of decency tolerated by a society and the conduct cause[d] mental distress of a very serious kind."[5] After reciting the facts, the court had no trouble at all finding that the conduct had been extreme and outrageous. The arguable right to bear arms aside, there can't be more outrageous behavior than firing a pistol in another person's general direction. Also, there was no question, and the court didn't address the issue, that Pearce had acted intentionally.

The last question was whether the Wilsons had suffered severe emotional distress. The court had little problem there, either, as Mr. Wilson had suffered actual bodily harm brought on by the emotional distress. As Pearce had been aware, Mr. Wilson had a heart condition for which he took medication. After Pearce began his campaign to have the fence removed, Mr. Wilson experienced chest and arm pain from the tension and stress.

Pearce's counsel attempted to capitalize on the caution with which courts treat claims under this tort. He argued that Mr. Wilson had served in the Marines as a young man and so undoubtedly had heard worse language there. If Pearce were guilty of the intentional infliction of emotional distress, so, then, were the

Marines. The court found the argument "preposterous."[6] Again making an argument based on the courts' traditional caution, Pearce's counsel suggested that Mr. Wilson might simply have turned his back on Pearce. Again this court disagreed, saying that "no one in a civilized society should be expected to take the kind of harassment the evidence shows the Pearces have forced upon the Wilsons over the course of at least eight years."[7] The court wondered if the Wilsons' holding out so long spoke not only to their patience but also to their fear of revenge. Given all of the evidence, the court concluded, the jury was correct to find for Mr. Wilson in his claim for damages under the intentional infliction claim.

As noted, only Mr. Wilson had prevailed on his claim. After hearing the evidence, the judge had directed a verdict in favor of the Pearces on Mrs. Wilson's claim, holding that she hadn't presented enough evidence for her case to be submitted to a jury—that is, no jury would be justified in finding for her. The court of appeals disagreed. Pearce had threatened to kill both her and Mr. Wilson, had threatened to arrest one of her children, and had threatened Mr. Wilson in front of her. Pearce knew that she took medication as well; she suffered from chronic obstructive lung disease and hypertension. Both could be aggravated by stress. With that evidence in hand, the court said, the jury should have been allowed to consider Mrs. Wilson's claim.

The court's finding in this case should come as no surprise. If any conduct is outrageous, it's the conduct that the jury found took place during the eight years before the suit was brought. If a court is to abandon its predisposition against claims for mere upset, this is the case in which to do so.

Here, as in the chapters on trespass and nuisance, the issues of one's land and house intrude. Pearce apparently could not bear the thought of that fence's encroaching on his property. Mr. Wilson apparently believed so strongly (and correctly, it turns out) that he had acquired the right for his fence to be there that no amount of harassment by Pearce would persuade him to move it or take it down. They, just like the Americans in the other cases, took their property rights so seriously that vindication of them crowded out any other concern. Matters of community were secondary to vindication of property rights. There is no community if one's physical place in it is challenged.

Still, the dispute—the mere location of a fence, the positioning of which hadn't bothered anyone else for over twenty years—seems out of proportion to Pearce's behavior. Thus the Wilsons' reaction, and the verdict by the court, and the affirmance by the court of appeals. At some point, uncivil behavior in the assertion of property rights goes too far.

* * *

Examples of such outrageous behavior abound far beyond the world of property rights. An example is a sad case from Maryland, *Harris v. Jones*.[8] William Harris worked in a General Motors (GM) plant where his supervisor was Robert Jones. Harris had an unfortunate stutter that worsened when he became nervous. Jones knew this and on a number of occasions made fun of Harris. Sometimes Jones would approach Harris, tell him not to get nervous, and then walk away. Harris objected and threatened to seek help from his union committeeman, one who handled employee grievances at the plant. But, made nervous by Jones, Harris stuttered, pronouncing the word "mmmitteeman," his head shaking up and down with effort. Jones seized on the incident, mimicking Harris's mispronunciation and calling Harris a troublemaker.

Harris filed two grievances against Jones, both of which GM management seemed to have resolved satisfactorily. However, taking their cue from Jones, others in the plant ridiculed Harris as well, making life miserable for him. Finally, Harris sued, alleging that Jones, and GM as Jones's employer, had behaved in an extreme and outrageous way, intentionally causing severe emotional distress.

Harris had begun an uphill battle. Though his case was tried in 1977, the Maryland courts still had not recognized the tort. Nevertheless, he managed to convince the trial court to send his case to the jury, and the jury entered a verdict for him, awarding him $3,500 in compensatory damages and $15,000 in punitive damages against both Jones and GM.

The defendants appealed, and the case was heard by a court of special appeals.[9] The court, in a very orderly and careful opinion, said that while the tort had not been recognized in Maryland before, thirty-seven other jurisdictions had done so in one form or another. The court believed that Maryland should adopt it as well. Then the court focused on the restrictions: The conduct complained of had to be truly outrageous; the defendant must have intended to inflict emotional distress; the plaintiff must have suffered true emotional distress; and the conduct had to have caused the distress.

The court had no trouble finding that Jones's conduct was intentional in that he intended to cause Harris emotional distress—why else would he walk up to Harris and tell him not to get nervous? The court also found that Jones's conduct was outrageous.

The problems with Harris's case were whether his distress was severe enough and whether Jones's conduct had actually caused the distress. Harris had suffered from his malady for quite some time, long before he met Jones. His wife testified that he had always been very nervous and withdrawn, and it was only after a certain amount of effort on her part that he would open up to her family and make new friends. She also said that when he began to have problems at work he grew ill-tempered, and he had started drinking heavily, even imbibing at a christening party. At one point he threw a meat platter at her. Finally they had separated for a two-week period.

Harris himself admitted that his bosses had always made him nervous. His condition had caused him to seek a doctor's help, and he had been taking Librium. Most of this occurred before he met Jones. So the court found that there was insufficient evidence that Jones's conduct had caused Harris's distress.

Further, the court doubted that Harris's distress was severe enough. It amounted to "nervousness" and "irritation."[10] That distress was simply not sufficient to allow Harris recovery. The court of special appeals reversed the judgments, entering judgment on behalf of Jones and GM.

Harris then took his case to the Maryland Court of Appeals, which affirmed the judgment of the court of special appeals. It agreed with the lower court that the new tort should be accepted in Maryland, and also agreed on the facts. Harris's distress was neither severe enough nor clearly enough the result of the ridicule heaped on him by Jones to warrant recovery. Along the way, the court quoted from a leading article on the tort by Chief Judge Calvert Magruder:

> Against a large part of the frictions and irritations and clashing of temperaments incident to participation in a community life, a certain toughening of the mental hide is a better protection than the law could ever be.[11]

In cautioning against allowing recovery too readily, Magruder implicitly expressed the fear that merely irritated and annoyed plaintiffs would clog the courts with petty disputes. It is the same kind of concern that led to the adoption of the Massachusetts rule in the trespass cases. Rather than litigate these petty matters, we should stiffen up and accept the minor irritations that arise in the natural, often uncivil state of society. In a further cautionary note quoted by the court, Magruder said that

> there is danger of getting into the realm of the trivial in this matter of insulting language. No pressing social need requires that every abusive outburst be converted into a tort; upon the contrary, it would be unfortunate if the law closed all the safety valves through which irascible tempers might legally blow off steam.[12]

But the court appears to have been pressing the wrong point. There was no question that Jones's behavior went beyond the trivial and that he wasn't using one of "the safety valves through which irascible tempers might legally blow off steam." Jones behaved outrageously enough, all right; it was just that Harris couldn't prove that the behavior caused him severe distress.

This case teaches that the law won't punish every incident of outrageous incivility. The courts are more demanding of the plaintiff than in, for example, the battery cases. In those, the plaintiff must have suffered merely unwanted or offensive contact, and she need not prove actual injury at all. In the intentional infliction cases, the plaintiff is going to have to suffer *severe* emotional distress. Further, the conduct complained of can't simply be more than a reasonable person should have to endure. According to the Restatement of Torts 2d, § 46, comment d, it must be such that, when one hears of it, one exclaims, "Outrageous!"[13] Because of the subjective nature of that inquiry—who would and who wouldn't exclaim "Outrageous!" over a particular set of facts?—these cases are heavily fact-dependent. In the right context, the worse the facts, the more willing the courts are to permit the plaintiff to recover.

Sometimes what is outrage is determined by the victim's state of mind. What might not seem outrageous, but merely "a large part of the frictions and irritations and clashing of temperaments incident to participation in a community life,"[14] becomes outrageous when we consider the person who hears the words. The defendants in *Zalnis v. Thoroughbred Datsun Car Company, et al.*, a case from Colorado, learned the hard way.[15]

In January 1978, Ms. Zalnis went to Thoroughbred Datsun and, negotiating with Mr. Cade, bought a 1978 model Datsun. Cade's supervisor, the president of the company, Mr. Trosper, approved the deal. But a few days later Trosper realized that Cade had miscalculated the purchase price and sold the car at a loss of about $1,000. Trosper told Cade and the sales manager to fix it: Either get more money out of Zalnis, take the car back, or make good the difference out of Cade's salary. (Hard cheese for Cade, when Trosper himself had originally approved the deal.) Another salesman, Mr. Anthony, had the bright idea of calling Zalnis and telling her that the car had been recalled and to bring it back.

Zalnis showed up with her new Datsun, but she cleverly refused to relinquish it until someone came up with a work order detailing the recall. Thoroughbred Datsun wasn't daunted; they took the car from her anyway. Zalnis claimed that the inventive Anthony called her a "French whore" and followed her around the showroom, screaming abuse at her and threatening her when she tried to get her car back.

Like the legendary prisoner with one phone call, Zalnis reached her lawyer, who called Trosper and apparently made him see the sense of returning the car. During the conversation, though, the equally imaginative Trosper told the lawyer that Zalnis had been "sleeping with that nigger salesman and that's the only reason she got the deal she got."[16] Trosper also told the lawyer that he had known Zalnis for years and had informed Cade and the sales manager that she was "crazy and she had watched her husband kill himself."[17] Trosper's venturing these opinions to Zalnis's lawyer seems to have been a mistake in judgment, for Zalnis promptly sued Thoroughbred Datsun and Trosper, alleging outrageous conduct by which they intended to cause her severe emotional distress. She also sued for slander.

The trial court granted the two defendants summary judgment—a judgment before trial—on the outrageous conduct claim, agreeing with them that, as a matter of law, the conduct wasn't outrageous enough to meet the standard under Colorado case law. Zalnis appealed.

Trosper and Thoroughbred Datsun had argued that their conduct amounted to "mere insults, indignities, threats, annoyances, petty oppressions, and other trivialities," and therefore was not outrageous. But the appeals court disagreed. They hadn't merely threatened and insulted her; they had taken away her car. Conduct that might not otherwise seem outrageous becomes so when the actor holds a position of power over his victim, as was the case here.

The defendants also argued that the law required that the conduct be outrageous to a person with ordinary sensibilities. Again, they claimed, the conduct didn't rise to that level. Again the court disagreed. Conduct that isn't otherwise outrageous could become so if Trosper had reason to believe that he was dealing with someone who was "peculiarly susceptible to emotional distress by reason of some physical or mental condition or peculiarity."[18]

Here, Trosper did indeed have knowledge that Zalnis might be particularly susceptible to the sort of abuse that Anthony heaped upon her. Though the court didn't explicitly say so, apparently Trosper hung himself in telling Zalnis's lawyer that he had told Cade and the sales manager that Zalnis was insane because she'd witnessed her husband commit suicide. Trosper couldn't have handed a better case to Zalnis had he intended to. Because Cade and the sales manager knew of her susceptibility—from a supposedly reliable source, their boss Trosper—a jury could find that they had acted at least recklessly, if not intentionally, to cause her severe emotional distress.

The defendants' last argument was that the court should distinguish between a single outrageous occurrence and a course of conduct that was outrageous. Here, they posited, was a single occurrence. While the distinction could be a factor, the court agreed, the rule was that one looked at the totality of the conduct to determine whether it was outrageous. In Zalnis's case, the court concluded, a jury should have been allowed to determine whether the totality of the conduct was outrageous. The court reversed the trial court's grant of summary judgment and sent the case back for trial.[19]

No doubt we agree with the court's reasoning, if only because the law shouldn't condone the defendants' bullying when they knew that it might be more successful with Zalnis than someone else. If part of civility is taking account of and respecting other people, then certainly we are charged with taking into account each individual's susceptibility. Here, the defendants are alleged to have taken Zalnis's susceptibility into account but for the wrong purpose: not to treat her with respect, but specifically to treat her without respect—to take advantage of her.[20]

The lesson to take from the *Harris* and *Zalnis* cases is that different courts may evaluate facts differently under the intentional infliction theory. And they should not be expected to seem entirely consistent, for whether conduct has been outrageous enough and whether the plaintiff has suffered sufficiently will always be complex, fact-dependent inquiries. The competing interests are too difficult to reconcile: We want to punish outrageous behavior, but we don't want to encourage potential plaintiffs to run to the courthouse every time their feelings are hurt.

One of the consequences of the inquiry's subjective nature is the uncertain result in any particular case. If precedent is unclear, the lawyer for a potential plaintiff may be more willing to take a chance with a close case, especially if the plaintiff is a sympathetic figure. The case could mean a jackpot trial verdict or, at least, a sizeable settlement. Thus the lawyer may encourage the potential plaintiff to bring the suit, and the potential plaintiff, suddenly affirmed in his grievance, may agree. An incivility can motivate the victim to gain revenge by trial.

Here's an example of how a pretty silly set of facts might strike a potential plaintiff as constituting a worthy claim. In October 1983, Irvin and Sylvia Ford sued the Valley Forge Towers Condominium Association, alleging that it had created a nuisance by placing a Dumpster outside of the suburban Philadelphia condominium building in which they lived. That lawsuit was settled in July 1985. However, universal harmony didn't ensue, as the Fords sued forty-one of their neighbors and closest friends in the condominium, alleging the intentional infliction of emotional distress and a civil conspiracy to commit that tort.[21]

The Fords claimed that the forty-one neighbors had engaged in a number of acts while the first lawsuit over the Dumpster was going on to try to make the Fords drop the suit, and, just to make the point, to punish them for bringing the suit in the first place. The Fords alleged that each of the forty-one had refused to talk to the Fords and turned their backs on them. Two spat in the Fords' direction on a couple of occasions. Several refused to shake their hands at the funeral of a mutual friend. While the first suit was pending, Ruth Isdaner "demanded to know what right plaintiffs had to sue her for $4,000 and stated that she and other people were going around to people in the condominium telling them not to speak to" the Fords. Finally, Sandra Lieberman, Sandra Klein, and Joan Blatstein told acquaintances that the Fords were suing them, so they shouldn't talk to the Fords. The plaintiffs also alleged that they had received phone calls at strange hours. The conspiracy consisted, at least in part, of some of the defendants' circulating a petition among the rest asking them all to agree to harass the Fords in the ways described. The Fords claimed that they had truly suffered, from "hypertension, anxiety, hernia, pulmonary interstitial fibrosis, anemia, tremor, fatigue and shortness of breath, duodenal ulcer, and mental depression."[22] Thus the Fords claimed that the Gang of Forty-One had by their extreme and outrageous behavior intentionally caused the Fords severe emotional distress.

The defendants moved to have this complaint, a complaint that had already been amended at that, dismissed because the allegations were too vague. The trial judge agreed and granted the motion. (This complaint, the court notes, was forty-five pages and two hundred and two paragraphs long. One wonders what specificity was lacking.) The Fords appealed. The court of appeals affirmed the ruling because, it said, the Pennsylvania Supreme Court in another case had stated that the tort of intentional infliction of emotional distress had never been adopted in Pennsylvania.[23] With no existing tort, the defendants had no tort to conspire to commit, so the conspiracy count failed too. Nevertheless, the court went on, even if Pennsylvania had adopted the tort, the Fords had failed to describe conduct outrageous enough to support a claim.

A concurring opinion disagreed with the court of appeals' reading of the supreme court precedent. This judge thought that the supreme court had only held that a plaintiff was required to present competent medical evidence of the intentional infliction of emotional distress. That disagreement aside, the concurring judge didn't believe that the Fords had alleged competent medical evidence of emotional distress. What we might find odd is both the fairly simply resolved confusion of the court of appeals on what its state supreme court had said and the finding that the sad list of medical complaints was insufficient to allege severe emotional distress.[24]

What shouldn't surprise us, however, is the majority's finding that the neighbors in this condominium had not acted particularly outrageously. If they had, then every junior high school student who ever felt aggrieved by his peers would have a good cause of action. The behavior may have been petty (and amusing), but we would be hard-pressed to find it outrageous. Nevertheless, the Fords took their case to the Pennsylvania Supreme Court, which swiftly decided to let the decision stand without comment.[25]

By the way, the Fords sold their condominium in June 1986. Though the court didn't vindicate them, they must have decided that they needn't put up with such uncivil neighbors. So much for Carter's sense of the shared values of the community.

This chapter has surveyed a number of the ways in which Americans treat each other with a profound lack of respect. The intentional infliction of severe emotional distress is a very personal tort, involving as it does another person's feelings and the studied intent of the defendant to hurt that person gravely. Given that, we would expect any humane court system to encourage the injured plaintiffs to come forward.

But our legal system is also wary of the plaintiff with his fragile feelings. So we have strict requirements for recovery. We will not punish every incivility, encouraging each other instead to toughen ourselves against the everyday irritations and annoyances. However, we are loath to allow a defendant to treat someone with extreme rudeness who he knows has a predisposition to the pain inflicted. All in all, then, the tort of intentional infliction of emotional distress is tailored to allow recovery for the worthy plaintiff.

The problem is that what finally constitutes suitably outrageous conduct, while usually defined in terms of the person of ordinary sensibilities, is generally left to the discretion of a jury, with its own predilections, prejudices, and emotions. Also, if the claim is that the plaintiff was predisposed to suffer, and the defendant knew it, as in the *Zalnis* case, the determinations of those facts are again necessarily subjective ones. So given the lack of sure guidelines and the uncertainty of how a jury will see the facts, the plaintiff cannot be assured of any outcome. The implication, of course, is that the potential defendant cannot fear certain censure. It's unclear how this cuts on two points: First, does the uncertainty necessarily keep plaintiffs from suing, or does it engender more litigation because the outraged plaintiff sees only the chance of vindication and not the chance of defeat? Second, does the defendant modify his behavior out of fear of litigation, or does the uncertainty make him less cautious?

Depending on how the actors view the law, our legal system could be accused, albeit unintentionally, of encouraging us to treat our neighbors with disrespect. Rather than come to a dispute with the requisite intention to treat our opponents respectfully, as Carter would have us do, we are allowed to behave with high devilry.

This analysis assumes, of course, that people act while knowing and considering the law. The Pearces' outrage over the Wilsons' fence, Jones's making fun of the stutterer Harris, the car dealership's attempt to intimidate Ms. Zalnis, the condo neighbors' shunning the Fords—it's safe to say that these defendants acted out of emotion and without much thought for the law at all.

Although the intentional infliction tort has arguably been crafted to be as effective as possible, once again the law does not appear to be a good tool for enforcing notions of civility that ought instead to be enforceable by respect for the other. The understanding brings us back to Stephen Carter.

Carter tells us that "we must come into the presence of our fellow human beings with a sense of awe and gratitude."[26] Only if we follow the Golden Rule—do unto others as you would have them do unto you—will we be able to reconstruct a civil world.[27] Carter admits that doing so is not easy, and, looking at these cases, it does not seem so simple an equation. Our sense of awe and gratitude ends exactly where we think that "part of God's creation," as Carter refers to individuals,[28] has begun to infringe on our rights or, in some cases, our mere desires. Thus, for a vindication of those rights or desires, we are thrown back on the law again, which, as we have seen, may not be willing to accept the task.

CHAPTER 7

Sticks and Stones Can Break Your Bones
Verbal Abuse

> Let your Conversation be without Malice
> or Envy, for 'tis a Sign of a Tractable and
> Commendable Nature: And in all Causes
> of Passion admit Reason to Govern.
>
> GEORGE WASHINGTON'S
> 58TH RULE OF CIVILITY,
> *Rules of Civility*
> *for the 21st Century*
> *from Cub and Boy Scouts*
> *from across America*

Unfortunately, the stresses of everyday life make President Washington's advice difficult to follow. Conflicts escalate; someone says something unforgivable. The shocked victim seeks recompense, because the insult, the sarcastic jab, hurts, is unnecessary, and it is certainly uncivil. And no one should have to put up with it. Yet remedies under the common law are generally not available for victims of mere verbal abuse. For instance, as we saw in the last chapter, verbal abuse seldom rises to the level of the intentional infliction of severe emotional distress. Nevertheless, the legislatures have tried to find a way to put reins on the runaway carriage of invective.

One legislative product came into play in the case of *Salvo v. Edens.*[1] In June 1956, Ms. Edens, a twenty-two-year-old married woman, went to see Dr. Salvo, a dentist practicing in Natchez, Mississippi, about her teeth. He examined her and found that she'd never had any dental care at all and had only eight teeth remaining. He proposed that he extract those, then create and insert a denture. She agreed, but, when he told her that his fee would be $100, and that he'd require a deposit, she told him that she'd have to come back later, as she didn't have the money. (By the way, she later testified that he said his fee would be only $75.) He suggested that for now he make an impression of her upper teeth. Then he could make the denture and have it ready when she was able to come back to have her last eight removed. She agreed, he took the impression, and she left, not to return for about ten months, until April 1957.

On her return, he extracted her last eight teeth and applied the denture. She looked in the mirror and saw a crack in the front with blood oozing out. She told Dr. Salvo, but he only advised her to go home and return later. She left and suffered all night from the pain, then called him in the morning to ask what he could do. According to Ms. Edens, he told her that if she didn't like the denture, she could take it out, and if she wanted to walk around "with her bottom lip touching her nose that would be all right with him, if she was that kind of people, and he thought she was that kind of people."[2] Imagine how his having said such a thing added insult to the injury he'd already inflicted. It should surprise no one that Dr. Salvo denied that the conversation ever took place. He did testify that she returned on two or three occasions for him to treat her further.

She testified, however, that her husband returned the denture to Dr. Salvo's office the very next Monday and asked what the charge would be. Dr. Salvo told him twenty dollars. Mr. Edens said that his payday wasn't until Thursday, and he'd bring the money then.

That very day, the Edenses claimed, the aptly named Dr. Salvo fired off the following round:

Mrs. B. D. Edens
Cemetery Road [This story becomes more lugubrious by the word.]
Natchez, Miss.
Dear Mrs. Edens:

I sincerely regret that you are without your denture, and your teeth. Had I suspected that you and your husband would have been satisfied with paupers' care I should have offered that to you. Had I also known that you and your husband had no aversion to your running around toothless and thereby loosing [*sic*] permanently your, until now, somewhat pleasant facial contours, I should never have suggested immediate denture service for you.

Your husband should not be blamed for his serious mistake but pitied for his understandable ignorance relative to dental care. (The seriousness of his mistake will only be fully realized at a later date.)

Since my generous offer of services (for such a negligible fee) has been so rudely declined I shall be moved nevertheless to overlook at this moment your rightful and legal indebtedness to me for denture-service as rendered to date. I shall mark it up as a profitable experience.

However, a statement of my fee for examination, diagnosis, medication, local anesthesia, and extraction of your teeth is enclosed herewith. Under the circumstances I shall appreciate prompt settlement so that we both can forget the whole matter.

Most sincerely yours,
/s/ E. W. Salvo, D.D.S.

encl. Statement Fee: $30.00
cc. Credit Assoc. Natchez Dental Society
EWS:bb[3]

Though Dr. Salvo noted a copy to the Dental Society, he didn't send one and only hoped that the reference would frighten Ms. Edens into paying his bill. When she didn't—and it's not as though his letter would have charmed her into doing so—he sued the Edenses in October 1957 for the whole $100. In December, Ms. Edens filed her own suit against Dr. Salvo, alleging libel and a violation of a Mississippi statute, then Section 1059 of the state code. The statute read, and, reenacted as Section 95-1-1, still reads in relevant part as follows: "All words which, from their usual construction and common acceptation, are considered as insults, and calculated to lead to a breach of the peace, shall be actionable."[4]

The statute was originally enacted in 1822, and its type is often referred to as an "anti-dueling statute." Its purpose was to provide a person who was insulted with a means of retribution other than challenging his tormentor to a duel or visiting some other violence on him. Instead, the offended person can bring suit under this statute. The statute is thus intended to function like the law of battery, which allows the victim of harmful or offensive contact to bring suit as an alternative to taking violent revenge. Under the anti-dueling statute, it doesn't matter whether the insulting language constitutes a true or a false statement. It's also irrelevant whether the words are spoken in anger. The language only needs to be "calculated to lead to a breach of the peace."[5]

The specific language that Ms. Edens complained of was in Dr. Salvo's letter: "Had I known that you and your husband had no aversion to your running around toothless and thereby loosing [sic] permanently your, until now, somewhat pleasant facial contours." The jury, to which the statute gives the task of determining liability, found for Ms. Edens, and Dr. Salvo appealed. (The court dismissed her libel claim, and she didn't appeal.)

The Mississippi Supreme Court disagreed with the jury, finding that the words that so bothered Ms. Edens didn't come within the reach of the statute. No doubt Dr. Salvo had written his letter in anger, but that wasn't relevant. To call her "toothless" wasn't to impute anything evil or degrading to her; he was merely calling attention to an existing condition. It might cause her embarrassment, but it wasn't calculated to lead to a breach of the peace. The court pointed out that Ms. Edens couldn't have been terribly compelled to react violently in response, as she waited seven months after receiving the letter not to breach the peace but merely to bring suit, and that, perhaps, only in response to Dr. Salvo's suit for his fee. "Toothlessness," the court concluded, "is a misfortune but not a disgrace."[6] The statute simply didn't apply to these words. Therefore, the trial court had made a mistake in allowing the jury to consider the claim at all.

So words that are simply insulting, that may merely hurt someone's feelings— words denoting disrespect—are perfectly all right as far as the statute is concerned. The short reach of the law is to words intending to provoke a breach of the peace. The law is in that way reminiscent of the tort of intentional infliction of emotional distress, for which the conduct must be outrageous, and mere insults don't qualify. Instead, the law hopes two things: one, that people will be governed by their respect for their fellow person, by etiquette and civility; and, two, that individuals who are merely insulted will shrug off any ill feelings. In refusing to reach further, the law limits itself, perhaps as Miss Manners would prefer. Unfortunately, in this case, the dentist could not restrain himself from making the gratuitous insult, and civility lost again, with no recourse under the law for Ms. Edens.

Remember Ms. Farpella-Crosby and her employment discrimination suit? The basis of her claim was that her boss had made so many offensive comments of a sexual nature as to create a hostile work environment, and that behavior gave rise to a claim for job discrimination based on sex. Because the language had been so pervasive and continuous, the court found that she'd been discriminated against.

Mr. Cariddi thought he had a similar claim based on his boss's insulting language. Cariddi was employed in the summer of 1972 by the Kansas City Chiefs of the National Football League as a supervisor of ticket takers. He had a day job as an assistant principal in the Kansas City school system. He had been hired by Mr. Wachter, the stadium director. At times Wachter referred to Cariddi as a "dago," and he referred to other Italian-American employees, perhaps in the collective, as the "Mafia." Cariddi worked the 1972–73 season and returned in the fall of 1973. Apparently, however, he ran afoul of the Chiefs' rules regarding use of the press box on game days, for the Chiefs fired him in September 1973.

He sued the Chiefs, alleging that Wachter's ethnic slurs constituted an unlawful employment practice under the law that prohibits discrimination on the basis of national origin.[7] After a trial, the judge found that Cariddi had not been discriminated against, and he appealed to the U.S. Circuit Court of Appeals for the Eighth Circuit.[8] The court had little trouble affirming the trial court. It was true, the court cautioned, that derogatory comments could in and of themselves be so excessive and offensive as to rise to the level of an unlawful employment practice. But here the trial judge had found that the derogatory ethnic comments made by Wachter were a part of casual conversation and weren't so excessive as to violate Title VII. There was also plenty of evidence that the Chiefs didn't otherwise discriminate. For crying out loud, the court nearly said, two of the Chiefs' six supervisors were Italian Americans, and Wachter had hired, on Cariddi's recommendation, eighteen ticket takers who were Italian-American. For good measure, the Chiefs also employed Cariddi's wife and daughter. Such a record didn't lead to the conclusion that the Chiefs discriminated against Cariddi on the basis of his national origin.

It's reasonable to conclude that Wachter's comments were inappropriate and offensive to Cariddi. Nevertheless, the court held that those comments weren't so pervasive and offensive—like the comments made to Farpella-Crosby—that they gave rise to a claim of employment discrimination. So the employment discrimination statute is concerned with preventing and punishing discriminatory activity in the workplace. But it is not designed to punish merely insulting language or to encourage civil speech there. As with the anti-dueling statute, the behavior has to rise to a certain level to be actionable. Below that level, civility and respect should govern, and, when they don't, the victim must endure the insults.

Anti-dueling statutes and antidiscrimination law seem inefficient vehicles by which to drive civil speech. To recover under the former requires language calculated to lead to a breach of the peace—a real duel or something like it. The latter law seeks to ensure that employment decisions are made and conditions maintained without derogation of the rights of a member of a protected class. Maintaining civil speech per se simply isn't a priority.

Miss Manners presumably believes that the force of etiquette ought to be sufficient. While she believes in the right, even the civil liberty, to be rude, she "wishes that so many people wouldn't exercise it so often."[9] Instead, she would prefer that people either decide to behave properly at any given event or take themselves away so as not to disrupt everyone else. In the rough and tumble world of everyday life, though, where the law refuses to reach, and etiquette is ignored, where do we turn?

We recall from chapter 2, in another context, Antioch College's Sexual Offense Prevention Policy (SOPP). The SOPP was an attempt to set down a quasi-law, a code of rules governing when and how students could explore and indulge their sexuality. It dealt both explicitly and implicitly with the nature and extent of respect that the students were expected to have for each other. The SOPP, then, can be said to have been an attempt to legislate respect. In much the same way, some other institutions have enacted speech codes—also quasi-laws.

The University of Pennsylvania's speech code, enacted in 1987, received national attention a few years ago. Penn's speech code attempted to legislate another manifestation of respect: the words the students used to speak of and to each other. The code made it a violation of university policy "to inflict direct injury" on someone by making a racial or ethnic insult. Those accused of doing so were charged and subject to the school's judicial process.[10]

In January 1993, a Penn freshman, Eden Jacobowitz, was studying in his room when he was interrupted by noise outside. He looked out and saw several female black students who appeared to be the source of the noise. He said that he yelled at them, "Shut up, you water buffalo, and if you're looking for a party, there's a zoo a mile from here." The women claimed that they heard him say, "Shut up, you black water buffaloes," and "Go back to the zoo where you belong."[11]

The women brought a racial harassment complaint against him under Penn's speech code. A few months later, however, they dropped it. They argued that one-sided media coverage had made a fair hearing for them impossible. Further, they claimed that Penn's system wasn't designed to protect their rights. They said that Jacobowitz had discussed the matter with the press, while they, in keeping with the code, had maintained silence. Penn's president, Sheldon Hackney, disagreed, saying that the defendant in such a case, Jacobowitz here, was allowed to speak about the case. Once he had done so, the plaintiffs could have joined in.[12] Whether that policy itself was wise, in that it allowed the adverse parties to try their case in and by the press when the school had a judicial process precisely for that purpose, is another matter.

In an editorial in the *Philadelphia Inquirer*, Deborah Leavy, the executive director of the American Civil Liberties Union of Pennsylvania, wrote that speech codes didn't address the real problem, which was not the racial epithet but the racial tension. Speech codes taught students not the usefulness of real debate or the importance of understanding other peoples, but to keep their mouths shut. She called for Penn to repeal its speech code, arguing that this case showed exactly why regulating speech was a poor way to try to improve relations among the races.[13]

Finally, in November 1993, Penn scrapped the code. It said that the school's judicial process would be replaced with a system of student-to-student talks and mediation. The new system, to be developed mainly by a committee of students, would be scheduled to be in place by the following June 30. Implicit in the announcement was that the present judicial system was immediately discontinued, and new cases would be managed through mediation. At that, a leader of

Penn's African-American Association was concerned that the African-American community wouldn't have sufficient input into developing the new policy.[14] In any event, Penn now has Guidelines on Open Expression, which seem mainly to express the sorts of reasonable time, place, and manner restrictions on public speech that are permitted under the case law developed according to the First Amendment respecting free speech. For instance, groups violate the guidelines if they "interfere unreasonably with the activities of other persons."[15]

The Jacobowitz incident illustrates Miss Manners's problem with speech codes. She notes that the professed goal of speech codes is to restrict dangerous conduct that might be provoked by offensive speech—that is, to prohibit "fighting words." But, she says, "For good reason, nobody believes this, not even those who claim it, which is why they are so easily intimidated when their own speech codes—which of course are intended to bar offensive speech—are challenged."[16]

Peck would almost certainly agree. Respect for the other doesn't come as easily as simply mandating it. One must instead, according to Peck, come to see the other as part of the same community. Once that revelation occurs, the need to regulate speech will appear ludicrous to the community members. That Peck's Foundation for Community Encouragement workshops could convince Jacobowitz and the female black students that they belonged to the same community, however, seems too much to ask.

Stephen Carter agrees with Miss Manners, and with Ms. Leavy, arguing that the solution lies not in outlawing hate speech but in applying social norms instead.[17] That is, treat the problem, not the symptoms. Hate-speech laws, he believes, are mainly further attempts to legislate civility.[18]

But *are* there situations in which a society can inform its members of a code of speech etiquette and enforce it effectively? Over the last decade, communication—business, government, personal—by electronic mail has become more and more pervasive. Scarcely fifteen years ago, it barely existed. Not surprisingly, there were no written rules immediately available. What rules, after all, would apply? E-mails aren't necessarily committed to paper, so aren't as formal. So should one start with a "Dear Sir"? Does one really have to bother with that bothersome grammar? And what if one isn't such a hot speller, well, it's only an E-mail, right? Anyone who receives E-mail regularly knows that each individual is likely to have evolved her own rules quite apart from anyone else's.

Still, somewhere along the way, some conventions—rules—began to evolve, and, in keeping with the egalitarian nature of the Internet, the people who use it are the ones promulgating them. Eventually some of the people thought it advisable to commit certain of the rules to paper, especially when adherence to the rules could make a difference. An example is the "E-Mail Etiquette Guidelines for Connecticut State Government—Version 1.0, Last Revised July 29, 1999."[19]

The Guidelines could hardly be more formal. There are two sections, "I. Guidelines for Effective E-Mail Communication" and "II. Guidelines for E-Mail Distribution Lists (LISTSERV®) and Newsgroups." Within those two sections are a number of subsections, starting from "Know Your Audience," and proceeding through composition guidelines, distribution conventions, and rules for sending attachments. Some of it sounds like common sense ("Avoid sending e-mail in anger or as an emotional response"), but some of it sounds like good warning for the unwary ("Be Aware of Copyright Restrictions"). The guidelines go on for eight pages.

For those who want a little less guidance, it's easy to find. Even one's local newspaper may run a short list of do's and don'ts.[20] Another set of practical guidelines was provided in *Information Technology Digest*.[21] Look out, the author warns, for "mixed signals," given and received because E-mail communication isn't face-to-face. The worst that can happen is that one party or the other will misunderstand and read reproach, anger, or annoyance where none was intended by an offhanded sarcastic but well-meant remark. The author notes, but doesn't endorse, the use of informal clarifiers such as "<grin>" or ":-)" to indicate good humor. Of course, not everyone understands these, and one's CEO might question the appropriateness of learning that the report she's been waiting for is going to be late—<grin>. Yet one does see these symbols in business communications.[22] To restate a theme from Mark Caldwell's *A Short History of Rudeness*, one of the problems with etiquette is that it's always changing. The smiley face that drew a frown yesterday may be returned in kind tomorrow.

Perhaps the effort to set down the rules for sending E-mails—rules that were informally understood at first—is an encouraging sign. An open society, Internet users, finds itself agreeing on the etiquette, the informal code, by which they, or most of them, agree to be bound. The rules don't carry the force of law, and they aren't part of a quasi-legal code, the violation of which will land the miscreant in a mediation facing a wronged party. Netiquette is self-government by implicit agreement to behave. To hearken back to Miss Manners, netiquette is an excellent example of how the lack of formal regulation—such as anti-dueling statutes—actually leads to more freedom. E-mail users following netiquette are free, within fairly loose bounds, to say what they wish how they wish.

Finally, though, abuse of E-mail can create problems of insulting language to which the application of netiquette isn't even the point, much less the solution. In September 1996, about sixty students of Asian descent at the University of California at Irvine received an E-mail that read as follows:

Hey stupid fucker

As you can see in the name, I hate Asians, including you. If it weren't for asias [sic] at UCI, it would be a much more popular campus. You are responsible for ALL the crimes that occur on campus. YOU are responsible for the campus being all dirt. YOU ARE RESPONSIBLE. That's why I want you and your stupid ass comrades to get the fuck out of UCI. If you don't I will hunt all of you down and Kill your stupid asses. Do you hear me? I personally will make it my life carreer [sic] to find and kill everyone one [sic] of you personally. OK?????? That's how determined I am.

Get the fuck out.

Mother Fucker (Asian Hater)[23]

The message was sent by Richard Machado, who, despite his being so determined, decided not to use his own name. His failure to do so illustrates a sad development. When one stands at a public meeting and insults another, he does it in front of a lot of people who now know who he is and what he stands for. An anonymous E-mail is another matter altogether.

However, Machado made the mistake of sending the E-mail from a university computer terminal in a lab in which a video surveillance camera recorded his actions. He apparently gave the camera plenty of opportunity to catch him at work. After he sent the messages, he logged off, then logged onto a different terminal to check for replies. When he didn't get a number sufficient to please him, he resent the message to the same group of about sixty. Now he did get a number of responses from some frightened, anxious, and angry people. Then he sent a third message, this time using his own name, but pretending to be a victim of the threat, writing, "Just keep an eye out for any suspicious person."[24]

With that video camera whirring away, the authorities had him cold. He was charged with violating a federal criminal law that reads in part

Whoever . . . by force or threat of force willfully injures, intimidates or interferes with, or attempts to injure, intimidate or interfere with—. . . (2) any person because of his race, color, religion or national origin and because he is or has been—(A) enrolling in or attending any public school or public college . . . shall be fined under this title, or imprisoned for not more than one year, or both.[25]

The law, passed in 1968, is comprehensive in prohibiting anyone from intimidating any other person due to his or her race, color, religion, or national origin from, generally speaking, attending college, applying for a job, serving as a juror, traveling interstate on the roads and rails, and staying in motels and other similar places. The clear purpose of the statute, passed with other civil rights legislation, was to ensure that the protected minorities were free from violence or threat of violence as they attempted to enjoy the fruits of American citizenship enjoyed by the white male majority.[26] The statute wouldn't quite appear to apply to Machado, as he doesn't exactly fit the stereotype of the southern redneck sheriff. Thus we can credit the U.S. attorneys involved in the case for being inventive enough to understand that the statute forbade his activities. It's also true that their inventiveness was the only means by which Machado could truly be called to account for his uncivil behavior. It is, sadly, the only law (or quasi-law) in this chapter that works to do so.

His first trial under the statute, during which he admitted sending the E-mails but said he was only bored and meant no harm, ended in a mistrial due to a hung jury.[27] (One wonders what the jury could have been confused about.) Ultimately, he was convicted on February 13, 1998, on two counts of violating the statute.[28]

Granted, the *Machado* case presents an extreme example. Most of the time, uncivil behavior rises only to the level of incivility, and not to criminality. Nevertheless, Machado's E-mails evince a true lack of respect not just for an individual but for people in general and people of Asian descent in particular. The horror is that technology enabled Machado to reach as many people as he did. Mavis Lee, an attorney prosecuting the case against Machado, was quoted as saying that she hoped that the conviction would serve as a deterrent to others who considered behaving the same way.[29] But, in part because this case is extreme, that may be naive. Machado's determination and state of mind remind us of the defendants in the intentional infliction of emotional distress cases. There, one didn't have the sense that the law would act as a deterrent to extreme behavior; the defendants weren't motivated by rational thought. Here, Machado seems truly to have been filled with such hatred that nothing would deter him, notwithstanding his defense that he'd merely been bored. The law's purpose, instead, at least for Machado, can only be to punish and give society its sense of retribution, of justice done. For the white male majority in 1968, the law clearly could work a broader deterrent effect. Nevertheless, even with respect to that white male majority, we are again left with a law's trying to stand in for society's inability to inculcate respect and tolerance for others. And again, the law may not be up to the task.

Even making allowances for the extreme case, we would appear to be left, then, almost nowhere. Efforts to legislate speech tend either to fail or to treat the wrong problem, if only because the ultimate goals or priorities of the law—the antidiscrimination statute, for instance—lie in other than promoting civility. The quasi-legal codes, such as Penn's speech code, tend to fail as well in that they fail to treat the underlying problem. We are mistaken if we look to the legal system to enforce civility in speech. Instead, we are left with the mere hope that we can treat each other with respect. The route takes us full circle; we are forced back on our etiquette-based restrictions on speech, but the failure of those restrictions is what gave life to the attempts to legislate against verbal incivility.

That's why the adherence to E-mail convention is such a hopeful sign, notwithstanding the Machados of the world. Senders and receivers of E-mails are asked to be sensitive to the impressions they're making and about the ways things are said to them. Of course, not everyone is on board, but that seems all right too. One of the rules often cited by guidelines regarding E-mails is not to be too annoyed with inexperienced E-mail users.[30] They have to learn too.

Penn's replacement of its speech code with a system for mediating disputes face-to-face with the aid of an objective third party, a mediator, also seems to be an encouraging step in the right direction. Mediation is a flexible tool that encourages each party in a particular dispute to see it from the other party's perspective. It is well suited for fact-specific matters that aren't addressed squarely by the legal system. Mediation systems can also help create a greater sense of community and connection by requiring individuals to sit down and talk. In many cases, one hopes, simple communication, aided by an objective third party, could go a long way toward resolving disagreements and, not coincidentally, teaching respect for others.

CHAPTER 8

Badgering
By Telephone, on the Street, and by Computer Chip

> November 30 . . . 7:56 P.M. A Hidden Cove
> resident reported that her ex-boyfriend
> had been harassing her by phone. The
> suspect was contacted and told to stop.
>
> "POLICE BLOTTER,"
> *Bainbridge Island (Washington) Review,*
> DECEMBER 13, 2000

We have long suffered harassment by people calling us on the phone, whether the ex-boyfriend in the quotation above, telemarketers, or people who repeatedly dial the wrong number with a stupid insistence that they have the right one. A newer form of incivility is the near-ubiquitous use of mobile phones in public places: street corners, buses, restaurants, and movie theaters. Due to the apparent lack of technical sophistication of devices requiring their users to shout, inadvertent eavesdroppers hear much more than necessary. Fortunately, of course, half of this consists of "Can you hear me? Can you hear me? CAN YOU HEAR ME NOW?" A good portion of the other half consists of conversations of the most private sort. One of the authors is unhappy to report that he knows all about the breakup of a marriage in Bremerton, Washington, due to the wife's unfaithfulness as reported by her friend on the Bainbridge Island ferry. Both authors are even more unhappy to report that lawyers routinely shout what must be confidential, attorney-client privileged (well, till then it was) information into their phones on the same ferry. Envy Queen Elizabeth: She has simply banned their use. A royal source was quoted as saying, "It is fair to say the queen was not amused when the phones started ringing incessantly."[1]

As Mark Caldwell points out in *A Short History of Rudeness*, circumstances and etiquette change.[2] There was a time when telephone conversations were held on neighborhood-wide party lines. The explicit etiquette was that one didn't listen in; the implicit understanding was that eavesdroppers did, but they were rude and nosy people. What's changed is that now unintentional eavesdroppers don't want to hear any mobile communications and are annoyed by the chirping interruption of the phones' ringing, but the people using the phones remain cheerfully unaware of their rudeness. Or do they? The sad possibility is, pointing back to Carter, that some cell phone users don't respect anyone else's right not to be bothered. They either simply don't care or have managed to convince themselves that the increase in productivity occasioned by being available all of the time outweighs anyone else's discomfort.

In any event, such nerve-jangling use of mobile phones in public may remind us of the *Cifarelli* case, in which Mr. Jacobs persuaded the State of New York to prosecute Mr. Cifarelli the drummer as a public nuisance. Had Cifarelli been convicted, it would have been of violating a criminal statute. Those of us bothered by the use of mobile phones may wish that we could get such public chattering condemned as well.

So we might stop at this point to ask, is the criminal law, with its very direct sets of penalties, perhaps better suited to enforce civility?

On sunny days the Chesapeake Bay gleams bright blue, and the parti-colored sails of the bobbing sailboats flap and soar like the wings of exotic birds. Entrancing is the view from the Chesapeake Bay Bridge, which connects Maryland's rustic Eastern Shore with the bustling western side near Annapolis. At the top of the bridge, one can imagine what the bay was like before Europeans busily intruded: silent and empty, a broad expanse of blue. It is a serene vision indeed that became horribly disturbed, at least for Mr. Richard von Lusch.

He lived in a house and ran an antique shop just north of U.S. Highway 50/301, which runs through Maryland's Eastern Shore, across the Chesapeake Bay Bridge, and west to Washington, D.C. On the Eastern Shore, a half mile east of the Bay Bridge, near Stevensville in Queen Anne's County, sat the Bay Bridge Airport.

When Queen Anne's county commissioners adopted a comprehensive zoning ordinance in 1964, they neglected to provide adequately for airports and landing strips. Some time later, a private group began operating the Bay Bridge Airport. Apparently, realizing that the land—which had been zoned M1, industrial park, for light manufacturing and agricultural uses—had not been zoned for an airport, the Board of County Commissioners amended the zoning ordinance. The amendment, in essence, legitimized the existing airport.

Von Lusch despised the airport with its insistently buzzing planes. When the board passed its amendment, von Lusch fought the decision bitterly, even litigating it into the Maryland Court of Appeals. He managed to have the board's amendment struck down on procedural grounds.[3] Eventually, however, the board got things right and its amendment to the zoning ordinance was upheld.[4] The airport could continue to operate.

But von Lusch couldn't tolerate the noise. On Sunday, May 5, 1974, he decided to complain to Mr. Julius Grollman, one of the county commissioners. At a trial that arose out of these events, the evidence was that von Lusch had called Grollman forty-three times that day to announce the time and yell, "Flight overhead!" There was also evidence that von Lusch knew that Grollman had a heart condition, and was trying to wear him down.

The next Saturday, May 11, von Lusch called Grollman fourteen times in the space of twenty-five minutes. On this second occasion, Grollman was attending to the general merchandise store that adjoined his home. Von Lusch complained that Grollman would hang up at the sound of his voice, or, if he did stay on the line, wouldn't listen to him and wouldn't answer his questions, which had to do with why the board wouldn't enforce the zoning laws. It's unclear from the record what law von Lusch thought was being violated.

Grollman, on the other hand, testified that on May 11 his store was open for business, and, when he realized that the caller was the persistent von Lusch, he hung up because he had customers to take care of. Even so, some left when he attended to the phone. Grollman testified that von Lusch was the one being rude, speaking in a loud and arrogant tone about the airplanes. Von Lusch claimed that their flying over his business was a trespass. Grollman said that it was von Lusch who was hanging up before Grollman could answer any questions.

All of this testimony was admitted in the criminal trial of von Lusch. He was eventually convicted of Section 555A of Article 27 of the Maryland criminal code.

We should stop to note the important differences between the civil common law and criminal law. One difference is in how we know what the law is. Civil common law often isn't codified in a state's statutes but is stated in the long history of the state's case law. Criminal law, however, is always as clearly written as possible in the state's statutes. As a constitutional matter, someone who may be charged with a crime must have it in black and white what the crime is. Another very important difference is that a plaintiff in a civil suit only needs to prove her case by a preponderance of the evidence—that her claims are more likely than not true. In a criminal action, the state must prove beyond a reasonable doubt that the defendant broke the law. This is, of course, a much higher standard to meet, and one that society insists on because of a final difference: While a defeated civil defendant may only have to pay monetary damages, the convicted criminal defendant may have to go to jail.

Back to von Lusch. The section of the Maryland criminal code in question provides that it is "unlawful for any person to make use of telephone facilities or equipment . . . for repeated calls, if with intent to annoy, abuse, torment, harass, or embarrass one or more persons."[5] Von Lusch was subject to a fine of up to $500 or imprisonment for up to three years, or perhaps both if the court thought it appropriate. In the end, he was sentenced to jail for three months on four different counts. The court suspended the sentence and placed von Lusch on probation for three years. He was also fined $500 on each count.

Von Lusch appealed to the Maryland Court of Special Appeals, which upheld the conviction.[6] Convinced that the trial judge had admitted evidence that he shouldn't have, among other points, von Lusch sought review by the court next up in the hierarchy, the Maryland Court of Appeals. It was more sympathetic and reversed the convictions.[7] The reversal was grounded on procedural matters, not on the facts, so the state was able to try von Lusch again, and again he was convicted. (We needn't get into the niceties of double jeopardy, but, suffice it to say that the general rule is that once a jury is impaneled, a criminal defendant may not be tried for the same crime again.) Again he appealed; again, the court of special appeals upheld the convictions.[8] There is no record that von Lusch appealed his conviction again.

At issue in the appeals was the language of the statute. For von Lusch to be convicted of a violation, he had to have made his phone calls "with intent to annoy, abuse, torment, harass or embarrass." Von Lusch argued that he had had more in mind than annoying people. He was out to rectify the wrong committed against him. The airport was operating illegally, he claimed, and he certainly had a right to bring that to the attention of Grollman, a county commissioner. Grollman had listened to his questions, he said, but had never answered them. Presumably, then, based on his version of the facts, von Lusch had the right to continue to call until his legitimate questions were answered.

But Grollman's testimony had been quite different. Because von Lusch would hang up before Grollman had a chance to answer, it was possible that von Lusch wasn't really interested in an answer. Grollman felt justified, then, in hanging up at the sound of von Lusch's voice, especially when he had customers in the store. Further, Grollman testified, von Lusch had never sought to meet with him as a county commissioner, and he had never asked for a chance to appear to argue to the county commission.

Of course, the court noted in one of the early appeals, if one holds public office, one has to expect to receive complaints, including angry phone calls. However, if von Lusch were making those calls with the required intent—to annoy, abuse, torment, harass, or embarrass—then it wouldn't matter that Grollman was a public official. A crime is a crime, and anyone can be a victim.[9] Other victims, by the way, included a number of airport personnel, though von Lusch was not convicted of calls he made to the airport. Still, he followed the same pattern with them: calling repeatedly, complaining of airplanes' flying too close to his house, and hanging up before anyone could speak. He also promised the people he called that he would tie up their phones all day.

Intent, the court noted, can't often be proven directly. How does one know what exactly is going on in someone else's head? Instead, we have to prove it by inferring thought from action. The court said that there were plenty of facts from which a jury could find that von Lusch had the intent to annoy or harass the people he was calling. Eventually, after two trials and three appeals, his conviction was upheld.

What we had, then, was a time-consuming and expensive lot of hoo-ha about calling an adversary on the phone over and over again. Von Lusch justified his adolescent use of the phone as a means to vindicate his property rights. The cases make embarrassing reading, yet the court seems at worst amused:

> The appellant, Richard von Lusch, felt aggrieved by a form of nuisance wrought initially by Orville and Wilbur Wright but inflicted ultimately upon him as traffic in and out of a local airport flew low over his Queen Anne's County home. The redress he sought, unfortunately, was by way of invoking another nuisance wrought initially by Alexander Graham Bell and inflicted ultimately upon Julius Grollman, a neighbor of the appellant and a Queen Anne's County Commissioner responsible in part for the presence of the airport which was the source of the appellant's chagrin.[10]

This court also indulged each of von Lusch's counsel's arguments, though it is possible to dismiss them easily. For instance, von Lusch tried to argue that the statute required that his *sole* intent be to annoy, harass, and so on. He cited cases that held to that effect. The court noted, however, that those cases had arisen under a different, federal statute that required that the actor's sole intent be to annoy or harass. The word "sole" didn't appear in the Maryland statute. So it didn't matter for purposes of the Maryland law whether von Lusch had another motive in mind, that is, calling to urge that some law be enforced, as long as he also had the intent to annoy, harass, and so on. (Did counsel not notice the absence of the word "sole" in Maryland's statute, or did counsel hope that the court wouldn't?)

This case, then, is an example of how far our system will allow people to push their rights. Despite von Lusch's methods, he apparently had right at least partly on his side, for in two of the five reported opinions, von Lusch won. He forced the board to go back and start over on its ordinance amendment, and he convinced the court of appeals to reverse his first conviction. His rights were at least partly and temporarily vindicated.

However, with respect to the criminal case, anyway, it boils down to a conviction for an uncivil act bordering on the juvenile. After the age of seven or nine, most people give up telephone games as a means of making mischief. Despite von Lusch's evident incivility, however, the courts looked carefully and considered all of the arguments before convicting him of a crime. The courts' deliberations were appropriate; in the meantime, the civil disobedience became very uncivil indeed.

The statute under which von Lusch probably wished he had been prosecuted was enacted in Massachusetts; the 1991 case of *Commonwealth v. Strahan* demonstrated its workings.[11] Strahan had been engaged in an off-again, on-again relationship with a woman. When they fell out, and she tried to break it off, he would call her frequently, trying to induce her to change her mind. Until the events described in this case occurred, the strategy had worked.

One night after they had parted ways again, the woman heard noises from outside the building and asked a friend to help her find out what was going on. The friend found Strahan outside, shouting and throwing an outdoor chair around. The friend told Strahan to leave, but he refused. The friend shut the door to the apartment and called the police, but Strahan opened the door and came inside. Why the friend hadn't locked the door is a mystery, though of course Strahan may have had a key. In any event, the friend kicked him in the stomach, which did convince him to leave. Even so, Strahan managed to engage the woman's housemate (evidently someone other than the friend) in conversation, an exchange that probably didn't calm any nerves.

The next morning, Strahan called his still-ex girlfriend approximately eleven times in seven minutes. The woman testified that Strahan told her that he only wanted to speak with her. He also left four or five messages on her answering machine.

The Commonwealth prosecuted Strahan under Massachusetts's version of a telephone abuse statute: "Whoever telephones another person, or causes any person to be telephoned, repeatedly, for the *sole* purpose of harassing, annoying or molesting such person or his family, whether or not conversation ensues . . .

shall be punished"[12] (emphasis added). At the close of trial, Strahan was convicted of having violated the statute. He appealed, arguing that no one could find beyond a reasonable doubt that the sole purpose of his telephone calls was to harass or annoy.

The Massachusetts Court of Appeals focused on the word von Lusch's counsel had so desired to bolster his argument: "sole."[13] The court concluded that the Massachusetts legislature had chosen to include the word to avoid any constitutional challenges based on the argument that the statute would criminalize all sorts of speech that had socially useful functions but that also had the tendency to harass or annoy. The legislature, the court said, didn't want a statute that would "criminalize the normal risks of unpleasant human intercourse emanating from neighborhood feuds, romantic rumbles, [or] family fall-outs."[14] So unless Strahan had called the woman with the sole intention of harassing or annoying her, he could not be convicted under the Massachusetts statute.

Looking at the facts, it seems an easy call. Strahan and the woman had established a course of courtship: She would break it off, and he would call up imploring her to give him another chance, and they would get together. Of course, he did make those eleven calls in seven minutes, but the calls may well have been motivated, *at least in part,* by Strahan's desire to make contact and get back together with her. That possibility, no matter how small, saves Strahan—his sole purpose was not, beyond a reasonable doubt, annoyance. Conviction reversed.

Once again, this time in the criminal law context, we see a law that tries to allow for those everyday annoyances of "unpleasant human intercourse." People must, to some extent, develop a tough hide and tolerate unpleasantness. The judge-made torts of nuisance and the intentional infliction of severe emotional distress have this feature in common with these telephone abuse statutes. Further, of course, society doesn't lightly stigmatize one as a criminal.

However, as a result, civility gains no ground. To boil down the facts: A man throws a chair around outside and argues with his ex-girlfriend's friend, prompting the friend to kick him in the stomach. The next day he makes eleven phone calls in seven minutes and leaves messages on an answering machine. For good reasons, no doubt, the court never tells us the girlfriend's name, but this fact seems emblematic. She and the respect that she ought to have been accorded are lost altogether; she becomes merely a cardboard character in this sordid play, during the last scene of which her tormentor must be acquitted.

A final note on this case: Our society's interest in encouraging free expression wins out over worries about incivility. The court had surmised that the Massachusetts legislature had included "sole" in order to fend off constitutional challenges. That is, without "sole," the statute might have been said to proscribe speech that is socially useful or at least neutral and not solely intended to harass. The First Amendment to the U.S. Constitution would arguably prohibit such a law. If the legislature had simply prohibited speech that might have tended to harass or annoy, it might have prohibited protected speech, such as that which expresses an unpopular political opinion. In this case, protecting Strahan's interest in exercising his free speech rights may seem a farfetched reason for his acquittal, but the point certainly underlies the court's analysis.

Incidentally, as we recall, von Lusch had tried to argue that, without "sole," Maryland's statute was unconstitutional because it would tend to prohibit protected free speech. The Maryland Court of Special Appeals rejected the argument, concluding that the "freedom of speech does not encompass the right to abuse the telephone with the specific intent to annoy and to harass the recipient of the call."[15] Thus, the extent to which the First Amendment requires us to tolerate such uncivil speech is a matter of some debate, at least among the legislatures and courts of Maryland and Massachusetts.

Von Lusch might be excused for looking enviously as well at the experience of a Mr. Caldwell. He, too, was convicted by a Maryland trial court under the same statute as von Lusch, and he, too, appealed. The complainant was a Ms. Breeding. At ten in the morning on January 16, 1974, she received a phone call at her job at the Caroline Nursing Home. As the Maryland Court of Appeals felt it important to quote Breeding's testimony, so shall we, in part, for to some extent it demonstrates that Ms. Breeding is her own worst advocate:

Q. And what was the substance of that conversation?

A. Well, it was a gentleman caller and he was calling to try to pick me up. In other words, he was saying that he would like to meet up with me and that he would meet up with me or talk to me before the day was over and he gave me all the information about hisself and I thought it was a joke. I thought it was somebody playing a prank on me and I was just . . . I just kept talking to him to try to find out who it was and he wouldn't give me his name. All he would say was "It was Jim."

Q. And how long did this conversation take, would you say?

A. Well, I kept on talking. I couldn't get rid of him. He kept talking and we had a new admission that came in at approximately eleven o'clock and then I did hang up, because the new admission I had to admit. . . . He wouldn't tell me who it was. He said that if I knew who it was that I would probably wouldn't want [as in original] anything to do with him and he just kept talking and talking and it was really very disturbing and upsetting because I didn't know who I was talking to.

Q. What other information, if any, did the caller give that indicated he knew your habits and whereabouts?

A. Well he said that he knew that I had a green Oldsmobile and that he had . . .
he knew that I worked out at the nursing home because he had asked his employees.
One of his employees knew me and he had asked his employee who I was and where
I worked; and he also told me that he had been by my house many times. He knew
exactly where I lived and he had been by there and looked it over many times, which
upset me quite a bit. . . . He said he could not find my phone number in the book
because he did not know my husband's name. . . . He said he had asked one of his
employee's [*sic*] who I was and where I worked so that he could get in touch with me.
. . . After two or three times who it was [*sic*] and he then said his name was Jim and I
said "Jim who?" and he would not give me his last name because he said if I knew
who it was that I would not talk with him anymore and I told him that I did not
particularly care to talk to anybody that I did not know anyway and he kept right on
talking and saying that he would either meet with me or call me again before my
quitting time. . . . Other than that he just kept saying that he wanted to meet up with
me and I asked him if he was having troubles with his wife or something.[16]

A corroborating witness, Wanda Lane, said that the first telephone conversation,
which did terminate when a new admission arrived, lasted between forty-five
minutes and an hour. A half hour later, a man walked through the nursing home
carrying a briefcase. He smiled at Breeding and left, then called her again to say
that she had now seen him and couldn't deny it. She testified that she told him
not to call her again.

Lynn Clark, a part-time receptionist at the nursing home and Wanda Lane's
daughter, polled her friends at school the next day and calculated that the mystery caller was Caldwell. (Several years earlier, he had called Lynn Clark to ask
her out and had spoken to her on the street.) The next day, Lane called Caldwell's
house, spoke to him, and he confirmed that he was James Caldwell.

At his trial, he denied making the two calls to Breeding but admitted receiving
the call from Lane, which prompted him to drive to the police station immediately to complain. His wife and business associate testified with alibis for the
times when Breeding said that she'd received calls from him.

Based on all of this evidence, the trial judge found Caldwell guilty of a violation of the statute prohibiting unlawful telephone calls made with the intent to
annoy, abuse, torment, harass, or embarrass. Caldwell appealed.

The Maryland Court of Special Appeals disagreed with the trial judge.[17] That
judge had said that "whether or not he made [the telephone calls] with intent to
harass and annoy her I don't think makes any difference because I think the
effect of it was."[18] That, the court of special appeals said, was the wrong approach. It made exactly all the difference whether he made the calls *with the
intent* to harass or annoy. (The rule requiring intent to commit a crime is pretty

much the point of what one learns in criminal law class in the first year of law school. That judges sometimes don't follow the rules is what one learns the first year in law practice.) In fact, the state must prove beyond a reasonable doubt that Caldwell had the requisite intent. That intent, as we saw above, can be inferred from the facts in appropriate cases.

Even if Caldwell made the calls (remember there were alibis), they did not amount to a large number over a small certain period, and, after Breeding told him not to call anymore, he didn't, though he certainly had the opportunity. His intent, from Breeding's own testimony, was to make contact with her and convince her to meet him. The conversation quoted in the testimony sounds flirtatious and perhaps a little silly, but Breeding did allow it to go on for up to an hour and kept up her end of the conversation, asking Caldwell about his wife, for instance. Her real remedy would have been simply to hang up, which she didn't do until her job (the arrival of the new patient) forced her off the phone.

Finally, the trial judge relied on the calls to Clark several years earlier from which to infer the requisite intent to annoy Breeding. The court of special appeals disagreed again; Caldwell was only trying to make a date with Clark, he was rebuffed, and there was no testimony from Clark that Caldwell's intent had been to annoy or harass her.

In short, the court didn't think that the facts added up to a case in which the state had proven beyond a reasonable doubt that Caldwell had intended to make a pain of himself over the phone. The court hastened to add that it was certain that Breeding was truly, extremely upset, as she had testified, but that fact standing alone wouldn't create intent on Caldwell's part. The conviction was reversed.

Here, then, is a case with a victim, of sorts, but no criminal. Our laws and courts are designed to take the utmost care not to convict and thus stamp as a criminal someone who hasn't committed a crime. Despite the anguish Breeding had suffered, and on which the trial judge had focused, Caldwell's case is an easy one, given the testimony. He had simply committed no crime.

The facts suggest another problem, though. Breeding testified that Caldwell had admitted that he knew where she lived and had driven by her house many times and that this knowledge upset her. Had Breeding known that it was Caldwell who was wandering around the nursing home grinning at her, what further fright might she have felt? Shouldn't she be protected against that sort of behavior?

Maryland tried to address those situations in two statutes, both enacted after the *Caldwell* case and so of no help to Breeding. First is its anti-stalking statute, which reads in part:

(3) "Stalking" means a malicious course of conduct that includes approaching or pursuing another person with intent to place that person in reasonable fear: (i) Of serious bodily injury or death.[19]

Maryland also has an anti-harassment statute, which reads in part:

(c) Prohibited conduct.—A person may not follow another person in or about a public place or maliciously engage in a course of conduct that alarms or seriously annoys another person: (1) With intent to harass, alarm, or annoy the other person; (2) After reasonable warning or request to desist by or on behalf of the other person; and (3) Without a legal purpose.[20]

Unfortunately, the criminal justice system is presented with real difficulties in enforcing laws like the anti-stalking and anti-harassment laws. *Pall v. State*, another case out of Maryland, is an example.[21] (Note that all but one of the cases in this chapter come out of Maryland. The authors don't think Maryland a particularly uncivil place—indeed, some of the defendants are acquitted—but believe that it's useful to compare different sorts of facts under the same law.) Mr. Pall was charged under the anti-harassment statute.

Ms. Etman claimed that Mr. Pall had followed her on May 16, 1996, in a store in Gaithersburg, Maryland. Frightened, she asked an employee of the store to escort her to her car. Then on July 2, 1996, she again saw Mr. Pall seeming to follow her in the Congressional Shopping Center in Rockville. She phoned the police, who arrived and told Pall to cease having any contact with Etman. In fact, the police said, if he saw her again, he was simply to turn the other way. Finally, on July 20, Etman saw Pall again in a Giant grocery store in Rockville. She immediately found a store employee, who took her into a back office where she called the police. By the time the police arrived, Pall had vanished.

Pall was charged and convicted of two counts under the harassment statute, and he appealed. The court of special appeals reversed the conviction. To be found guilty, the court said, Pall would have to have contacted her "(2) After reasonable warning or request to desist by or on behalf of the other person." At the first incident in Gaithersburg, if he had seen someone escort her to her car, then maybe he could have surmised that she didn't want him hanging around her. But there wasn't even any evidence that he saw her escorted away, much less that he intuited that he was the reason for the escort. Even if he had, was that a "reasonable warning" on which to base a criminal conviction? We've already seen in the other cases in this chapter how careful the courts are to require strict proof of the elements of the proscribed conduct before convicting someone of it.

The only real warning Pall received was from the police after the second incident, the one at the Congressional Shopping Center in Rockville. Therefore, the conviction had to have been based on Pall's third contact with Etman at the Giant grocery store. The problem was, the court found, that there was precious little evidence of that third contact. Etman herself testified that as soon as she saw Pall she hightailed it off to find a store employee. The only evidence was that he was shopping at the Giant store, turned a corner, and saw her. That he had vanished by the time the police arrived could very easily be taken as his compliance with the order to leave her alone. He was not required, the court nearly said, to chase after her to tell her not to be afraid, that he was leaving now. He appears simply to have left. The court therefore reversed the conviction.

The outcome of this case indicates how difficult it is for the criminal law to control activities that society has deemed uncivil enough to prohibit, such as harassment. There's no real basis for speculating that Pall's behavior violated the statute, as the court ultimately found. But assume another situation with another person. Under the statute, an Etman needn't actually call the police to administer the warning. She could do it herself. But proving that warning in a criminal case would be a lot more difficult than if the police had given it—the testimony would simply be Etman's word against Pall's. Further, an Etman might not feel safe in administering the warning herself. Someone being harassed must, as a practical matter, involve the police. Then, once the warning has been given, someone truly bent on harassing his victim—and perhaps even more so in revenge—will simply do so with more prudent stealth. Pall may very well have left the Giant store voluntarily, anguished by the bad fortune of an incidental meeting. But one bent on trouble could make the same easy getaway and obtain the same result in court. So the anti-stalking and anti-harassing statutes exist, but they appear to be of little help in preventing the uncivil behavior that they contemplate, except in the extreme case.

And the next, sad step: In 1996, Gary Dellapenta, a fifty-year-old security guard in Los Angeles, met a twenty-eight-year-old woman in church. Apparently finding her attractive, he tried to start up a romance, approaching her a number of times and sending her flowers and cards. She wasn't interested and told him so, even writing him a letter to that effect. But he wouldn't back down and continued his aggressive ways until she finally complained to the church elders. They banned Dellapenta from their congregation.[22]

Then, in April 1998, Dellapenta began to take his revenge. He started to post personal ads in her name on the Internet, on sites such as America Online and Microsoft's Hotmail. When men responded to the ads, Dellapenta answered them, saying "she" was "into rape fantasy and gang-bang fantasy." He told a number of men everything: her address, her physical description, and her phone number.[23]

Men began to appear at her door—six of them within a short period. The victim was mystified. She didn't even own a computer. So how was she being targeted by all of these people? Worse, how did they get the idea that she wanted to be raped? When she found out about the personal ads, she posted a sign on her apartment door saying that they were fake.[24]

When Dellapenta discovered that, he began e-mailing ad respondents that the note on the door was only part of the fantasy; she wanted to be taken by force. To aid in that goal, he even offered to provide instructions on how to foil her security lock. Being a security guard, he apparently knew how.[25]

Finally, investigators from the FBI, the district attorney's office, and the Los Angeles Sheriff's Department, with the help of the woman's father, who posed as an ad respondent, tracked Dellapenta down. They copied the ads and E-mails and then obtained records from the Internet service providers on whose sites the ads had been posted. Finally they discovered his identity, and he was arrested. He was ordered to stand trial on charges of computer fraud, solicitation of sexual assault, and stalking.[26]

The last charge, with respect to stalking by computer—cyberstalking—was new under California law. As amended, the law punishes someone who "willfully, maliciously, and repeatedly follows or willfully and maliciously harasses another person and who makes a credible threat with the intent to place that person in reasonable fear for his or her safety."[27] A "credible threat" is a "verbal or written [*sic*] threat implied by a pattern of conduct or a combination of verbal, written [*sic*], or electronically communicated statements and conduct."[28] And we can guess the last step, added by the recent amendment: "electronically communicated" includes by computer.[29]

Dellapenta was sunk, and he eventually pleaded guilty. The judge gave him the maximum sentence, six years in prison.[30]

For the record, the bill that amended the criminal stalking law also amended California's Civil Code to make cyberstalking a tort for which the victim could recover both general and punitive damages.[31] (Here is an example of civil law being codified in a statute. As we have noted, not all civil law is common law; remember the employment discrimination statutes.) There is no indication that the victim in the Dellapenta case has sued him, and why bother? At the time, he was living with his eighty-year-old mother and likely had few assets to pursue. Anyway, the victim has the satisfaction and security of knowing that he had gone to jail.

The facts of this case are truly awful. Dellapenta was quoted as saying that he had an "inner rage" against his victim that led him to behave as he did.[32] But it's just no excuse for the utter lack of respect that he had for his victim's feelings and privacy and the threat that he created to her safety. She probably counts herself very lucky indeed that she didn't encounter someone else who had other awful fantasies to act out.[33] We have, in any event, come very far from the young man whom Miss Manners described earlier: the one who, receiving a negative response to a romantic gambit, recoils in embarrassment, never to bother the young woman again. At the core of Dellapenta's behavior, of course, is a profound lack of respect for the other person, "inner rage" notwithstanding.

It is at least as difficult to enforce appropriate behavior under the criminal justice system as under the civil system, for, as we noted earlier, the state must prove beyond a reasonable doubt that a person charged with a crime actually committed it. In tort law, the plaintiff need only prove his case by a preponderance of the evidence—that is, show it's more likely than not that he suffered damages. Criminals generally must be shown to have criminal intent, which, although it can be inferred from their behavior, is still difficult to prove. Furthermore, we see the courts in these cases bending over backwards to make sure that the criminal defendants are afforded every opportunity for exoneration. Finally, as the telephone statutes especially bear on free speech issues, they must be written narrowly to avoid violating First Amendment rights.

Should the state have been put to all of this trouble in these cases? Again, we see persons behaving in ways that ought to be governed by simple rules of etiquette and respect. One man calls a public official over and over again to tie up his phone and his time. Another badgers a former girlfriend in his hope for reconciliation, and another calls to propose a meeting of questionable purpose. The common courtesy and respect with which we ought to treat each other should have prevented or at least moderated these folks' behavior, even if that behavior didn't rise to the level of a criminal act, as in Mr. Strahan's and Mr. Caldwell's cases. The stalking and harassment statutes were written to address a situation so simple as one in which one person follows another around specifically to threaten or annoy; it's worse than rude to follow people around to scare them. In the last few years, those statutes have had to be amended to take into account the same sort of rudeness acted out in another venue, the cyber world. But it's the same old incivility: badgering someone needlessly.

The interesting irony is that this latest manifestation, cyberstalking, is in some cases easier to prove than the stalking that takes place on the street. Whereas a person like a Caldwell can quickly drive away, or someone like a Pall can duck out the grocery door, the cyberstalker leaves more indelible tracks, such as those of Dellapenta's that the police found. While Dellapenta's behavior is dismaying, at least the law was able to catch and punish him.

Aside from Dellapenta's "inner rage," however, which seems to spring from a much scarier impulse, these are situations that Miss Manners might consider properly beyond the scope of the law. Adhering to society's expectations for telephone use—mere etiquette—would minimize the need for the telephone-abuse statutes. Respect for another's peace of mind on the street ought to mean that we don't need anti-stalking and anti-harassment statutes. However, the actors in this chapter are motivated by forces stronger than the desire to adhere to society's rules of etiquette. Because the behavior is all too common, the law must step in, sometimes unsuccessfully, where it is ill suited to intervene. And the criminal law, unfortunately, is no better match for this poor behavior than the civil law.

CHAPTER 9

Nasty Words
Blasphemy, Obscenity, and Cursing

> Use no Reproachfull Language against
> any one neither Curse nor Revile.
>
> GEORGE WASHINGTON'S
> 49TH RULE OF CIVILITY,
> *Rules of Civility*
> *for the 21st Century*
> *from the Cub and Boy Scouts*
> *from across America*

In the nation's distant past, some state legislatures banned another kind of speech they found objectionable: blasphemy. For example, Maryland's criminal statute read as follows:

> If any person, by writing or speaking, shall blaspheme or curse God, or shall write or utter any profane words of and concerning our Saviour Jesus Christ, or of and concerning the Trinity, or any of the persons thereof, he shall on conviction be fined not more than one hundred dollars, or imprisoned not more than six months, or both fined and imprisoned as aforesaid, at the discretion of the court.[1]

Mr. West was convicted of having violated the statute. It's really a shame that the opinion of the court is silent on the facts. All we know is that West was convicted of blasphemy, disorderly conduct, and resisting arrest. He doesn't appear to have appealed the other convictions, so it sounds as if he had been acting unruly, an officer of the law tried to arrest him, and he took vocal and physical issue with the process. In a post-conviction motion, West argued that the statute was unconstitutional. The trial judge agreed with him and set aside his conviction. The State of Maryland appealed this judge's ruling to the Maryland Court of Special Appeals, which decided the case in 1970.[2]

The origins of the statute, the court noted, go back three hundred years. The language has remained remarkably the same, though the punishment has changed. In 1723, before there was a U.S. Constitution or even a United States, the statute was amended to provide that, upon conviction for the first offense, one would be "bored through the tongue"; for the second offense, one would be "stigmatized by burning in the forehead with the letter B"; and, finally, Maryland imposed a three-strikes-and-you're-out penalty enough to give any miscreant prone to cussing serious pause: He would "suffer death without the benefit of the clergy."[3] The purpose of this statute, said the court, was to "preserve the sanctity of the Christian religion; and the sanctions invoked by the statute demonstrate the depth and earnestness of [the statute's drafters'] feelings toward the Christian religion."[4]

But the drafters of the Constitution had another priority. The First Amendment states in part that "Congress shall make no law respecting an establishment of religion, or prohibiting the free exercise thereof."[5] It is commonly understood that while the majority may profess one brand of religion, and Americans may think of themselves as a religious people, the Constitution's authors were acutely aware of the dangers of forcing anyone to profess a belief in one faith. So what has become known as the Establishment Clause ("Congress shall make no law respecting an establishment of religion") prohibits the support of one or another religion by the state, and the Free Exercise Clause ("or prohibiting the free exercise thereof") guarantees the right of each individual to practice her faith free of coercion by the state.

The trial judge in West's case had found that the statute empowered the state to arrest and jail persons speaking out against Christianity. Therefore, Maryland's statute violated the Establishment Clause by providing protection to the Christian religion, thereby establishing it as a favored denomination.

On appeal, the state argued that the statute, originally written in aid and support of Christianity, had secular purposes. The state could help citizens to worship unbothered by speech they would find offensive. Also, there are few subjects about which individuals have such strong emotions as religion. The state argued that blasphemous speech could incite the wrath of a churchgoer outraged enough by such language. Thus persons speaking blasphemously threatened the public peace.

The Court of Special Appeals disagreed. One had to read a lot into the statute to find those purposes. It didn't say anything about a breach of the peace; instead, it went a lot further, prohibiting Mr. West from blaspheming at all, even if he were all alone in his room. Finally, the plain, obvious purpose of the statute was to protect and preserve the Christian religion. The Establishment Clause forbade any state from protecting Christianity or any other religion. The state's position regarding any and all faiths must be neutral. This statute violated that rule, and thus it was unconstitutional.

The outcome in this case was plainly correct. One wonders why, as late as 1970, the State of Maryland even bothered trying to enforce the statute. (Maybe Mr. West put up a helluva fight, and the state was just annoyed with him.) The court was simply fixing a state of affairs that had originated before the Constitution was enacted. The statute was struck down, and Mr. West was acquitted.

In the process, of course, the holding doesn't do much to discourage uncivil speech. But Miss Manners would probably say that we shouldn't need the statute anyway. People living side by side should respect each other's beliefs sufficiently that mere etiquette should cause us to keep our mouths shut. If religion is one matter about which people become most exercised, then we should understand that others can easily become offended by the wrong words and we should avoid speaking them.

Though prohibiting blasphemy is unconstitutional, simply relying on people to behave well when they have become emotional or upset, however, seems a losing proposition. One of the problems of human nature revealed by the cases in this book is that people can't seem to resist bedeviling each other. In the battery chapter, Hough kept at Mooningham, the electrician, until the latter bashed him with a shovel. The Hays had to have their fences; the Stevenses abhorred them. In the intentional infliction chapter, Jones couldn't stop making fun of Harris's stutter. Add the presence of anger or frustration to a difficult situation, along with an absence of respect for another's feelings, and reliance on etiquette simply isn't enough. Yet here the law is obviously, and quite rightly under the Constitution, powerless to do anything about it.

While it's pretty clear that the state can't regulate blasphemy, what it may do about obscenity is a much tougher issue. Take, for instance, the case of Mr. Baker, a truck driver in Alabama who was annoyed by a campaign to monitor truck drivers' behavior on the road. His specific gripe was with bumper stickers on trucks reading, "How's My Driving? Call 1-800-2-Advise," by which motorists were encouraged to snitch on truckers who drove offensively. To illustrate his annoyance, the next time he was in Panama City, Florida, sometime in September 1987, he picked up a bumper sticker that read, "How's My Driving? Call 1-800-Eat Shit." He stuck it on his back bumper and kept on truckin'.

Unfortunately for Baker, Officer Glover of the Alabama State Highway Patrol caught a glimpse of it. He believed that it violated an Alabama statute that read, "It shall be unlawful for any person to display in public any bumper sticker, sign, or writing which depicts obscene language descriptive of sexual or excretory functions."[6] He stopped Mr. Baker on Highway 231 outside of Dothan and told him that he was in violation of the statute, and he needed to remove the bumper sticker. Mr. Baker covered it up, but then subsequently sued in the Federal District Court for the Middle District of Alabama, challenging the constitutionality of the statute. He argued that the statute infringed his First Amendment right of free speech.[7]

The State of Alabama put forth several reasons that it ought to be allowed to enforce its statute and ticket Mr. Baker for displaying the bumper sticker. First, the sticker was obscene, both to adults and to children. Furthermore, the bumper sticker constituted "fighting words." Third, more important from a practical standpoint, the sticker was likely to distract other motorists and interfere with highway safety.

The federal district court examined these arguments carefully in light of the law on obscene speech as laid down by the U.S. Supreme Court, which has held that obscene speech is not protected by the First Amendment. Because the legislatures must be careful not to limit free speech, the U.S. Supreme Court defined obscenity very carefully and narrowly in the case of *Miller v. California*: Obscenity is "limited to works which, taken as a whole, appeal to the prurient interest in sex, which portray sexual conduct in a patently offensive way, and which, taken as a whole, do not have serious literary, artistic, political, or scientific value."[8]

The *Baker* court mentioned analogous cases, including *Cohen v. California*.[9] In that case, Mr. Cohen was convicted under a California statute for wearing, in a courthouse, a jacket with the words "Fuck the Draft" on the back. The Supreme Court said, "It cannot plausibly be maintained that this vulgar allusion to the Selective Service System would conjure up such psychic stimulation in anyone likely to be confronted with Cohen's crudely defaced jacket."[10] Further, the statement was clearly a political one and so enjoyed the protections afforded free speech.

In the truck driver's case, the state argued back that some people do find some sexual interest in excrement. Perhaps, the court conceded, but the four-letter word in question was part of a facetious message. The court was not persuaded that a single profane word in this context could be viewed as causing such sexual interest.

Besides, this language failed another part of the *Miller* test. The bumper sticker had literary and political value. Granted, the literary value wasn't extensive, but it did have the intent and content of parody. For instance, the medium was essential to the message. To parody a bumper sticker, one best uses a bumper sticker. The seven letters mirrored the seven digits of a phone number. The message humorously conveyed Mr. Baker's strong feelings. Also, the bumper sticker certainly had political value. It was a protest against the Big Brother mentality that encouraged people to report misbehaving truck drivers. The political content of the bumper sticker no doubt protected it under the *Miller* test.

The court continued to address the state's arguments. It had disposed of the notion that the bumper sticker was obscene to adults, for, like "Fuck the Draft," this one four-letter word was highly unlikely to appeal to anyone's prurient interest in sex. Likewise, it was hard to see how the bumper sticker could appeal to minors' prurient interest in sex.

The state had also argued that the bumper sticker constituted "fighting words," which is another category of speech not protected by the Constitution. In the landmark case from 1942, *Chaplinsky v. New Hampshire*, the U.S. Supreme Court had permitted the prohibition of language that would "by [its] very utterance inflict injury or tend to incite an immediate breach of the peace."[11] (That language should remind us of the anti-dueling statutes discussed in chapter 7.) Thus the Supreme Court held that First Amendment protection did not extend to language that would incite a riot. But the *Baker* court didn't think that this bumper sticker amounted to "fighting words." In the words of the *Cohen* court, "No individual actually or likely to be present could reasonably have regarded the words . . . as a direct personal insult."[12] Put in those terms, one has to agree. They may be annoying words, and the use of the four-letter word may be offensive to some people, but no one was likely to want to shed Baker's blood over them.

Finally, the state had argued that the statute was valid because the sticker was likely to distract motorists and cause accidents. Thus the statute regulated traffic, and so it was a valid use of the state's police power. No, the court disagreed, there was nothing in the record that revealed that either the statute or its application was supposed to regulate traffic. The language of the statute spoke expressly about obscenity, not ten-car pile-ups. The court saw no support for the idea that this bumper sticker was more likely to distract motorists than other bumper stickers.

Finally, then, the court concluded that, as to this bumper sticker, the Alabama obscenity statute was an impermissible restriction on Mr. Baker's right of free speech. The language was unlikely to evoke erotic thoughts in anyone; it couldn't be proscribed as "fighting words"; and it didn't exercise the state's power to regulate traffic. Mr. Baker could continue to display his bumper sticker in Alabama.[13]

The law must weigh society's complex interests regarding free speech. No doubt a number of people would be offended by the language on the bumper sticker. Nevertheless, as the court stated in *Cohen*, their remedy is to avert their eyes.[14] Nothing prevents us from acting as our own censors, and, in fact, that option is preferable to prohibiting offensive speech that also has useful political or literary content. The First Amendment protects offensive speech, including in-your-face statements like "Fuck the Draft" and "Call 1-800-Eat Shit." Because the interest in protecting speech is so great, we are expected to put up with the incivility that may accompany the speech.

This old battle goes on. On August 15, 1998, Timothy Boomer, Jr., was canoeing on the Rifle River in Arenac County, Michigan. The Rifle River is a popular tourist attraction in summer, and there were a number of boaters on the river. At some point Boomer fell out of his canoe. No doubt shocked by the water's chill and annoyed with his fate, he blasted a string of curses. Unfortunately for him, some county deputies were nearby and heard the shouting.[15] They cited him for violation of a hundred-year-old Michigan statute that read, "Any person who shall use any indecent, immoral, obscene, vulgar or insulting language in the presence or hearing of any woman or child shall be guilty of a misdemeanor."[16]

When Boomer realized that the case and its attendant inconvenience weren't going to go away, he contacted the American Civil Liberties Union, which agreed to represent him in the case. His attorney, William Street, said that the law was one that "a court should just take behind the barn and put a bullet in."[17] His argument was on the expected constitutional grounds: Boomer's speech wasn't obscene, and it didn't constitute fighting words. Therefore, it was constitutionally protected. Street wondered in his brief to the court how one could find Boomer's language obscene when much worse could be found on MTV and in Ken Starr's report to the Congress.[18]

Nevertheless, Boomer was convicted by a jury in a district court. At least the judge did find unconstitutional, and sever from the statute, the part that referred to using bad language in the presence or hearing of a woman.[19] In one hundred years, we had at least come that far. Boomer appealed his conviction on the grounds that the statute, even as maimed by the trial court, was overly broad and vague.[20] His conviction was confirmed by a circuit court, so he appealed to the Michigan court of appeals. That court reversed the conviction, finding that the statute was too vague to give people fair notice of what might be a crime for which they could be convicted. The argument is, essentially, one of due process: If the statute doesn't tell me exactly what is illegal, then I could be arrested for any number of acts, based purely on the arbitrary discretion of the police. However, the court said, such a reversal needn't implicate First Amendment free speech concerns. The court reversed, it said, purely on the basis that the statute was vague. Nevertheless, it still managed to go on to say that the statute offended the First Amendment because it prevented constitutionally protected speech, such as insults.[21]

Whatever the legal implications, the columnist Mitch Albom defined the debate for the purposes of civility in an editorial in the *Detroit Free Press*.[22] Certainly, he concedes, one doesn't want one's children exposed to this sort of language. But do we want the law to intrude? No, he argues; this behavior is not for the law to govern, because the law is more concerned with matters of free speech. The real issue, he thought, was that the cursing occurred in "a small town that gets overrun by drunken tourists every summer."[23] The deputy sheriff wasn't there to enforce a one-hundred-year-old statute but to look for drunken and too-boisterous boaters. Thus, according to Albom, the issue wasn't dirty words or free speech and the laws that governed them, but simply civil behavior. Civility, he said, had to be taught by parents, schools, and religious leaders.

The cases in this chapter illustrate the ways by which society chooses to allow rather than prohibit uncivil language. We may not like language that takes the names of our respective deities in vain, but the states may not legislate against it, for to do so would be to offend the Constitution's guarantees respecting religion. Here, society made a choice of individual freedom over civility in everyday speech.

The First Amendment to the Constitution provides perhaps the most serious hurdle to legislating civil speech, as it prohibits the enforcement of laws that limit freedom of speech. Language must be extreme to amount to obscenity that can be proscribed, and that language must lack any serious literary, political, artistic, or scientific merit. The exception permitting the regulation of fighting words is similarly narrow. As the law has priorities that trump civil speech, then, we are once more left facing each other. We are thrown back on either policing ourselves so as to avoid expressing incivilities or relying on the common sense of the populace to ignore the incivilities.[24]

This and the two previous chapters have surveyed the problems that the law has when it comes to matters of uncivil speech. In chapter 7, we looked at the difficulty that the civil law has in regulating insulting language. Neither the anti-dueling statutes, nor the federal employee discrimination laws, nor even a quasi-law—the University of Pennsylvania's speech code—was up to the task. The statutes were enacted for purposes more extreme than regulating the occasional mere insult. Penn's speech code was criticized as doomed to failure because it was designed to deal with specific violations of a code rather than treat the problems underlying it. A hopeful development was the evolution of netiquette, informal rules by which one sends E-mails. Yet these rules involve little penalty if they're broken. Nevertheless, netiquette seemed to come closer to a model Miss Manners would prefer: informal, flexible manners that provide a certain amount of freedom.

In chapter 8 we explored whether criminal laws were any more effective in enforcing civil behavior, this time involving issues not only of speech but of simple interaction. Again we saw the law running into difficulties. For one, the criminal law contains strict conditions under which its sanctions can be imposed, thanks to society's care not to brand lightly an individual as a criminal. For another, the First Amendment to the U.S. Constitution protects all manner of speech that we might otherwise find objectionable. Finally, then, the criminal law was an unwieldy tool to use to force people to behave with respect toward each other.

The protection of free speech was the major impediment to the application of the criminal laws discussed in this chapter. Laws attempting to regulate blasphemy, obscenity, and foul language run up against the very strict rules regarding what sorts of speech can be limited or prohibited outright. Society has decided that it wants to listen to too much rather than too little, wary of chancing that its regulation tips over into the area of prohibiting too much. Thus the protection of free speech protects much uncivil speech.

We've seen that society's interests in encouraging civil speech run up against a number of other societal interests that are built into the legal system. Thus, as much as society would like to encourage civil speech, it cannot forbid certain kinds of uncivil speech. In that regard, the legal system's hands are tied. Instead, individuals must rely on themselves and each other to exercise their rights to free speech in as civil a way as the moment, their emotions, and their circumstances will allow.[25]

The next chapter will complete our examination of issues regarding civil speech, but we shall give up on the application of criminal law and return to the world of torts. Instead of looking at what uncivil language people will speak *to* each other, we'll look at how terribly they will speak *about* each other.

CHAPTER 10

Gossip Gone Bad
Defamation

> Be not hasty to believe flying
> Reports to the Disparagement of any.
> GEORGE WASHINGTON'S
> 50TH RULE OF CIVILITY,
> *Rules of Civility*
> *for the 21st Century*
> *from Cub and Boy Scouts*
> *from across America*

In 1981 the Bechtel Power Corporation contracted with the Washington Public Power Supply System (WPPSS) to assume the engineering management and safety functions of the construction of its nuclear power plants. Some of these duties consisted of operating first aid stations. Bechtel would supply the nurses, and WPPSS (derogatorily pronounced "whoops") would provide the space and equipment.[1]

Bechtel was assuming these duties from another company, which had employed three nurses, Ms. Funderburk, Ms. Lang, and Ms. Sams, at one of the aid stations. All three applied to be kept on when Bechtel took over. However, Bechtel required its nurses to be certified emergency medical technicians and to have a certification in cardiopulmonary resuscitation. Only Ms. Sams held those certifications, and Bechtel offered employment to her only, in early 1981.

In May 1981 Mr. Elledge from Bechtel met with four safety officials at WPPSS and complained about the state of the aid stations. The eye examination chair was inadequate. The lack of partitions compromised patient privacy. The supplies were disorganized. Elledge also claimed that the stations were dirty, and the floor covering was cracked and some pieces were missing. In general, Elledge said—and here there was dispute over the terms used and to whom or what they were applied—the stations were either a "whore's nest" or a "boar's nest."

One of the participants, Mr. Caster, who was with WPPSS but was shortly to be terminated for reasons unconnected to the meeting, spoke with a safety official of Bechtel's predecessor, Mr. Geihm, about the meeting. He claimed that Elledge had said, "The reason Bechtel did not hire the nurses at Unit 2 was because they were a bunch of whores, and it was nothing but a whore's nest." Geihm repeated this to two of the nurses. They sued Bechtel, claiming that Elledge's statement defamed them and caused Bechtel not to employ them.

The legal commentator Dean Prosser defines defamation as "that which tends to injure 'reputation' in the popular sense; to diminish the esteem, respect, good-will or confidence in which the plaintiff is held, or to excite adverse, derogatory, or unpleasant feelings or opinions against him."[2] To recover, a plaintiff, under the common law, needs to show that a defamatory statement, as Dean Prosser describes it, was made about the plaintiff and was published. Publication means that the statement must reach someone other than the plaintiff. The defamatory statement was assumed to be false; thus it's a defense to a claim of defamation that the statement made was true.[3] Not as old as nuisance, trespass, or battery, defamation began to appear in the English common law courts by the sixteenth century. It was met with some alarm by the common law judges, who felt cornered by the valued concern for ensuring freedom of speech. So those judges corralled defamation law with restrictions that survive today.[4] Transported to America, defamation law became even more complicated when it ran up against the Constitution's written codification of the protection of free speech in the broadly worded First Amendment. In this chapter, we will look at how those restrictions complicate the law and make it difficult for one who feels he has been defamed to recover.

Back to the nurses' suit. In response, Bechtel claimed first that Elledge, who was speaking for it, was referring to the station, not the nurses. Second, he called it a "boar's nest," not a "whore's nest."

The case was tried to a judge, who found that Elledge had indeed used the term "whore's nest," but that he was referring to the condition of the station, not the nurses' sexual activities. Further, the judge held that everyone at the meeting understood that Elledge was referring to the station, not the nurses. The judge at least implicitly relied on testimony that Caster had misstated what Elledge had said because of the ill feelings Caster had toward Bechtel. With these findings of fact, the judge granted a verdict for Bechtel. The nurses appealed to the Washington Court of Appeals, but, in a rare procedural twist, the Washington Supreme Court ordered the case transferred directly to it for hearing and decision.[5] The only question to be decided was whether there were facts sufficient for the trial judge to make the finding that he did.

The supreme court examined the facts. The only reason that the nurses thought that the term was intended to refer to them was Caster's statement to Geihm that "the reason Bechtel did not hire the nurses at Unit 2 was because they were a bunch of whores, and that it was nothing but a whore's nest." Caster didn't testify at the trial, but there had been evidence of his grudge against Bechtel. Taylor, a WPPSS official present at the meeting, testified that Elledge had used the term to convince WPPSS to allocate some funds to upgrade the station. Taylor and Fisher, another who had been present at the meeting, testified that Elledge hadn't called the nurses whores. Taylor, Fisher, and Hood (yet a third present) each testified that there had been no reference to the nurses at all. Finally, all of the testimony was that the persons at the meeting understood that "whore's nest" referred to the nurses' station, not the nurses.

This last evidence was crucial. The purpose of defamation law is to determine liability for a person's statement that "tends to injure 'reputation' in the popular sense; to diminish the esteem, respect, goodwill or confidence in which the plaintiff is held."[6] So the central question is how the statement in question was understood by the persons who heard it. If they didn't understand Elledge's statement in such a way as to "diminish the esteem, respect, goodwill or confidence" that they had for the nurses, then there could be no viable action. The overwhelming testimony was that the three men did not think that Elledge's statement even referred to the nurses. The supreme court couldn't find any defamatory statement under those circumstances and affirmed the trial judge's verdict.

We can't quarrel with this holding. The facts don't lend themselves to a finding that Elledge had defamed the nurses by referring to their morals. Bechtel's predecessor employed the nurses, and there's no statement in the opinion that Elledge even knew the nurses. It would be an odd circumstance indeed that would lead him to comment on their morals. The case may strike one as a lot of puffing and shouting about very little at all. Though of course if the nurses felt that Elledge's statement had damaged their reputation, then we can certainly understand their motives for bringing the claim.

Actually, though, several things seem amiss. What did they claim had caused Bechtel to decide not to employ them? Elledge's statement. Yet Elledge was employed by Bechtel. Elledge was speaking and acting on behalf of Bechtel. So how could Bechtel's own statement cause Bechtel not to hire them? Bechtel is entitled to form its own opinion, and, under these facts, it did so through Elledge with no input from anyone else. The court doesn't address this issue, possibly because, no matter who was making the statements, they weren't defamatory.

What the court does say is that only Sams held the certifications required for employment by Bechtel. However, there's no statement in the opinion that Bechtel raised the other nurses' shortcomings as a defense. Again, perhaps the court felt that it didn't have to reach this issue.

Finally and most importantly, the court held that Elledge was referring not to the nurses but to the condition of the aid station. There was plenty of evidence that the stations were a mess—a whore's nest, perhaps, if that means a dirty, disorganized place. If Elledge were referring to the stations themselves, the nurses would have had no claim at all, because another defense to a defamation claim is that the statements made were true. Thus, the nurses were stuck with a pretty tenuous claim: Calling the aid station a whore's nest means that Elledge was calling us whores.

Though the parties pursued this case doggedly to the Washington Supreme Court, it appears upon close examination to be about nothing much at all. The irony is that the nurses not only did not win vindication, but they also exposed their work to the sort of examination just completed. Perhaps they would have been better advised to have left well enough alone. That they didn't sounds again the theme that Americans tend to sue when they feel that they have been insulted. All of that time, money, and effort spent because the nurses felt defamed because someone had referred to their aid station as a "whore's nest." So imagining this litigation working its way through discovery, a trial, and an appeal to the Washington Supreme Court is disheartening. One hopes that the litigation was actually a desperate attempt to recover damages to cover lost wages.

Certainly, if Elledge did call the aid station a "whore's nest," it was at least a thoughtless, and perhaps offensive statement to make. Certainly it was a statement of opinion; anyway, the court said that no one could think that Elledge was actually making a factual statement that the nurses were whores. Would an apology have eased the nurses' hurt? Whether or not the nurses received an apology, the question again arises as to whether this sort of dispute is something Americans ought to be litigating. Some matters might call instead for a wave of the hand, a turn of the back, and a turn of the other cheek. As with the law of intentional infliction of emotional distress, defamation law, partly by limiting the types of action that can be brought, forces potential plaintiffs to put up with some insulting language. It's an appropriate result for the legal system, though a loss for the cause of civility.

*   *   *

A case from North Carolina will further our discussion. Again, the facts are quite simple. Ms. Donovan and Ms. Hunter sued Mr. Fiumara for saying, in January 1990 and again in June 1990, that they were "gay and bisexual." The three were coworkers for a telecommunications company at which Fiumara was in a higher-level position. One comment was made in a parking lot and the other inside the building in which they worked. The two women hadn't been present when the comments were allegedly made, but, of course, under defamation law, the statements had to be made to third parties, and the women didn't have to be present. Though the two women pursued an internal grievance proceeding, Fiumara vehemently denied making the statements, and Donovan and Hunter felt strongly enough that he had and that they'd been defamed to bring suit.[7]

Fiumara moved to dismiss their complaint, arguing that it didn't state a claim for which relief could be granted. That is, the facts that they alleged didn't add up to a good claim under defamation law. The trial judge granted the motion, and Donovan and Hunter appealed. The North Carolina Court of Appeals took their case.[8]

First, the court carefully distinguished slander per se from its cousin, slander per quod. Though judges and lawyers have hopelessly confused the concepts in some contexts, we can try to boil them down. Slander per se involves a false statement that is so egregious or affects such an important interest of the plaintiff that all by itself it forms the basis of an action, and the plaintiff doesn't even have to prove damages. Slander per quod involves a statement whose harmful character doesn't appear on its face but only becomes clear once facts are shown to demonstrate the damaging effect. In that case, some damages must be proven. For slander per quod, that means money—one can't recover for emotional suffering under defamation. Unfortunately, Donovan and Hunter didn't plead money damages, so, the court concluded, they were apparently claiming that the statement constituted slander per se.

In North Carolina, only three kinds of defamatory statements are so egregious that they can constitute slander per se: one that charged Donovan and Hunter with a crime involving moral turpitude, one that impeached them in their trade or profession, or one that imputed to them a loathsome disease.[9] The court eliminated the last two quickly. Being "gay and bisexual" didn't bear at all on one's trade or business, and it didn't impute any loathsome diseases. Donovan and Hunter didn't contend otherwise.

However, the two argued, engaging in some activities practiced by homosexuals was a felony in North Carolina.[10] Therefore, falsely stating that they were "gay and bisexual" imputed to them the commission of a crime, which, of course, is the first category of statements that constitute slander per se.

The court didn't agree. The statute in question stated: "If any person shall commit the crime against nature, with mankind or beast, he shall be punished as a Class H felon."[11] The court unflinchingly stated that crimes against nature in North Carolina can include acts with animals and certain acts between humans, including sodomy, buggery, and cunnilingus, no matter by whom committed and which genders involved. However, Donovan and Hunter didn't allege that Fiumara had said that they had committed any criminal acts. They only alleged that he said that they were "gay and bisexual."

The North Carolina court wasn't necessarily hairsplitting, for courts from other jurisdictions had held the same way: "A simple statement descriptive of an individual's alleged sexual orientation does not as a matter of law impute to that individual commission of a crime."[12] For instance, the Illinois Court of Appeals had held that the defendant's calling the plaintiff a "fag" only asserted that he was homosexual, not that he had committed any specific act.[13]

Then the North Carolina court slapped down the trump card. The Court of Appeals for the District of Columbia Circuit had just invalidated a Department of Defense directive that had barred homosexuals from serving in the armed forces: "The secretary's justification for the gay ban presumes that a certain class of persons will break the law or [military] rules solely because of their thoughts and desires. This is inherently unreasonable."[14] Even if Donovan and Hunter were gay or bisexual, that didn't mean that they were committing felonies.

There were analogous cases. A North Carolina court had reviewed a case arising out of a labor dispute in which truck drivers, union members, were accused of being "gangsters." The court held that the statement amounted mainly to name-calling and didn't mean that they had committed a "specific crime for which they could be indicted or punished."[15]

So, because Fiumara hadn't said that the two had committed this or that specific crime, they couldn't avail themselves of slander per se's rule of damages being assumed. Because they hadn't alleged any actual damages, they didn't have a viable claim one way or the other. So the trial court had been correct to dismiss the complaint.

The court would have quit there, it said, except that Donovan and Hunter had made another argument that the court wanted to address. They had argued that a recent North Carolina Supreme Court case had actually created a fourth category of slander per se, a statement that held the plaintiff up to disgrace, ridicule, or contempt.[16] The court disagreed. In essence, it said, the North Carolina Supreme Court had only been listing the *elements* of what you had to prove to win a slander per se claim, not the *categories* of slander per se.

Nevertheless, the court went on. (Courts do, on occasion, like to go on. Remember the New York judge in the *Cifarelli* case who said that not only did the state lose this public nuisance case, but if Jacobs had brought the case as a private nuisance case, which it wasn't, Cifarelli still would have won.[17]) Statements that held Donovan and Hunter up to "disgrace, ridicule or contempt" did not constitute a fourth category of slander per se. However, *if there were* such a fourth category, they still wouldn't win. The court noted that an Illinois court had found that because times had changed it was no longer sufficient for the plaintiff to allege merely the statement that he had been called homosexual. A false accusation of homosexuality did not constitute slander per se.[18]

Hilariously enough, the North Carolina court stated that "as North Carolina progresses through the mid 1990's, we are unable to rule the bare allegation that an individual is 'gay' or 'bisexual' constitutes an accusation which, as a matter of law and absent any 'extrinsic, explanatory facts' . . . per se holds that individual up to 'disgrace, ridicule or contempt.'"[19] As North Carolina progresses, indeed. The court disregarded the fact that the state, as of this writing, criminalizes—as a felony, not just a misdemeanor—virtually all sex acts except intercourse between a man and a woman. In fact, effective January 1, 1995, North Carolina amended the statute, leaving its language unchanged except to reclassify the felony to make those convicted under it eligible for a vacation in North Carolina's jails for a lesser period. That's progress.

So Donovan and Hunter were out of luck, and it appears that North Carolina wasn't the only state in which they would have been unsuccessful. The decision seems correct on a very strict reading of the law. But wasn't Fiumara really saying that he believed that Donovan and Hunter were engaging in specific acts that, in North Carolina, anyway, were felonies? Why, then, would a court stand on such ceremony?

For one thing, crediting the plaintiffs' claim would put the court in the uncomfortable and politically incorrect position of affirming that a statement that one was homosexual was damaging to a person's reputation. Also, generally, the court may be working to avoid finding a claim here because the courts are exceedingly unwilling to make new law in the defamation arena assisting plaintiffs to recover absent a showing of real damages. Again, the burden is put on the plaintiff. Free and open speech claims the day, even if civility suffers.

At any rate, this isn't the first time we've seen the law address priorities other than civil speech. We've just finished looking at cases in which courts condoned all manner of speech, as long as it wasn't truly obscene or didn't amount to a serious invitation to fight. Obviously, though, if Fiumara had made the statement—and again, he had vigorously denied doing so—the court's decision would do nothing to punish him for a statement that was at best indiscreet and at worst mean-spirited gossip.

Another limitation on the claim for defamatory statements is that statements of opinion, as opposed to fact, are generally protected. The interest in fostering public debate and the exchange of ideas wins out over suppressing opinions, no matter how offensive they may seem.

A case from Illinois provides a good selection of strong opinions that were held to be protected. In one case, Rick Baker wrote an article in the Peoria *Journal Star* on October 26, 1984, expressing his opinion about a transaction between David Horowitz and the Mayor of Peoria, Richard Carver. Baker had described the facts behind his opinion in an article published a couple of days earlier. Apparently, according to Baker, Carver had, on behalf of "a friend," bid on used bricks being offered for sale by the city at a price of twenty-five cents a brick. The terms Baker used in the second article to express his opinion were "sleazy," "cheap," "pull a fast one," "secret," and "rip-off." Horowitz sued Baker and the newspaper for libel. Horowitz argued that the clear implication was that he had obtained bricks from the city in an unlawful manner. Those statements, he believed, defamed him.

The Illinois Court of Appeals disagreed.[20] The rule is that opinion is constitutionally protected provided that the facts underlying the basis for the opinion are disclosed. Baker had disclosed the underlying facts in the earlier article. In fact, the second article began, "Now that we know to whom Richard Carver planned to secretly and cheaply sell public bricks . . ." Baker was stating right out that the public was aware of the underlying facts.

Of course, there is no protection for a false statement of facts. Horowitz argued that Baker's statements imputed unlawful behavior to him. It was true, the court agreed, that had Baker said, "Horowitz bribed Mayor Carver to get cheap bricks," that would certainly be a defamatory statement. In fact, accusations don't have to charge the criminal offense so directly. But here, given the context, the average reader would conclude that Baker's statements only constituted his opinion of the transaction. The terms he used to characterize those facts constituted opinion and amounted only to "rhetorical hyperbole." Not very nice opinion, the court thought, but opinion all the same and therefore not actionable.

The court's interest is in preserving the robust marketplace of ideas, even at the expense of civil speech. "Rhetorical hyperbole"—or just plain name-calling—is tolerated, if not actively encouraged.[21]

The issue becomes even more complicated when the opinions are stated about a public figure. Ms. Julia Lampkin-Asam wrote a book about her frustrations with what she termed the "cancer establishment." The problem, as she saw it, was that the establishment had disparaged her as a cancer scientist, and, as a result, she had been unable to obtain grants for research. Without those grants, she had been unable to develop a cure for cancer. She voiced her grievances in a book, *Malignant Intrigue*, which, whatever shortcomings its 753 pages might have had, certainly had a catchy title. In her book, Lampkin-Asam named her former supervisor, Dr. Wilhelmina Dunning, as the one who'd done the most to damage her career.

Lampkin-Asam took her book to Ms. Terry Johnson King, the lifestyle editor of the Miami *News*, in an attempt to gain some publicity for both her book and her plight. King read the book and, before publishing a review of it, thought she'd better get Dunning's view of the allegations against her.

Then King wrote her column; overall, she didn't much credit Lampkin-Asam's theory highly. King went as far as to say that Lampkin-Asam's charges were "almost paranoical."[22] She also quoted Dunning as follows:

> To which the highly respected Dr. Dunning says, "She (Asam) is very emotionally disturbed, and has no qualifications to do cancer research. She may have gotten her doctorate from George Washington University, but I suspect they gave her the degree to get rid of her."[23]

It may come as no surprise that Lampkin-Asam sued Dunning, the Miami *News*, and King, alleging defamation. The trial court, however, granted summary judgment in favor of all of the defendants. Summary judgment means that the court found that, as a matter of law, the facts that Lampkin-Asam presented were so insufficient to make a claim for defamation that there was no reason to submit the case to the jury—that is, no reasonable jury could find for her. Lampkin-Asam appealed, though she failed to get her appeal filed in time with respect to Dunning, so it was only the action against the Miami *News* and King that survived. The Florida Court of Appeals took up the case.

The court first took up the issue of whether Lampkin-Asam was a public figure, as determining that would go a long way to establishing whether the newspaper could be liable. The court took note of a number of her activities: She tried to arouse public attention and tried to influence the allocation of public funding for cancer research. She participated, at least through her book, one imagines, though the court doesn't say, in the public debate on health issues. She published her book, wrote other materials, and made speeches in an effort to publicize her plight. All of these activities together made her, the court held, a "public figure" for the purposes of defamation law.

What did that mean? In the landmark case of *New York Times v. Sullivan*, the U.S. Supreme Court established a more difficult standard for public figures to meet to prove that they had been defamed.[24] A public figure or official has to show, with convincing clarity, that the maker of the statements either knew they were false or made them with a reckless disregard for their falsity. The rationale for the rule is the importance of permitting criticism of public officers, and, by extension, persons who may have some role in determining public policy. The court felt that Lampkin-Asam, by thrusting her own plight into the debate about cancer research, had made herself into a public figure. The priority, as we have seen, is to foster robust debate, perhaps at the expense of excusing some statements that might otherwise be damaging to the public figure's reputation. To slide in the other direction would be to allow public officials—government officers—to threaten to quell public dissent by filing defamation actions. Americans don't like the sound of that, smacking as it does of government censorship of a free press.

So the question was, did King make statements she knew were false, or did she act with a reckless disregard for their truth? The court turned to the newspaper columnist's testimony. King swore that she had accurately quoted Dunning. Dunning testified that she wasn't sure that she'd made such statements, and she was certain that she would not have made them in such a form. Perhaps, she allowed, a succession of questions might have elicited the information from which the quoted material might have come. Dunning did admit that she could have said that Lampkin-Asam wasn't qualified to do independent cancer research. Further, it was indeed her opinion that George Washington University might have donated Lampkin-Asam her degree just to get rid of her. Finally, though, Dunning insisted that if she had made such comments, she'd made them facetiously, and King hadn't been given permission to quote them as she did.

So did King set out to print a falsehood, knowing that Dunning hadn't intended her statements other than facetiously? King swore she'd quoted Dunning accurately. Was there "clear and convincing" evidence that King had intentionally stated a falsehood by quoting Dunning inaccurately? No, the court said, it was just King's word against Dunning's, and that's hardly "clear and convincing" evidence. To get to "clear and convincing," King probably would have had to admit to punching up Dunning's statements to make a catchier quotation.

To take the next step, did King misunderstand Dunning's intent? Possibly. But, the court asked, did she make the mistake recklessly, without caring whether she'd gotten it right? Again, there was no clear and convincing evidence that King had acted recklessly with a knowing disregard for the truth.

Now, now, the court went on to say, by quoting a case from the U.S. Fifth Circuit Court of Appeals, we're not condoning careless journalism.[25] But we do have these other priorities mandated by the public interest. While we want to protect public officials and figures against libelous statements, we also don't want to hold liable a journalist who merely makes an honest mistake. Instead, the public's interest has to be considered, and the public has an important right to a free and uncensored press. Better the public figure suffer the sting of an inaccurate statement than the free press—protected by the First Amendment—suffer unnecessary restraints.

Here, then, the press's rights win out. There was no clear and convincing evidence of a statement made either with the knowledge that it was false or with a knowing disregard for its accuracy. The worst that could be said was that Dunning made the statements, but made them facetiously, and King misunderstood her. Summary judgment for the newspaper defendants was affirmed.

There was a second issue that this court raised in its footnotes. King wrote that Lampkin-Asam's charges were "almost paranoical." Such a statement constituted an opinion, and the court stated the general rule about opinions that we saw in the *Baker* case out of Illinois: As it was based on facts set forth in the column, it was entitled to absolute constitutional protection. The court went on to quote the U.S. Supreme Court in *Gertz v. Robert Welch, Inc.*: "Under the First Amendment, there is no such thing as a false idea. However pernicious an opinion might seem, we depend on its correction not on the conscience of judges or juries but on the competition of other ideas."[26] Therefore, this court said, King's opinion was protected against a charge of defamation. The only question was whether, in quoting Dunning, King had made a defamatory statement about a public figure, and we just saw how that came out.

Vindicating one's reputation under the American law of defamation is, as we have seen, a tough proposition. The plaintiff must prove that a statement was made that diminished her reputation among the people to whom the statement was made. It matters most how people who heard the statement understood it. The statement has to have been false. And unless the statement was one of a few narrow sorts, she has to prove exactly what damages she suffered. If the statement is merely a matter of name-calling, or if it constitutes an opinion, she loses. If she's a public figure, she has to prove that the person who made the statement either knew it was false or made the statement with a reckless disregard for its falsity.

The bottom line is that the courts will allow American society to remain a cacophony of sometimes rude, offensive, opinionated, shrill, unreasonable, and unreasoning voices that sometimes make statements that are flat-out wrong. Verbal incivility is destined to be tolerated in our society, at least as far as the legal system is concerned. Yet the only people who would ever criticize the way the priorities have been set are likely to be those losing plaintiffs. Virtually everyone else stands by the freedom of speech and of the press.

The lessons learned in this chapter differ only in degree from those in the prior chapters relating to speech. As we saw, the rules limiting purely abusive speech are tailored to very specific sorts of remarks, such as the fighting words prohibited by the anti-dueling statute. To be actionable, insults regarding national origin have to be so extensive as to amount to employment discrimination. The criminal statutes that deal with more serious violations relating to speech— harassment by telephone and computer—can impose sanctions only on those whose activities rise to a certain level and can be proven beyond a reasonable doubt to have occurred. Statutes regarding blasphemy, obscenity, and vulgar language are subject to careful scrutiny. Finally, of course, we have just seen the limitations that the Constitution and the courts have, in order to preserve freedom of speech, placed on defamation actions.

It's not surprising, then, to see that our Anglo-Saxon traditions work against civility in speech. Americans' first instinct is to bristle at any perceived limitation on our right to speak our minds. If it's offensive to the listener, so be it. We insult, annoy, and sometimes defame first, and then try to avoid apologizing later. American history is about an immense respect for and protection of the freedom of speech. The trade-off is that we're more than willing to sacrifice civility along the way.

Incivility Incarnate
Litigation

> In disputes, be not so desirous to
> overcome as not to give liberty to each
> one to deliver his opinion and submit to
> the judgment of the major part, espe-
> cially if they are judges of the dispute.
>
> GEORGE WASHINGTON'S
> 86TH RULE OF CIVILITY,
> *Rules of Civility*
> *for the 21st Century*
> *from Cub and Boy Scouts*
> *from across America*

A view commonly expressed is that children receive a warped view of violence from television.[1] Physical wounds and death become unreal and inconsequential. The same kind of numbness may suffuse anyone reading a good number of these cases. A couple of courts hint at the pain and suffering the parties inflict on each other by the very act of litigating. But read enough of these, and one forgets that real people had to spend real time, money, and energy to have their disputes heard and decided. Let us not mistake or underestimate what this means.

A good example is the "whore's nest" defamation case described in the previous chapter. Remember that this case involved three nurses who sued Bechtel Power Corporation, claiming that one of Bechtel's employees had defamed them by referring to them as whores. The court held that the worst interpretation of the events was that the employee was complaining about the condition of the workstations that the nurses had been charged with maintaining. The court held that the nurses' claim that the comment had defamed them was without merit.[2] The nurses appealed, and the Washington Supreme Court affirmed the verdict for Bechtel. Let's examine the events in the context of taking the case to trial.

The monetary cost to the individuals would have been substantial. The case had to be explored by the attorney (or attorneys) on each side at a cost, no doubt, of $90 an hour and probably much more, even in the early 1980s. (Fees would have been much higher had the lawyers been from Seattle instead of Richland and Yakima, Washington, smaller cities with a lower cost of living. Today it would cost more like a minimum of $150 an hour.) It's possible that the nurses' attorneys took the case on a contingency basis—that is, they would take as a fee some percentage, typically anywhere from twenty-five to forty percent, of whatever the court finally awarded the nurses, if anything. Bechtel, on the other hand, was no doubt paying a full hourly cost billed on a regular basis. In addition to the fees, the expenses of filing the lawsuit with the court, mailing correspondence, calling long distance, copying documents, and any traveling (transport, food, and rooms) are all generally passed directly to the clients. Often, the lawyers charge something like their hourly rate for the time taken to drive or fly or otherwise get where they're going.

Each side was entitled to and probably did take depositions—oral testimony under oath before trial—of the potential witnesses. The purpose of the deposition is to determine what the other side's witnesses are going to say at trial. The lawyers aren't trying so much to score points as to pin the other side down. Thus every possible fact to which an individual might testify has to be established, starting from name, address, education, and so on, in mind-numbing detail. (Once when one of the authors was attending a deposition on behalf of his client, during a break, the lawyer conducting the deposition grinned at him and said, "I know it seems boring, but it's going very well.") The testimony doesn't even have to be of the quality that would be admissible at trial but only has to lead to admissible evidence.

Despite the routine nature of this questioning, however, it's still part of an adversarial proceeding, and the atmosphere is generally tense and strained, if not openly hostile. While a deposition can be taken in a couple of hours, lawyers routinely schedule no more than one for each half day, and many seem to itch from a compulsion to fill the time. So, it's no picnic. On top of that, while only one lawyer is needed to conduct the questioning, if the client doesn't object to the extra cost involved, that lawyer is often likely to want to have another lawyer assisting, listening hard to make sure nothing is forgotten or left confused. Thus there are not two but sometimes four lawyers to argue with each other. If there are multiple plaintiffs or defendants with their own counsel who also want to ask questions, the time expands and the costs multiply.

The testimony must be recorded, of course, in order to compare it against any inconsistent statements that the witness might make at trial. A court reporter performs this task, and his or her work is generally the most interesting thing going on. The reporter sits just off the table recording the questions and answers, often in a kind of shorthand on a small keyboard. (A reporter might also use another method, whispering into a dictating machine, a mask fitting over his face to muffle the sound.) The shorthand code is printed on about a three-inch-wide tape that feeds through the machine and winds its quick way onto the floor. The amazing thing is that if one of the lawyers wants a question or answer read back, the court reporter is usually able to finger her way quickly to the exact spot where, minutes before, the words were spoken. When the deposition is over, the court reporter winds the tape up, takes it away, and transcribes it in a matter of days, or, if necessary, more quickly and at a higher cost. Obviously a person with this sort of skill must be paid a fair wage as well, and these fees are billed directly to the client.

More recently, some depositions have been videotaped, especially if the witness would likely be unavailable to testify at the trial. Videotaping a deposition is more elaborate and cumbersome than using a court reporter. At times, in fact, one suspects that the videotape technicians believe that the deposition is being held strictly for their benefit, so directly do they appear to control the proceedings. Of course, someone must pay for the videotaping as well.

In *Bechtel*, we can imagine a good number of depositions: certainly the three nurses—Sams, Funderburk, and Lang. Elledge actually spoke the words at issue, so the nurses would certainly take his statement. The opinion refers to testimony by Taylor, Hood, and Fisher from Bechtel, so it's likely that their depositions were taken too. Caster was at the meeting, and he repeated Elledge's remarks to Geihm. Though the court doesn't say so, and though Caster didn't testify at trial, it's possible that those two were deposed as well. That gives us, of the people mentioned in the opinion, at least seven and perhaps nine depositions to pay for. It's entirely possible that the nurses also took the deposition of a corporate representative of Bechtel, what many jurisdictions call a 30(b)(6) deposition, after the Federal Rules of Civil Procedure (or corresponding state court rule) to which it refers. The point of that deposition is to get the corporation's official word on the issues. If the nurses made any comments about the dispute to anyone, those folks might have been in for questioning as well.

Each side was also entitled to propound written questions to the other. One kind is known as written interrogatories, which are designed to elicit specific factual information regarding the other side's claims. Bechtel would undoubtedly ask what words, exactly, the nurses thought were defamatory. It would also ask the nurses to quantify their damages and how they suffered them. While there are stock forms of interrogatories, they have to be customized for each case, so someone has to draft, review, and revise them. Lawyers can be so creative in finding things to ask that some courts have taken steps to limit the number of interrogatories that can be propounded so that the answering party isn't overwhelmed unnecessarily. The questions are often, in the first asking, useless anyway, as lawyers routinely object to the scope as being unreasonably broad, too onerous to answer, or too unclear to understand. Eventually, the lawyers end up on the phone asking each other exactly what it is the other wants to know and then negotiating how to supply it.

Each party is also entitled to make requests for admissions, which are designed to get the other side to admit the existence of this or that fact and thereby eliminate some facts for the jury or court to have to find at trial. If some facts can be established, then theoretically no one will have to be asked about them, and the trial will go more speedily. Bechtel might ask the nurses to admit that they lacked certain professional certifications; the nurses might ask Bechtel to admit that Elledge was speaking on its behalf. While it's unlikely that Bechtel would have asked the nurses to admit that they were whores (thereby providing an excellent defense to a defamation suit), Bechtel probably would have asked them to admit to some deficiencies in the way the workstations were kept. Again, lawyers must draft, review, and revise these requests, and the time is too often not well spent due to the opposing lawyers' skill in evading direct questions.

Each side was also entitled to request copies of the documents that the other side expected to introduce into evidence at trial. The nurses would want to know what documentation Bechtel had with respect to how the workstations were kept—no documentation, maybe no proof of defects. Bechtel might ask for any correspondence that the nurses had written to anyone about the incidents, perhaps hoping that they had admitted that they hadn't really done much of a job of keeping things up. These documents are requested in writing, again requiring drafting, reviewing, and answering. These requests are also subject to objection and negotiation until the parties agree on what's to be disclosed. Eventually, of course, documents would be exchanged—and reviewed, discussed, and copied.

Though probably not in the *Bechtel* case, in a number of the other cases in this book, the parties engaged the services of expert witnesses, the cost of whose time and expenses had to be paid up front also. Sometimes, if they're known to make very good witnesses and command high fees as professionals in their regular line of work, like actuaries and doctors, they can cost even more than the lawyers.[3] These fees are passed directly to the client.

Finally, the attorneys had to write various documents for the judge: briefs on the legal issues (the law of defamation in Washington, for example) and lists of the witnesses to be called and documents to be introduced. At some point, as the trial went forth, each side would also have drafted proposed findings of fact and law for the judge to consider at the trial's conclusion. There didn't appear to be a jury in the *Bechtel* case, but, if there were, each side would also have prepared jury instructions for the judge to consider.

Often, one side or the other will file motions to be heard before trial, such as a motion for partial or complete summary judgment. Bechtel might have filed a motion to the effect that there was no material question of fact that Elledge's comments referred only to the nurses' stations and not to the nurses themselves. The parties might also have filed motions to preclude certain evidence as inadmissible for this or that reason. Caster didn't testify at trial, so testimony at trial on what he told Geihm would have been hearsay. The parties might well have filed motions to find that hearsay to be admissible or to keep it out. These motions would also probably have had to be argued, and counsel would have had to prepare for the arguments.

Conscientious counsel also prepares notes for conducting the direct and cross-examinations of the witnesses. Finally, of course, each lawyer prepares opening and closing arguments. Before the jury is charged, they also anticipate arguing about the exact text of the jury instructions and the proposed findings of fact and conclusions of law.

Someone, perhaps a paralegal whose time could also be billed to the client, has to make copies of the documents to be introduced at trial: a copy for the clerk to go into the record of the trial, one for the judge to look at, and one for opposing counsel, who has obtained a copy during discovery, but as a matter of courtesy has to be given another one now. If it's a document that the jury ought to see, then copies must be made for them as well. Costs of copies, of course, are billed directly to the client.

The parties try their cases to either a jury or a judge. As we noted, *Bechtel* appears to have been tried to a judge. With no jury involved, matters are less complicated, because there's no worry about whether the jury is likely to hear something that the judge will subsequently decide it shouldn't have heard. If the judge accidentally hears inadmissible testimony, it is presumed that he's smart enough to disregard it. When a jury's involved, an astounding amount of time goes into arguing the propriety of what's to be said and not said in front of it, with two or three or five lawyers huddled up at the bench whispering frantically and insistently to the judge, who's glancing over their heads to make sure that the jury isn't catching any of it.

If the case is tried to a jury, the lawyers must agree on the jury members. Depending on how critical the makeup of the jury is to the case, picking a jury adds at least a half a day in the best of circumstances. Obviously, in criminal trials in which life or liberty is at stake, the collection of people who will decide the questions is extremely important, so days and even weeks can be swallowed up in the process. In those cases, as well as in complex commercial litigation, the lawyers may hire expert consultants to advise them on the sorts of people whom they want to fill the jury box. The worlds of marketing and law have collided: Sometimes lawyers will even try the case to a mock jury to learn how their show played to the focus group. Fortunately, however, it is unlikely that such an expensive undertaking was necessary for any of the trials in this book.

The *Bechtel* trial shouldn't have been too complicated, as it turned on just a few issues, but it might well have lasted two to three days, from arguing pretrial motions to disputing the findings of fact and law. To focus on the cost of simply this part, assume two lawyers for Bechtel billing at a very conservative average of $100 an hour each. Due to the preparation for each part of the trial, from the pretrial motions to the drafting of the judgment, they're working not only during the hours court is open, perhaps from nine to noon and one to four, but for hours before and after, easily ten hours a day. Over three days, that would amount to a bare minimum of $6,000 (again, in early 1980s rates and dollars). And the trial has probably been the least expensive part of the lawsuit, as the pretrial discovery would have gone on for months.

When the judge found for Bechtel, the nurses could have filed various post-trial motions, such as for a new trial or for judgment notwithstanding the verdict. These motions, though, generally challenge the findings of a jury, so as a practical matter wouldn't have helped much in *Bechtel*, in which a judge made the find-ings—he's certainly not going to reverse himself. But in a typical trial to a jury, the loser does make those motions to protect her grounds for appeal. Again, those motions must be drafted, briefed, and argued. This exercise is typically a waste of time, as the judge is unlikely to overturn a jury's findings unless they were just plain loony. The general rule is that the appellate court will not substi-tute its judgment for the jury's on matters of fact, so why should the trial judge? Still, the motions must be made in order to preserve an appeal after they've been denied.

Once the judgment was final, the nurses would have had to file their notice of appeal. Then the lawyers had to agree on what the record of the trial for review by the court of appeals would consist of. The record would include a transcript of the court proceedings (cost and copies passed on to the client) as well as more copies of everything introduced as evidence at trial.

Then each side had to write, rewrite, and polish a brief for the appellate court. The Washington Supreme Court might well have allowed oral arguments, which would have required the lawyers, who lived in Richland and Yakima, Washington, to drive to Olympia, a few hours away. (On occasion, the Washington Supreme Court has sat in other cities, but we'll presume Olympia now for the sake of simplicity.) Then the lawyers probably waited for their chance to argue, as the court would have been hearing cases besides theirs. Oral argument generally consists of counsels trying to set forth, as quickly and clearly as possible, their theory of the case to a panel of judges who interrupt to ask questions. The questions are theoretically contemplated to clarify the judges' understanding and to probe at the weakness in an argument.

Finally, after what is to the litigants an agonizing wait of many months, the appellate court will issue its holding. In *Bechtel*, that would have been the end of it, for the Washington Supreme Court would be the last stop for this type of state law matter. As it happened, Bechtel was vindicated, and the nurses were left without a remedy—in fact, we saw, they had suffered no injury that deserved a remedy. Their disappointment at having funded the direct expenses of the litigation must have been keen. Bechtel must have felt pleased to have won, but certainly annoyed that it had spent so much money and effort on a case that really did not seem, in the end, to stack up to much.

One can only guess what *Bechtel* cost the litigants. It might not have been very expensive, as cases go, because, as noted above, there were not that many witnesses testifying, and only a few issues. But it is not far-fetched to say that, from filing suit through arguing at the supreme court, Bechtel could have paid its lawyers fees and expenses anywhere from $50,000 to $70,000 in 2003 dollars. (The nurses' lawyers, as noted, perhaps had the case on a contingent basis, though the nurses would have paid the expenses incurred.)

In a number of the cases in this book, and as is the usual progression, the parties would appeal to their state court of appeals before taking the case up to the state supreme court. As the second appeal may amount to not much more than a rehash of the first, the cost may not be too much more, relatively speaking. But a brief must still be written, tailored to disagree or agree with the lower court of appeals, and often the higher court will allow oral argument. All of this costs money. After expending all of that money, someone will finally win.

The cases discussed in this book have little monetary worth. Recall, in fact, that some of the torts—battery, trespass, and one form of defamation—don't even require the plaintiff to show that he has suffered any physical, economic, or other injury. Recall that in one of the trespass cases the court actually comments on how hard the lawyers worked, considering how little money was at stake.[4]

More painful to consider than the monetary cost is what the litigation must have felt like. The *Bechtel* case is actually different from most of the cases in this book in that a corporation was involved. Generally, we see a person suing his or her neighbor or another individual—forcing that person to spend the same kind of money, all the while living, in some cases, just a few yards away. We cannot begin to calculate the energy lost to anxiety, sadness, and anger. While a corporation facing off against another or against an individual would seem insulated from a neighbor-to-neighbor reaction, in some ways the costs are just as painful. The business of the corporation is disrupted, and enormous sums of money— funds often not budgeted for the purpose—have to be spent. And the emotions of the individual officers and other managers are still very much engaged, especially if the litigation has been caused by their decisions or courses of conduct.

We shouldn't discount the stress of the parties' actually having to face each other during the process, either. Though one party doesn't have to attend the deposition of the other, there's nothing to prevent it. Of course everyone will attend the trial. Watching each other testify—and by such testimony implicitly claiming that the other is a liar—is only part of the strain. During breaks, the parties wait in the same hallways, ride the same elevators (or maneuver not to), park in the same lot or garage, and accidentally lunch at the same diner. That's an awful lot of working not to catch each other's eyes.

Just as painful to consider is the loss to the community. If, in the trespass and nuisance cases, the litigants' property lines created disputes between them, each probably had other adjoining neighbors. Were they enlisted by the disputants in support of their causes? If the neighbors were not aware of the litigation, then no community existed to begin with. But if the neighbors had at least some minimal contact, we can bet that they discussed the dispute—it's a rare person who will refuse at least to hear gossip about his neighbor. The litigants were so adamant and obstinate with each other in these cases that it is difficult to believe that they wouldn't badger and lobby their neighbors for support. Choosing a side or choosing not to take sides entails its own risks and stress.

So there is incivility inherent in the system. It is, after all, an adversarial one. But one of the goals of the legal profession is to ensure that this adversarial system works to arrive at resolutions of disputes in fair and evenhanded ways. To aid in reaching that goal, each state has enacted rules of professional responsibility, often modeled on those suggested by the American Bar Association. Each lawyer must be trained and tested on the rules and is constrained to follow them on pain of being disciplined by his state bar.

For example, one rule states: "A lawyer shall make reasonable efforts to expedite litigation consistent with the interests of the client"—that is, no messing around with delaying tactics just to forestall the inevitable defeat.[5] Another states: "A lawyer shall not . . . (d) In pretrial procedure, make a frivolous discovery request or fail to make reasonably diligent effort to comply with a legally proper discovery request by an opposing party."[6] That is, when it's time to discover the facts, don't waste everyone's time and money asking for what you don't need or refusing to tell what ought to be told. Do the right thing.

Further, the systems of civil and criminal procedure are designed to bring some order and civility to the resolution of disputes. That's why the legislatures and courts enact the various rules of court and rules of procedure that the lawyers must follow. They govern how the lawsuit proceeds, from the summons served on the defendant, to the form and, to some extent, to the content of the pleadings, through the discovery procedure, the trial, and the posttrial activity, including appeals. The point is to minimize uncertainty about the process; everyone knows the drill.

But the lawyer's real goal is to win. That's what the client hired him for, and that's really all the client cares about.

Too often in recent years, the battle to win has become nasty. There is increasing concern in the legal profession about a perceived decline in civility among lawyers.[7] It is nearly axiomatic that the profession is no longer gentlepersonly. Examples abound: A lawyer will refuse to grant her opponent a routine extension of time, will schedule depositions without conferring with the opposing party, will fail to provide copies of documents that were required to be produced, or will intentionally schedule a hearing knowing it will be inconvenient for the other side. Indeed, some actions border on the unethical, such as writing a letter to confirm a conversation (which is a routine matter), but making the letter intentionally inaccurate.[8]

In addition, some lawyers simply behave rudely as a means of trying to establish an advantage. The following is a transcript of the deposition of Hugh Liedtke that was taken in Texas by an attorney named William D. Johnston in the case of *Paramount Communications Inc. v. QVC.*[9] A Texan lawyer, Joseph D. Jamail, defended the deposition on Mr. Liedtke's behalf. In quoting from the transcript in its decision on the case, the Delaware Supreme Court stated:

> Mr. Jamail abused the privilege of representing a witness in a Delaware proceeding, in that he: (a) improperly directed the witness not to answer certain questions; (b) was extraordinarily rude, uncivil, and vulgar; and (c) obstructed the ability of the questioner to elicit testimony to assist the Court in this matter.

The transcript, as quoted by the court, read as follows:

MR. LIEDTKE: I vaguely recall [Mr. Oresman's letter]. . . . I think I did read it, probably.

MR. JOHNSTON [Delaware counsel for QVC]: Okay. Do you have any idea why Mr. Oresman was calling that material to your attention?

MR. JAMAIL: Don't answer that. How would he know what was going on in Mr. Oresman's mind? Don't answer it. Go on to your next question.

MR. JOHNSTON: No, Joe—

MR. JAMAIL: He's not going to answer that. Certify it. I'm going to shut it down if you don't go to your next question.

MR. JOHNSTON: No. Joe, Joe—

MR. JAMAIL: Don't "Joe" me, asshole. You can ask some questions, but get off of that. I'm tired of you. You could gag a maggot off a meat wagon. Now, we've helped you every way we can.

MR. JOHNSTON: Let's just take it easy.

MR. JAMAIL: No, we're not going to take it easy. Get done with this.

MR. JOHNSTON: We will go on to the next question.

MR. JAMAIL: Do it now.

MR. JOHNSTON: We will go on to the next question. We're not trying to excite anyone.

MR. JAMAIL: Come on. Quit talking. Ask the question. Nobody wants to socialize with you.

MR. JOHNSTON: I'm not trying to socialize. We'll go on to another question. We're continuing the deposition.

MR. JAMAIL: Well, go on and shut up.

MR. JOHNSTON: Are you finished?

MR. JAMAIL: Yeah, you—

MR. JOHNSTON: Are you finished?

MR. JAMAIL: I may be and you may be. Now, you want to sit here and talk to me, fine. This deposition is going to be over with. You don't know what you're doing. Obviously someone wrote out a long outline of stuff for you to ask. You have no concept of what you're doing. Now, I've tolerated you for three hours. If you've got another question, get on with it. This is going to stop one hour from now, period. Go.

MR. JOHNSTON: Are you finished?

MR. THOMAS (counsel for Paramount): Come on, Mr. Johnston, move it.

MR. JOHNSTON: I don't need this kind of abuse.

MR. THOMAS: Then just ask the next question.

MR. JOHNSTON: All right. To try to move forward, Mr. Liedtke. . . . I'll show you what's been marked as Liedtke 14 and it is a covering letter dated October 29 from Steven Cohen of Wachtell, Lipton, Rosen & Katz including QVC's Amendment Number 1 to its Schedule 14D-1, and my question—

MR. LIEDTKE: No.

MR. JOHNSTON: —to you, sir, is whether you've seen that?

MR. LIEDTKE: No. Look, I don't know what your intent in asking all these questions is, but, my God, I am not going to play boy lawyer.

MR. JOHNSTON: Mr. Liedtke—

MR. LIEDTKE: Okay. Go ahead and ask your question.

MR. JOHNSTON: —I'm trying to move forward in this deposition that we are entitled to take. I'm trying to streamline it.

MR. JAMAIL: Come on with your next question. Don't even talk with this witness.

MR. JOHNSTON: I'm trying to move forward with it.

MR. JAMAIL: You understand me? Don't talk to this witness except by question. Did you hear me?

MR. JOHNSTON: I heard you fine.

MR. JAMAIL: You fee makers think you can come here and sit in somebody's office, get your meter running, get your full day's fee by asking stupid questions. Let's go with it.

Anyone's stomach ought to be queasy after reading that exchange. The Delaware court found Jamail's "unprofessional behavior to be outrageous and unacceptable." It had other problems with Jamail, including his appearance at the deposition, that we needn't take up now. In any event, the court concluded:

> This kind of misconduct is not to be tolerated in any Delaware court proceeding, including depositions taken in other states in which witnesses appear represented by their own counsel other than counsel for a party in the proceeding. Yet, there is no clear mechanism for this Court to deal with this matter in terms of sanctions or disciplinary remedies at this time in the context of this case. Nevertheless, consideration will be given to the following issues for the future: (a) whether or not it is appropriate and fair to take into account the behavior of Mr. Jamail in this case in the event application is made by him in the future to appear pro hac vice in any Delaware proceeding; (footnote omitted) and (b) what rules or standards should be adopted to deal effectively with misconduct by out-of-state lawyers in depositions in proceedings pending in Delaware courts.

The court was inviting Jamail to suggest why it shouldn't bar him from ever appearing in a case in a Delaware court again.

Granted, this was high-stakes war: hostile takeover litigation involving a lot of high-powered New York and Delaware firms. A lot of money was at stake, and the loser wasn't going to be very happy about it. But the court clearly finds Jamail's behavior unacceptable. So should we all.

Other examples that are just as awful abound. In one case, attorney Lawrence Clarke was attending a deposition in which an adversary was represented by a female attorney, Beth Rex. The transcript of the deposition revealed that he made the following comments either to or about her in front of other lawyers, the witness, and the court reporter: "I don't have to talk to you, little lady," "Tell that little mouse over there to pipe down," "What do you know, young girl," "Be quiet, little girl," and "Go away, little girl." At a hearing to determine whether sanctions should be levied against Clarke, Rex testified that while making the comments he flicked his fingers or the back of his hand at her dismissively. Clarke defended himself by stating that he was only engaged in "name-calling." As might be expected, the court let him have it.[10] What's especially amazing is that a lawyer not only behaved abusively, but spoke in a manner that, had it been in an employment context, might have subjected his employer to a claim of sex discrimination.

Lawyers aren't abusive only to opposing counsel; sometimes they go after the judge as well. In another case, a Lewis Stanley apparently took issue with several of the court's rulings. He was accused of a number of acts, including insisting on interrupting the judge. He'd stop what he was saying to make a "rude grimace" at the judge. Rather than question witnesses, as is the form, he'd engage in discourses of his own, despite the judge's admonitions to stop. When the judge made a ruling he didn't like, he'd laugh or even say "Oh, boy" under his breath. The judge admonished Stanley during the trial, but he wouldn't take the hint. Finally, at the conclusion, he delivered an apology that the judge found insincere and refused to accept. The state disciplinary board had no trouble finding that Stanley should be publicly reprimanded for his behavior.[11]

So why does this sort of behavior take place? There are a number of theories. There is a demonstrably larger number of lawyers than in generations past, and those lawyers must compete for clients. Thus they are treating the practice of law more as a business than a profession, and the civility of a profession is forgotten. Law firms advertise and maintain Web sites, as well as provide coffee cups, pencils, and all of the other paraphernalia of a going commercial business. Because there are more lawyers, some may figure that they will never see the other in a case again and so are free to behave as badly as possible with no ramifications for the future.[12]

There is anecdotal evidence to suggest that rapid technological change has made a lawyer's life more stressful and complicated. When the authors began in practice, word processing barely existed, and e-mailing a document was only in the foreseeable future. Now documents can—and the expectation is that they will—be received in the blink of an eye, reviewed, revised, and returned, again in the blink of an eye. There is no reflection in tranquillity.

Finally, for a lawyer to appear reasonable may be to appear weak to a particular client, who may well take her business elsewhere if she perceives an advocate less than willing to fight as fiercely as she wishes. Fighting fiercely isn't the only criterion, of course: The lawyer must also win, and winning at any cost becomes a temptation. It should come as no surprise that civility has become lost in the shuffle.

Alarmed at this recent perceived rise in incivility at the bar—and from the bench, as well—various state bars and the American Bar Association's section on litigation have drafted proposed rules of engagement.[13] One duty, for instance, states: "We will not obstruct questioning during a deposition or object to deposition questions unless permitted under applicable law."[14] Another reads in part, "We will refrain from acting upon or manifesting bias or prejudice based upon race, sex, religion, national origin, disability, age, sexual orientation or socioeconomic status toward any participant in the legal process."[15] Messrs. Jamail and Clarke, take note. Unfortunately, these proposed duties do not carry the weight of law and only amount to standards to which lawyers should aspire. However, they are a beginning, and, one hopes, a good one, toward reestablishing civil relations among members of the bar.

One question remains: With clients like some of those in this book, how can some lawyers avoid getting their hands dirty? Suing one's neighbor or friend is not a civil act. As Carter says, "Civility has two parts: generosity, even when it is costly, and trust, even when there is risk."[16] Many of the citizens in the cases in this book seem to be litigating for either or both of two reasons: because they can't or won't back down, and because they can afford it. Few or none of them are being generous, showing trust, or seeking compromise. They would rather incur the cost of litigating than the cost of being a good citizen. In the process, of course, whatever there is of being a conscious member of a community is lost.

The lawyers are only following along, but that doesn't excuse them. One of the best and most important roles a lawyer can fill for his client is that of an advisor. Washington Rule of Professional Responsibility 2.1 reads:

> In representing a client, a lawyer shall exercise independent professional judgment and render candid advice. In rendering advice, a lawyer may refer not only to law but to other considerations such as moral, economic, social and political factors, that may be relevant to a client's position.[17]

And why not? A lawyer is in the best position to give such advice, knowing, if he does and as he should, every possible fact about the matter to be litigated. In pursuing a position that may be untenable for any reason, whether moral or otherwise, both the lawyer and the client are allowing themselves to walk into a situation that can't help but grow more uncivil by the moment. By counseling his client to give up an untenable position, the lawyer takes a step toward removing them both from a situation out of which no good can come for anyone. In the process, everyone can save time, money, and pain. And they can take a step toward instilling some civility in the uncivil act of litigation.

CHAPTER 12

Revenge by Litigation
Wrongful Civil Proceedings

> Wherein you reprove Another be
> unblameable yourself; for example
> is more prevalent than precepts.
>
> GEORGE WASHINGTON'S
> 48TH RULE OF CIVILITY,
> *Rules of Civility*
> *for the 21st Century*
> *from Cub and Boy Scouts*
> *from across America*

After eleven chapters on the various ways in which Americans can act uncivilly to each other and how the legal system does or doesn't address those acts, it should not surprise anyone to learn that some lawsuits can trigger a lawsuit in retaliation.

Here's an example of just how nightmarish American litigation can become. In 1932 Mr. Kaufman sued his very own brother-in-law, Mr. Ackerman, for malicious prosecution, more correctly known as wrongful civil proceedings. Malicious prosecution is the correct term for a response to a criminal prosecution; the two torts are otherwise quite similar. Courts are just as likely to use "malicious prosecution" to describe both, so we will too. Ackerman had sued Kaufman and had lost, and so Kaufman brought his claim for malicious prosecution.

The elements that Kaufman would have to prove were simple: Ackerman had initiated a civil action against him, the action had terminated favorably for Kaufman, Ackerman had lacked the probable cause necessary to bring the action and brought one for an improper purpose, and Kaufman had suffered damages.

The only damages Kaufman sought were the $500 in legal fees that he'd spent.

He also sought a permanent injunction against Ackerman's suing him again. The verdict was in Kaufman's favor, and Ackerman appealed to the Arizona Supreme Court.[1]

The supreme court discussed the prior litigation between the parties that consisted of the following:

1. The parties had moved to Tucson, Arizona, sometime before 1911. In December 1912 Ackerman sued Kaufman for the return of documents that Ackerman claimed Kaufman had obtained from him by fraud. Kaufman won.

2. A few months later, Ackerman sued again, this time alleging that a woman named Esther Felix had forged Ackerman's name to documents that benefited Kaufman. Ackerman asked for $6,000 in damages. Kaufman won again.

3. In July 1913 Ackerman sued Kaufman yet again, alleging the same facts and adding that Kaufman had been annoying him and stealing his property. Ackerman again asked for $6,000 in damages, and yet again Kaufman won.

4. Kaufman, apparently having had enough, sued Ackerman for $5,000 and an injunction against further actions. (This is not the case first described above—not yet; we're only halfway through.) The verdict was for Kaufman, but only in the amount of $500.

5. In 1927 Kaufman sued Ackerman for $204 that Kaufman claimed he'd spent on Ackerman's behalf. Ackerman counterclaimed, asking $10,000 in damages. Kaufman won.

6. In February 1931, apparently having caught his breath, Ackerman went on the attack again, suing Kaufman based on facts going back to 1911, including all of the facts from the lawsuits that he'd already lost. His complaint, a rambling first-person narrative, added that while he was in Europe, Kaufman had embezzled $9,000 from him, alienated his wife's affections, and kidnapped his daughter. Kaufman's motion to dismiss the complaint was granted. Ackerman refiled the complaint, and again it was dismissed.

7. A few days later, Ackerman filed essentially the same suit again, and it was dismissed yet again.

In the lawsuit for malicious prosecution that Kaufman then brought (yes, we've finally gotten to the main case), the court alluded to the following set of slightly earlier, somewhat unrelated cases that it had also heard. One was *Ackerman v. Southern Arizona Bank & Trust Co.*[2] Of Ackerman's complaint against the bank, the court wrote, "In all our experience we have never seen a pleading like this." The pleading consisted of forty-three single-spaced typewritten pages of excerpts of conversations, the story of how the City of Tucson had condemned one of his buildings, his experiences with Kaufman in collecting rents, and balances of accounts between Ackerman and the bank and Ackerman and Kaufman.

The trial court had dismissed the suit, and Ackerman had appealed the dismissal to the Arizona Supreme Court.

In the earlier pleadings of the case, the court said, it was clear that Ackerman hadn't had the assistance of a lawyer, because nothing filed in his name followed the court's rules. It was clear that he had since found a lawyer to help, as the papers looked a little spiffier, but only Ackerman had signed the brief. The court noted, "The record shows he [Ackerman] is a very thrifty man and possessed of considerable means." Unfortunately, however, the trial court had been right—the complaint was not a concise statement of facts, as required by the rules of the court, but merely an "unloading on the court a world of grievances, business and domestic, against the bank and his kinsfolk, especially the latter." The supreme court affirmed the dismissal by the trial court.

Another case not mentioned in the list above was a companion case to the bank case, printed immediately adjacent in the case reporter. This one was confusingly also named *Ackerman v. Southern Arizona Bank & Trust Co.*[3] This was an action by the bank against Ackerman for amounts due under two promissory notes. The court found for the bank, and Ackerman appealed. Ackerman's answer in this action consisted, said the court, of all of the same material that was in his complaint in the companion case, and much more, "involving many divers transactions wholly unrelated in subject matter and time." In this opinion, the court speculated that Ackerman hadn't had the assistance of counsel because "he has no rights to protect or wrongs to redress" such that a lawyer would take the case. The court affirmed the judgment of the trial court.

Two other opinions on the next page of the same case reporter, *Ackerman v. Kaufman* and, of course, *Ackerman v. Kaufman*,[4] merely affirmed the dismissal by the trial court of two of the cases described in the numbered list above.

With that background in mind, we turn to the court's discussion in Ackerman's appeal of the verdict for Kaufman in his malicious prosecution action, the very first suit mentioned in this chapter. The court noted that, again, Ackerman had no assistance of counsel, despite the fervent advice of all of the courts that he obtain some. Ackerman's brief to the court was garbled, violated the rules of the court, and failed to cite any errors made by the trial court, except that it had failed to give him ultimate justice. Nevertheless, the court sighed, it would bend over backward to see if it could figure out what his defenses were.

The court wasn't the only one trying as hard as it could to be fair to Ackerman. In order to avoid taking advantage of Ackerman's not having had the benefit of legal counsel, Kaufman's own lawyer raised a point that was unclear in Arizona law. In malicious prosecution actions, did Arizona follow the English or the American rule?

To answer that question, it's useful to look at the theory of this tort. The courts have put significant restrictions on it because one of our most cherished rights is to seek redress of grievances in courts. We especially want the plaintiff of modest means who is honestly aggrieved to bring her action without undue fear that, if she loses, her wealthier defendant will lash back with a lawsuit of his own for malicious prosecution. Thus, the winning defendant isn't given an easy way to make a claim for malicious prosecution.

In a sizeable minority of states, one of the restrictions is that a plaintiff in a malicious prosecution action—that is, the defendant in the prior action—must have suffered some special, calculable, or concrete damages beyond the usual expenses of litigation, especially attorneys' fees. Generally, one suffers "special injury" when the first suit works an immediate interference with person, property, income, or credit. One example would be the creditor who brings suit against the debtor and garnishes the debtor's paycheck to pay off the debt. If it turned out that there had been no debt, then the debtor could bring an action for malicious prosecution. Likewise, a creditor might bring an attachment action through which he would file a lien on the debtor's property. That lien would prevent the debtor from selling the property without paying off the debt. Again, if the debt didn't exist, the debtor could bring an action for malicious prosecution. There are other certain special circumstances. For instance, someone wrongfully instituting insanity proceedings could be liable for malicious prosecution, as the outcome could well be loss of liberty for the one whose sanity was questioned.[5] States that require a showing of this sort of damages are said to follow the "English rule."

In England itself, the seemingly strict nature of the English rule is mitigated somewhat in that the winner *in any lawsuit* recovers her attorneys' fees from the loser. So, if Arizona decided that it followed the English rule, then Kaufman would lose his malicious prosecution case because he had suffered no special damages. However, he could recover his attorneys' fees from his brother-in-law.

The majority of American courts reject the English rule and allow recovery of less concrete or easily calculable damages, such as to reputation, and emotional injury, as well as the cost of litigation. Those costs do include attorneys' fees because, most of the time, each American litigant pays only his own lawyers. An exception is that the winning American litigant can generally recover attorneys' fees if a statute provides for it.[6] Also, lawyers often draft contracts with a clause providing that in any litigation between the parties the loser pays all of the fees. But the general course of things is that each party pays his own fees. Therefore, under the American rule, it makes sense that the winner in a malicious prosecution action can recover attorneys' fees.

Whether Arizona followed the English or the American rule was an important point, because Kaufman hadn't suffered any damages except the expense of litigation (though we can be sure there was plenty of that). If Arizona followed the English rule, Kaufman would lose his malicious prosecution suit, as he had no special damages such as an arrest of his person or interference with his property.

The court understood the reason for the English rule. In English courts, a winning defendant is compensated for everything he would have lost: his court costs and his attorneys' fees. Therefore, the typical English defendant has no money damages in the face of an action filed in bad faith. In America, as we saw, the winning defendant typically does not recover his attorneys' fees. Therefore, the defendant suffers damages simply by being put to the trouble of defending a suit. If that suit were in bad faith, should the defendant have to suffer? The court understood the argument about not wanting to discourage worthy plaintiffs who might fear a retaliatory suit if they lost. However, the court also felt that an honest plaintiff, one who filed a suit in good faith, should have nothing to worry about. Arizona, said the court, would follow the American rule. Kaufman didn't have to allege and prove special damages in order to prevail.

With that settled, the court didn't worry too much more over the elements of the tort. Kaufman could easily prove that Ackerman had initiated a civil action against him, the action had terminated favorably for Kaufman, Ackerman had lacked the probable cause necessary to bring the action and brought one for an improper purpose, and Kaufman had suffered damages. The court merely said that the "recital of facts is sufficient to convince any fair-minded jury that defendant in this case is either mentally unbalanced or that his action was malicious."[7] The court neglected to consider one other possibility: These fellows were brothers-in-law. In some families, that could be explanation enough.

So justice was finally done for poor Kaufman. But he had to suffer over a twenty-year period before the court put an end to the misery. And what might have been the outcome if the court had adopted the English rule? Because Kaufman couldn't have proved special damages, Ackerman would have had no incentive to amend his litigious ways. However, if ever there were an instance of the facts determining what the law was going to be, this is that instance. It's difficult to imagine the court's not wanting to adopt the rule that would create victory for Kaufman, if only so that they wouldn't have to keep reviewing trial courts' judgments against Ackerman.[8]

In the meantime, the parties—family, at that—beat up on each other for a good number of lawsuits before Kaufman finally pleaded with the court to put an end to Ackerman's plague of paper. Ackerman appeared to be either an annoying pest or, as the court suggested, somewhat unbalanced. Yet, no matter

Ackerman's problems or motivations, the fact remains that he filed these suits *in bad faith*. He meant to do a bad thing, over and over again, including, it appears, against the advice of people who bring lawsuits for a living.

Yet the courts, as they are bound to do, gave him every benefit of the doubt, time after time. Because the legal system is so careful to afford every citizen his right to seek justice, achieving real justice in this set of circumstances took a long time. The Ackerman-Kaufman litigation is an excellent example of how the legal system isn't designed to curtail the incivility of litigation. The trade-off is, as the Arizona court implied, that an honest litigant needn't fear a suit for wrongful civil proceedings. Because that's so, we err on the side of allowing greater access to the courthouses, even for those who act in bad faith. But the cause of civility is not served.

The painful results of the English rule were evident in the case of *O'Toole v. Franklin*.[9] In that case, in July 1974, a Mr. Mathis sued Dr. O'Toole and his partners in a Medford, Oregon, clinic, alleging malpractice in prescribing medicine two years earlier. The doctors told Mr. Mathis and his attorneys that they hadn't treated Mr. Mathis at all, much less treated him negligently. They repeatedly asked that the suit be dismissed. Nevertheless, the suit was allowed to linger until January 1975, about six months after it was filed. Though the opinion doesn't make this clear, one would like to think that during that time the lawyers on both sides didn't take much action and so not much money was spent or effort expended—indeed, Mathis's lawyers simply realized that they had the wrong guys.

When Mathis finally did dismiss his complaint, the doctors sued Mathis and his lawyer, alleging malicious prosecution—that they had maintained the action knowing that the doctors hadn't prescribed any drugs for Mathis. The doctors asked for $50,000 in damages for "special injury," specifically, injury to their professional reputations. They also asked for punitive damages in the amount of $200,000. The doctors added a second count in negligence, against both Mathis for failing to tell his lawyers the true story and the lawyers for failing to investigate the case properly and for inciting Mathis to begin the malpractice action. The doctors also asked for $50,000 in general damages for "emotional disturbance and anguish."

Mathis and his lawyers moved to have the action dismissed, arguing that the allegations failed to state a proper claim against them under the law of malicious prosecution. The trial court granted the motion. Its holding was apparently based on Oregon's following the English rule, which of course required that they claim that they had suffered one of those special injuries. The court felt that the doctors hadn't been able to do so. As we've noted, special injury must be a concrete, calculable one beyond the effort, expense, and other trouble usually visited on a litigant.

The doctors appealed the decision to the Oregon Supreme Court. They argued that the allegation of damage to their professional reputations arising out of the inaccurate allegation of malpractice was a sufficient special injury.

The court conceded first that "'special' was not the most self-explanatory of terms."[10] Still, cases that provided examples had come from the Oregon courts earlier. They included the injuries suffered when the first suit interfered with person, property, income, or credit. Examples are the creditor's garnishing a paycheck to pay off a nonexistent debt, and insanity proceedings to have someone committed who was as sane as can be. The court had also left open the possibility of the existence of other special circumstances in which the defendant in the first suit was individually, uniquely vulnerable, beyond the usual hardship of litigation. This case, however, was not one of those cases.

The doctors had other arguments. The plaintiff in a malpractice action, as well as in any other court proceeding, enjoyed an absolute privilege against defamation actions arising out of statements made in litigation. That meant that a plaintiff could allege anything he wanted, in complete and utter bad faith, and still be invulnerable to attack. This was so even if the plaintiff managed to destroy a doctor's reputation. The doctor had no remedy against such bad-faith trash talking. The remedy, according to the doctors, ought to be an action for malicious prosecution. If a doctor didn't suffer special injury arising out of that kind of bad faith, they argued, then he could never suffer special injury.

The court conceded that other states, about twenty-three, had dropped the special damages requirement of the English rule, while only seventeen states kept company with Oregon in retaining it. Further, the Restatement of Torts followed the American rule. Yet further, Dean Prosser argued against the requirement of the English rule that one must show special damages, agreeing that while honest litigants should be welcomed to the courthouse, "surely there is no policy in favor of vexatious suits known to be groundless, which are a real and often a serious injury."[11]

Critics of the English rule also argued that it was tough enough to establish that the plaintiff in the original suit had acted with a lack of probable cause and an improper purpose; requiring special injury was piling too many burdens on the successful defendant. The Oregon Supreme Court, though, believed that that argument invited a weighing of interests. What was more important: preventing frivolous suits, or encouraging the honest assertion of rights? And the English rule did give a plaintiff concrete, specific notice of the kind of claims that, if made wrongfully, would subject him to a subsequent suit: interferences with property, like garnishment and attachment, and interferences with person, like insanity proceedings.

Prosser also described other justifications for the English rule. One was that we needed a significant restriction on the right to bring a claim for malicious prosecution, or else each such suit invites a third in return, and then a fourth back again, and so on. Even the most litigious American bound on revenge probably wants the battle to stop somewhere.[12]

The Oregon Supreme Court finally concluded that the trial court had been correct to dismiss the count of malicious prosecution. The doctors were without a remedy.

By the way, it's interesting to see how the court disposed of the negligence suit, which was based on Mathis's and his lawyers' alleged carelessness in bringing and maintaining the action. The facts supporting the negligence and malicious prosecution claims were more or less the same. The court believed that the doctors could be trying to use the negligence claim to recover the damages refused them under malicious prosecution. The court felt that would be a pretty sneaky end run on the requirements of malicious prosecution. Why should the doctors be able to recover by alleging mere carelessness when they couldn't recover under the tougher standards imposed by malicious prosecution? The court wouldn't allow that to happen, and affirmed the dismissal of the negligence count as well.

The *O'Toole* case demonstrates that the English rule may encourage frivolous litigation and its attendant costs to society. While Mathis had notice of the kinds of claims that would buy him a malicious prosecution suit if he lost, he also knew what actions he could bring without fear of reprisal—for instance, the instigation of this suit without proper investigation of the facts.

States that have adopted the English rule put stringent restrictions on the ability of someone wronged by an action brought in bad faith to recover. It's another situation in which our legal system supports interests inconsistent with societal civility—or, perhaps more precisely, finds the risk of incivility outweighed by other concerns.

So the English rule allows the attack, but, in the interest of drawing a line somewhere, does not permit the counterattack except in certain narrowly defined circumstances that these doctors couldn't meet. While we might argue that there's nothing civil about the counterattack, it remains true that, without the counterattack, we are countenancing more frivolous, nonmeritorious litigation up front. As we have seen time and again in this book, Americans don't need any more encouragement to sue each other. Thankfully, for the sake of civility, the English rule is not followed countrywide, and, in fact, is only followed in a minority of states. In a majority of states, the Medford doctors could have recovered.

Let's look quickly at one last case that shows another way that a defendant can be put to the exasperating trouble of defending a meritless suit. In June 1971 Mr. Minasian, a lawyer, sued his client Mr. Sapse for $300 in fees owed. Minasian employed a process server to serve the complaint on Sapse. The process server served the complaint on Mrs. Sapse. Then, on August 12, Sapse filed a counterclaim. A counterclaim is just what it sounds like; a defendant in a suit may bring an action against the plaintiff, provided, essentially, that the defendant's claim arises out of the same transaction or occurrence on which the plaintiff's suit is based. Sapse alleged in his counterclaim that Minasian's process server had behaved so badly that Mrs. Sapse became so agitated and shocked that she suffered severe hypertension and died. Sapse wanted $50,000 in damages.

Then, on August 16, Sapse's lawyer filed an amended counterclaim to the effect that, oops, no, Mrs. Sapse didn't actually die, but she was still feeling pretty bad. Now Sapse wanted only $6,000.

Over the next two years, Minasian didn't hear another peep from Sapse, and, presumably, did not receive payment of those $300 in fees. In December 1973 Minasian moved for dismissal of Sapse's counterclaim on the grounds that he had failed to prosecute it—that is, he had simply let things slide for more than two years. So the drowsy counterclaim ought to be put to sleep formally. The motion was granted.

Then, Minasian filed a suit for malicious prosecution. The trial court dismissed Minasian's lawsuit, holding that Sapse's counterclaim had not terminated in favor of Minasian. We recall from the *Kaufman* cases that the suit has to terminate in favor of the defendant (in this case, the defendant to a counterclaim). The decision didn't sit well, and Minasian appealed to the California Court of Appeals.[13] By the way, the court didn't question whether a defendant's bringing a counterclaim constituted bringing a civil proceeding. When Minasian sued and Sapse brought his counterclaim, that counterclaim acted just like a complaint. Minasian had to answer it, and Sapse (had he been so inclined) would have been entitled to take discovery and ask a jury or a judge for damages, in this case, for his wife's ill health. Therefore, there was no reason not to treat Sapse's counterclaim as anything other than the institution of a civil proceeding.

Minasian's argument was that the whole point of the malicious prosecution action was to compensate the winner for having been damaged by having to defend himself against a claim that shouldn't have been brought. Minasian didn't have to pay Sapse anything, so he must have won on Sapse's counterclaim; the inquiry should end there. Sapse argued that there was no termination on behalf of Minasian *on the merits*—that is, Minasian didn't exactly win. Sapse had simply failed to prosecute his claim. No prosecution, no decision, no favorable termination.

The court of appeals agreed that, if a termination was such as to indicate lack of liability on Minasian's part, then it was a favorable termination. If the dismissal had come about by merely technical means, or for a procedural reason, or for any other reason that wasn't necessarily consistent with lack of liability, then the termination wouldn't be favorable. For instance, if the trial court had found that it didn't have jurisdiction to hear the counterclaim, a dismissal on that ground wouldn't be on the merits. That finding would simply have been that the party wasn't subject to suit for some reason. The finding wouldn't have anything to do with whether or not he had performed the acts cited in the complaint. Sapse argued that the same applied here: A dismissal for failure to prosecute was exactly *not* on the merits. So this dismissal sounds like one on technical grounds.

But the court disagreed. Sapse brought his action for money damages. Questions would "arise from the natural assumption that one does not simply abandon a meritorious action once instituted."[14] That is to say, one doesn't leave $6,000 lying on the table if one has a reasonable expectation of recovering it. Sapse, then, must not have had a good-faith belief that he was going to be able to recover that $6,000. Dismissal of his counterclaim for failure to prosecute, then, carried with it the strong implication that Minasian would have won had Sapse pursued the claim. The court reversed the judgment of the trial judge.

If Sapse didn't expect to win, then what was his motivation for bringing the counterclaim? The implication is that his motivation was wrongful. Perhaps he brought the claim merely to put pressure on Minasian to drop his claim for his fees. A first, natural instinct on being sued is to ask, What can I blame *that* guy for? One purpose of the tort of malicious prosecution is to put some reasonable restraints on people whose first instinct on thinking that they've been wronged is to fire off a complaint—or, in this case, a counterclaim, whether it has any merit or not. Doing so is, unfortunately, close to our litigious American hearts. The problem is that one who prevails in his defense of such a claim receives nothing for suffering the loss of time, waste of effort, emotional stress, and considerable expense of defending against a frivolous claim. Such a state of affairs cries out for some kind of remedy. Thus, the availability of the tort of malicious prosecution.

What is especially sad about this case, though justice eventually was done, is that the counterclaim went out not with a bang but with a whimper. Sapse and his lawyer let the claim sit for over two years with apparently no intention whatsoever of doing anything about it. It's not just an example of malicious prosecution, but something beyond—wrongful civil coercion, or maybe just a case of failed blackmail. Whatever it is, bringing that frivolous action was an act of disrespect of Minasian—and a refusal to approach the litigation system with a sense of how citizens are to use it: as a means of resolving good-faith disputes within the confines of a set of agreed-upon rules.

As we have often seen in this book, the rules have evolved to accommodate a weighing of interests. The English rule of malicious prosecution provides protection to the worthy, honest plaintiff, but it also provides protection to a plaintiff maliciously filing a suit in bad faith, because he knows that, unless he's threatened the defendant's property or liberty, he's not going to be subject to a subsequent suit for malicious prosecution, at least not one likely to be successful.

On the other hand, under the American rule, if one brings a lawsuit in bad faith, the winning defendant will likely be licking his chops in wait for the judgment to be entered so he can serve his complaint for malicious prosecution the next morning. The only deterrent is the memory of the awful experience just ended: The next morning may bring a surge of vengeful emotion, but it's going to be tempered by the hangover of the last couple of years of litigation. Who wants to go out drinking again after a night like that? If his attorneys' fees were high enough, and the defendant were angry enough, though, he just might want to give it a try.

So what do we do? Perhaps we ought to think harder in America about adopting the English rule with respect to attorneys' fees, which allows the winning party in litigation to recover his attorneys' fees from the other side. Then parties would think more than twice about beginning or continuing with litigation in bad faith. Unfortunately, such a solution goes against the grain of one of our cherished concepts, that of keeping the courthouse door open for worthy plaintiffs. Under this rule, even a worthy, good-faith plaintiff will have to pay the defendant's fees if a judge or jury should look unkindly on her case. A poor plaintiff would think twice before bringing suit, and Americans do not want that.

Of course, the real solution has been there all along. Rather than tinker with the litigation system and its procedures, why shouldn't Americans be asked to stop and think before litigating at all? Or is this too much to ask? Perhaps. Nevertheless, the law of malicious prosecution, or wrongful civil proceedings, is not the solution to the problem of our bringing lawsuits in bad faith. It's not the solution to the problems of incivility in American society as a whole or in the legal and litigation system in particular. In this sort of situation, malicious prosecution treats the symptoms but does nothing to cure the illness. Again we see the legal system able to go only so far. Instead, Americans must learn to approach each other with some mutual respect, trust, and generosity in their disputes.

One more case summarizes our themes. Mr. Silvino Gomez was employed in April 1978 as a supervisor at the Shawnee County, Kansas, fairgrounds. His immediate boss was a Mr. Kanatzer. One evening that month they were readying the grounds for a horse show when they discovered a break in a water line. Breaks apparently occurred fairly often.[1] They went to Kanatzer's office to call a contractor to come out and repair the line. They encountered Mr. Roland Hug, a member of the Board of County Commissioners, and a Mr. Corbett.

Hug immediately asked Kanatzer, "What is that fucking spic doing in the office?" Hug repeated his question, then ordered Gomez to approach him, again calling Gomez a "fucking spic." Gomez asked what he meant by that, and Hug answered, "You are a fucking spic." Gomez repeated his question, and Hug replied, "A fucking Mexican greaser like you, that is all you are. You are nothing but a fucking Mexican greaser, nothing but a pile of shit." According to Gomez in his deposition testimony in the ensuing litigation, Hug continued to assert his opinion, then raised his fist and asked, "Now what are you going to do about it?"

Hug continued in this vein; nothing is gained by repeating the same words over and over, so suffice it to say that Gomez believed that this invective continued for from five to fifteen minutes. Along the way, Hug continued shaking his fists in front of Gomez's eyes and pounding on the desk. He also challenged Gomez, calling him a coward. Finally—and one wonders why the others allowed this to go on so long—Kanatzer escorted Gomez out of the office and home.

There is, apparently, little explanation for Hug's behavior. That the water line tended to break frequently wasn't Gomez's fault, and he wasn't sneaking out and intentionally breaking it. A reasonable explanation was that Hug was a county commissioner, a person of some power, and Gomez was not. The constantly breaking water line was merely a convenient excuse. Thus Hug could feel free to treat Gomez with as little respect as he pleased.[2] And it seemed to please him a lot to behave as cruelly as he wanted.

Gomez was understandably upset by the incident. Apparently, this encounter with Hug was not Gomez's first of this sort,[3] and he began to suffer medical problems. He consulted a family physician, a neurologist, and a psychiatrist. The latter two believed that Gomez's medical problems were related to the incident with Hug.

Gomez sued both Hug and the county, alleging assault, intentional infliction of emotional distress, slander, and denial of civil rights—that is, several of the claims examined in this book. The trial court granted the defendants' motion for summary judgment (that is, a judgment before trial to the jury), and Gomez appealed to the Kansas Court of Appeals.[4]

The first issue was the assault. Could a reasonable jury decide, on these facts, that Hug had assaulted Gomez? We recall that an actual touching needn't occur; an assault, the court said, was "an intentional threat or attempt, coupled with apparent ability, to do bodily harm to another, resulting in immediate apprehension of bodily harm."[5] Words by themselves aren't enough, but words together with other acts or circumstances could suffice. In fact, remember from chapter 2 the scene Dean Prosser posited: the highwayman sitting perfectly still but holding a gun and demanding money. There was no overt act, but, Dean Prosser felt, that situation felt a lot like an assault.

The court of appeals noted that Gomez had testified that Hug repeated the ugly language over and over while shaking his fists at Gomez and pounding on a table. It is significant that Gomez testified, "I was froze because I was afraid of the man."[6] The court considered some additional facts, significantly that Gomez and Hug had a history, including problems that had resulted in other litigation.[7] The court had to say that a reasonable jury could find that an assault had occurred. The trial court was reversed on the assault count, and Gomez was allowed to pursue his claim at trial.

Next was the intentional infliction of emotional distress claim. The court cited the law of Kansas, which follows our discussion of the tort in chapter 6—Hug must have engaged in extreme and outrageous conduct that either intentionally or recklessly caused severe emotional distress to Gomez for Hug to be liable for the emotional distress and any bodily injury resulting from it. The court took note of the relative positions of the parties, which we recall was an important issue in the *Zalnis v. Thoroughbred Datsun* case.[8] (The car sales manager had reason to know that Ms. Zalnis, due to her husband's suicide, was particularly vulnerable.) Here, Hug was the employer, Gomez the employee. Hug had been speaking in this way for several days, and Gomez testified to being afraid of Hug and afraid for his job and his family.

Furthermore, the court did seem truly offended by the language. While it felt that the courts shouldn't intervene every time someone's feelings are hurt, that our society still had rough edges, and that one ought to be allowed to blow off steam, this language went well beyond that point. "It is not a burden of American citizenship in the State of Kansas," the court intoned somewhat ponderously, "that such vitriolic bullying as was turned by Hug against Gomez, and its emotional and physical consequences, must be accepted without possibility of redress and accepted as often as it amuses the speaker to utter it. Kansas courts are not so impotent."[9] In any event, the court found that a reasonable jury could find for Gomez on this claim and reversed the trial court again and allowed Gomez to proceed with his claim at trial.

The court dealt more quickly with the slander count. Slander, we recall, consists of false statements that tend to diminish the plaintiff's reputation—the esteem and respect in which the plaintiff would otherwise be held in the community. Here, there was simply no evidence that Gomez's reputation had been harmed. In fact, one can imagine that Gomez might well have become the object of some sympathy and even regard in the eyes of Kanatzer and Corbett. The court quickly decided that the trial court had correctly granted summary judgment on this claim.

Next, had Gomez been denied his civil rights? He had sued under 42 U.S.C. § 1983, which provided that

> every person who, under color of any statute, ordinance, regulation, custom, or usage, of any State or Territory, subjects, or causes to be subjected, any citizen of the United States or other person within the jurisdiction thereof to the deprivation of any rights, privileges, or immunities secured by the Constitution and laws, shall be liable to the

party injured in any action at law, suit in equity, or other proper proceeding for redress.

The court dealt quickly with this claim as well, as there was controlling case law. Verbal abuse simply didn't support an action under 42 U.S.C.S. § 1983. (Remember from chapter 7 that Mr. Cariddi, the Kansas City Chiefs ticket taker, also had no claim under the statute governing discriminatory employment practices, 42 U.S.C.S. § 2000e *et seq.*) Summary judgment for the defendants was affirmed.

That was pretty much that. Gomez could go back to the trial court and bring his claims for assault and the intentional infliction of emotional distress. However, he could only proceed against Hug, not the county. The court held that Hug, as a county commissioner, was an elected official. The rule was that elected officials were public officers and not the agents of the corporate body, in this case the county. Therefore, Hug was not acting as an agent for the county, but only in his individual capacity. The decision was a significant setback for Gomez, for the deep pockets of Shawnee County were out of the picture. And while Shawnee County had agreed to pay the defense of lawsuits brought against its county commissioners, that agreement certainly wouldn't extend to paying for any judgment against Hug for an intentionally wrongful act.[10] Thus the only pocket now was Hug's; if he carried liability insurance, it probably didn't cover him for intentional acts like assault and intentional infliction of severe emotional distress. Therefore, Gomez's chance of actually recovering damages arising out of this unfortunate incident were much narrowed.

There is no subsequent history of the case because nothing else happened. The case was remanded for trial, and at that point the parties settled. Remember that Shawnee County had the obligation to pay for Hug's defense. At that point the county apparently decided that it made more sense for it to pay Gomez something now than to pay Hug's legal fees through trial.[11] Thus Gomez was paid some amount in settlement, though undoubtedly less than he had hoped.

This case includes three of the torts that we discussed earlier: assault, the intentional infliction of severe emotional distress, and slander. Each claim arises out of Hug's failure to behave civilly—with respect—toward Gomez. Apparently, the mere incentive to behave with respect for another person wasn't sufficient for Hug. Something about Gomez set him off, and he was unable to quell the desire to treat Gomez badly.

Therefore, Gomez turned to the law. Yet the likelihood is that Gomez's ultimate satisfaction, if any, was small. If the county hadn't settled, Gomez would have had to drag Hug through a trial with all of its attendant costs (including the stress of facing his adversary in court) and likely gain little monetary relief, even if he had won. So Gomez's only available recourse, the legal system, wouldn't provide much in the way of satisfaction. With this case, depressingly typical of many that we've seen, in mind, it is useful to consider where we've been.

A SUMMARY

We saw that battery, assault, and trespass are simple actions. The torts implicitly accept that individuals will behave uncivilly toward each other. These very old torts developed with such minimal requirements, in part, to invite an easy recovery in court and thus preclude a violent response. Also implicitly accepted is that litigation can easily arise because so little is required to recover. Nevertheless, litigation, though it can be an evil itself, is presumably preferable to retaliatory bloodshed.

The battery involving unwanted sexual contact is troublesome. The rules grow more complex because the context is so complicated. What starts out as a consensual touching may rapidly turn into a battery. These matters definitely seemed better governed not by law but by etiquette; however, perhaps due in part to a perception of changing sexual mores, the etiquette seemed either to have changed or to have simply been ignored. Thus the legal system was called in: Federal law was passed prohibiting sexual harassment in the workplace, and a victim could vindicate her rights in court. The bottom line, however, is that the legal system is ill suited to setting policy regarding sexual activity. A compromise to litigation was the more flexible intervention of Antioch College's Sexual Offense Prevention Policy, a quasi-legal code inviting various levels of mediation.

The tort of nuisance is a more complicated cousin of trespass. The lesson is that everyone must expect to be a little bit bothered—just not too bothered. At that, whose inconvenience is worse? The person being annoyed, or the person who must stop causing the annoyance? We see the law struggling to adjudicate situations involving members of a community who see their individual interests as more important than another's and so are unwilling to compromise. The warring neighbors instead demand that the legal system create a compromise for them. No one works to advance the causes of civility and community.

The balancing of the litigants' interests that occurs in nuisance also takes place in determining whether recovery is warranted under the tort of intentional infliction of severe emotional distress. One person has behaved truly abominably toward another, and the courts feel compelled to provide redress. Yet the courts must balance the behavior against an uncertain measure: How much annoyance should one be expected to endure? How close may the court come to excusing brutality, and how close to encouraging mere whining? The torts of nuisance and intentional infliction of emotional distress thus take the battery/assault/trespass trio a step further: Not only do the courts expect that a certain amount of incivility will occur, but they declare that we will all have to put up with it.

We began our look at speech by discussing some of the laws that attempted to enforce civil speech. The reach of those laws was limited to certain extreme sorts of circumstances, such as fighting words. Otherwise, people are free to insult each other as they please. We also looked at another alternative to litigation, a quasi-legal attempt to enforce civil speech, the University of Pennsylvania's speech code. Generally speaking, society and its institutions will be extremely sensitive to the notion that Americans must be free to speak their minds. Civility loses out in the balance.

We turned next to a discussion of some criminal statutes to examine whether those, society's most direct sorts of sanctions, were more effective in enforcing notions of civility. Some laws forbade harassment by telephone, and others were enacted to prevent people from stalking or harassing each other on the street and by computer. Each law ran up against another of society's most important interests: that we not lightly brand individuals as criminals. In the end, the criminal laws, though well intentioned, are inefficient methods by which to enforce civil behavior.

We continued with a look at some laws that attempt to restrict speech simply because of the kind of speech it is: blasphemous or obscene speech, or public curses. Many would agree that such talk is uncivil. However, the courts would rather err on the side of allowing manifestly uncivil speech than make the mistake on the other side: prohibiting speech that may be unpopular but that has some useful social value. These laws implicitly recognize that uncivil speech must be tolerated.

Finally, with respect to speech, we surveyed cases involving defamation—language that tends to injure someone's reputation. To speak ill of another person is to speak in an uncivil way. But society also has an overwhelming interest in ensuring that its citizens may express their opinions freely, without fear of sanction by the government through the courts. Therefore, those of whom ill is spoken are hard put to recover. The interest is in ensuring that unpopular opinions may be expressed freely. While it doesn't serve to regulate uncivil speech, there appears to be no alternative if society is to give its citizens freedom to voice their opinions.

After reviewing the full and glorious panoply of ways by which Americans can mistreat each other, and how such mistreatment could lead to litigation, it's important not to neglect the uncivil nature of litigation itself. The sometimes-considerable monetary cost is only part of the issue. Larger, more important costs are borne by the community. The litigants must expend time and emotional effort to fight their battles. The essential nature of the disputes described in this book are personal—invasions of property, of person, of dignity. In virtually no case can one person say to another, "Don't take it personally. It's only business." And in a good number of the cases, the litigants were neighbors. Living close to a sworn enemy can't be pleasant. And, like countries adjacent to countries at war, the peaceful neighbors presumably can't help being nervously caught up in their neighbors' battles. No one wins, and no one can rest easy. Litigation, by its adversarial nature, is an uncivil business.

Finally, we examined a cause of action in which an angry defendant who has won her case sues in retaliation for having endured litigation pursued in bad faith. One can argue that it's only justifiable revenge for the act of bad faith worked by the plaintiff in the first place. But the second lawsuit is likely to be as rancorous as the first, or worse. As a consequence, of course, what little community existed is finally sundered, and along the way society's time, efforts, and resources are expended doubly in the pursuit of incivility.

THE IMPLICATIONS

So where does it leave us—all of these cases of people's behaving badly toward each other and then suing and being sued?

First, it is clear that recourse to the legal system is not the best means by which to enforce society's notions of civility. Many of the formulations of the torts and statutes that enable litigation assume incivility. Then we must worry over the next step: With how much incivility shall we require people to live? How much should one individual be forced to put up with the uncivil actions of another? Further, what other societal interests interfere? Society has interests in protecting free speech and robust expression of opinion, for example, that override the notion that the government should enforce civility in speech. Sometimes, then, enforcing civility isn't the top priority of the law.

Yet society has too great an interest in maintaining control *not* to step in, through the government, with laws in cases in which it is clearly necessary. In recent years, we have felt it necessary to enact new legislation regarding, for example, sexual misbehavior, stalking, and, finally, cyberstalking. Civil behavior *will* be legislated if the stakes are high enough and the incivility extreme enough.

Quasi-legal procedures, such as the Antioch College Sexual Offense Prevention Policy, may have some place in helping maintain civility. Often, such procedures include some element of mediation that, as we'll elaborate below, may have value in addressing incivility that has already occurred. But such mechanisms don't work in every context—the University of Pennsylvania's speech code was viewed as censorship and finally abandoned.

So we are left with mixed results. The legal system can be too clumsy, cumbersome, expensive, and ineffective for what are often essentially emotional disputes. Further, no one much likes using the legal system to enforce mere etiquette. Too often, however, mere etiquette isn't up to the task. The quasi-legal attempts to enforce civil behavior may or may not work. What other options do we have?

MEDIATION?

Each of our three main commentators, Miss Manners, Peck, and Carter, advocates our listening with the utmost respect to one another. Further, for debate to be useful, it has to change from a shouting match into an occasion in which each person not only lets the other have his say, but actually listens to it, respects it, and seeks to understand it. One has the sense that Miss Manners, understanding our penchant for rough-and-tumble talk, would prefer that most public encounters be governed by Roberts's Rules of Order.[12] There may just be something to this. To that end, there is a dispute-resolution method other than litigation that we can explore, one to which we have alluded earlier: mediation.

We saw that each of the various torts we considered tended in one way or another to encourage individuals to litigate over uncivil behavior. That litigation was itself uncivil, and, because the laws developed as they did, sometimes uncivil behavior was to some extent condoned. Results achieved through the legal system in cases involving incivility are bound to leave a sour taste in the litigants' mouths.

Why not, then, do what we can to avoid the traditional adversarial legal system for these disputes over civility? A number of devices are available. "Alternative dispute resolution," as it's generally known, tends to be either "arbitration" or "mediation." Arbitration, often imposed by contract (such as those between stock brokers and their clients or construction companies and property owners), is a means by which each party gives up its right to litigate in favor of a decision by the arbitrator that is binding and can be entered at the courthouse as a judgment. Arbitration is a formal procedure, usually akin to a trial, though sometimes it doesn't adhere to the rules of evidence.[13] Because that form of dispute resolution is usually imposed by contract in a business context, it wouldn't be a likely method of dispute resolution for the cases in this book. Therefore, we'll exclude arbitration from this discussion.

Mediation, on the other hand, is much more informal, as we'll describe below. But first we should note that many states and federal court systems have mediation procedures in place. Sometimes the court will order a mediation, and sometimes the parties will simply agree to engage in one. However, these procedures apply only after the lawsuit has been filed. Such a mediation has disadvantages. Both parties have hired lawyers, and, depending on how far along the process is, have already sunk a good deal of money and time into the process and so are invested in a winning outcome. The further along the process is, the less willing they are to give in. So we'll also exclude discussions of mediations conducted after the lawsuit has begun, as the point is to resolve a dispute before that point.

So let's assume that the parties agree to mediate before any lawsuit is filed. The procedures can vary, and some are exceedingly informal. Opposing parties with the authority to settle the dispute must be present; whether either or both of them has engaged a lawyer can vary. The most important point is that the mediator be an objective third party who will promise to keep confidential everything that happens in the mediation.

That outside third party is a main advantage of mediation. It forces an individual to view objectively the dispute in which he's engaged. Unfortunately, when he simply hires a lawyer and directs her to file suit, the lawyer may have little disincentive to derail the process, especially if she knows she's going to get paid on an hourly basis. Then, with the lawyers' collaboration, the litigants are thrown into the morass of time, money, and energy spent and wasted on a dispute possibly engendered by someone's behaving badly, not apologizing, and not backing down. No one gains any perspective on the other person's view because no one is forced by an objective third party to listen. A mediator, however, is more likely to make the two parties listen to each other in good faith.

One problem, though, is finding that mediator. A number of nationwide companies exist simply for the purpose of resolving disputes. The yellow pages also list local mediation services. In Seattle, Washington, for example, there are at least seventy. A good number have to do with family-related matters like divorce, but others are oriented more generally. Some gear their services toward interpersonal relations, while others are clearly tilted toward helping to mediate matters of law. Some mediators are retired lawyers and judges. As they are in the business of providing these services for a fee, those fees can escalate if the dispute is complicated. As an example, JAMS/Endispute, which mainly handles business disputes, charges an hourly rate comparable to that charged by an experienced business attorney. Mediators who focus on family-oriented or other individual-to-individual disputes may begin in a lower, more affordable range. So mediation is unlikely to be cost-effective for disputes with little money at stake—though, of course, the low stakes didn't prevent a lot of the cases described in this book from being litigated, so that may not necessarily dissuade the parties.

There are other resources, fortunately. A large number of community-oriented and -based organizations exist. The National Association For Community Mediation claims 260 programs in forty-five states, and a large number of the mediations it conducts involve the sorts of disputes litigated in the cases in this book.[14] The mediators in those actions are volunteer citizens trained in mediation. What better way to reinstill the sense of community, of neighborhood, than to encourage common citizens to volunteer their time to help mediate disputes?

We would be remiss if we failed to note that there is extensive criticism of mediation as opposed to outright litigation.[15] For example, it is argued that mediators, working in an informal venue, have a much more personal relationship with the parties than does a judge, and thus prejudices—overt racial or sexual biases—can flourish. Judges, on the other hand, keep a real physical and psychological distance, sitting up on the bench and mainly speaking only to the lawyers.[16] But it is also true that judges, being human, are prey to dangerous prejudices. In the worst case, they may know and trust one lawyer more than the other and thus give more weight to that one's arguments and objections. Just as easily, too, a judge can become annoyed with one lawyer, perhaps unjustifiably, and be unable to hide his annoyance from the jury. Thus the playing field is tilted. Critics of mediation also argue that litigation provides a public venue in which the parties are separated by their lawyers who advocate for them; the lawyers can act as a buffer between the parties so that the weaker-kneed warrior needn't face the tougher one. A party who must represent himself in mediation, however, may dread having to confront the other party.[17] While this argument does have some merit, it ignores the point that we made in chapter 11, that the parties in litigation do indeed face each other in court and out of court daily, day after day.

There is another, more fundamental problem with any form of dispute resolution, be it litigation or mediation. Simply put, Americans are not good at compromise. That part of American culture and myth that holds that we are all equal is that very part of our culture that makes us so difficult to live with. Peter insists on standing up for his rights at least as strongly and vociferously as Dan does for his. Further, it is ironic that our culture's reverence for the right to have and express an opinion allows both Peter and Dan to forget that the other has an opinion that may very well be just as valid.

Unfortunately, Peter and Dan are the very folks who people the pages of this book. How often would mediation be useful in these cases? We can leave out the intentional infliction of emotional distress cases right away. The defendants in those cases won't be amenable to any third-party meddling, and the plaintiffs aren't going to want to be in the same room with the defendants anyway. Leave out the sexual battery cases as well, for obvious reasons. You can probably omit most of the nuisance cases also: The Gormans aren't going to listen to reason when they've been blasting the radio at the Sabos for years. Mediation seems doomed in the cases in which the parties believe that their property rights have been trampled. We are left with despairingly few candidates for a rational, useful mediation. Perhaps Squyres and Phillips, the two women who had the fender-bender in the bank drive-through, could have been made to see the possibility of a compromise; perhaps not.

So if mediation isn't the final answer, and we know that litigation is often a destructive process, where do we go?

A CALL TO CIVILITY

Litigation and mediation both address the symptoms but not the underlying sickness, which is incivility. The problem with the sickness is that it appears to have always been with us. Stephen Carter asserts that incivility began to increase when Americans lost their sense of community circa 1965. Rather than assuming that incivility has increased, we have argued that the longevity of the torts tells us that we have always been, to some degree, an uncivil people. That is, the evolution of the intentional torts suggests that incivility is inherent in Anglo-American culture.

However, for the sake of argument, let us accept that Carter and Peck and Miss Manners are right, that there has been some increase in our inability to treat each other with the sort of respect that our forebears exercised and experienced. What, then, do we do about it? As we suggested above, neither mediation nor litigation provides a complete answer. While these resolution devices can provide some measure of conclusion, they begin only after an incivility has occurred. How do we instead prevent the incivility before it happens?

The answer doesn't lie with Carter's call to a return to Christian values, certainly not for everyone. American society is so diverse that such a solution is unworkable, if not insulting to those who have other beliefs or simply no belief at all in a higher authority (to use Peck's term). One may be glad for Carter, who has such a strong individual faith, but one suspects that it will not do for all as a foundation for civil behavior.

Nor does the answer lie with Peck-type workshops. We have all been to enough workshops to know that the effect is usually ephemeral, even assuming that the participants buy into the concepts that they're being sold. As soon as everyone gets back to work (and Peck posits the usefulness of his workshops for corporations), it's hard to maintain the spirit of the workshop when that malcontent down the hall is invading one's turf. We perceive the stakes as entirely too high with respect to our own destinies to be constantly mindful of the other person. It's our own place that matters most. So Peck and others like him, while performing a perhaps useful service conceptually, don't provide any lasting solution. Anyway, like mediation, his workshops are treating only the symptom, not the disease.

Just for the record, Miss Manners doesn't present us with a coherent scheme by which incivility can be overcome either. She instead simply observes society and comments on what does and doesn't constitute civil behavior. Cogent, useful, and insightful comments they are, but she doesn't purport to present a cure for incivility.

Perhaps a start toward addressing the problem would be to revisit the definition of civility given in the introduction. We said first that civility is manifested by respect for the others with whom we must live in our crowded society. Second, civility is a commitment to accommodate our own interests to the greater good of the community. Our best interests are most realized when integrated with those of the community. In exchange, individuals in the community should generally be expected to subjugate their interests to the greater good of the community as well. Finally, civility is a respect for society's rules, whether etiquette, tradition, or the law. We must be both willing to follow those rules, and, again in exchange, able to expect that others will follow them, too.

That definition may guide us toward a solution. For a solution to work, it must resonate with everyone living in America. It must grow out of our understanding of what it means to be an American. And not just a Christian American, or one with a belief in a higher authority, or one who ascribes to the rules of etiquette that existed even in the last decade, for we are welcoming new Americans every day from countries, cultures, and traditions very different from our own.

We have noted that one of the apparent reasons for all of this incivility is that our society's laws emphasize our individual rights with respect to our person, our property, our beliefs, and our speech. America celebrates individual achievement and self-reliance; a necessary corollary is that we fiercely protect our individual rights. For instance, the Slairds, who created a garden in their backyard, fought in court against the swimming pool that they believed violated their property rights.

We also have the wherewithal to protect those rights. America is a very fortunate country. Aside from the Civil War, we have had a remarkable history of political stability. While we are often annoyed (or worse) by our government, we are comfortable that it will not be dissolved by a military coup or by the power of a cult dedicated to an individual. Further, for much of our history, our geographical isolation and friendly neighbors have insulated us from the wars that exhausted and destabilized other continents. Thus we've always felt secure from threats such as most European nations have from time to time visited on one or more of their neighbors. Finally, we are a rich country, made wealthy by immeasurable natural resources that we have fully exploited. Our individual initiative and free-market system, which have attracted vast numbers of eager, capable, competitive immigrants, no doubt have contributed to our being able to build this wealth. True, there is poverty and unemployment out of which has grown much despair. But the general prosperity of our citizenry is remarkable, even among other developed countries.

There is a downside to all of this good news. In short, our more fortunate citizens haven't had enough real problems to worry about. With so much material comfort and safety, each of us has been allowed to focus on our own place in society, our own status, our own rights. We might do well to consider the words of another set of commentators on the American state of mind, the authors of *Habits of the Heart: Individualism and Commitment in American Life.*[18] The book, originally published in 1985, was an exploration of who we are as Americans and an examination of how we were living as a society and how we ought to live. By the mid-eighties, the generation of Americans coming of age had abandoned or been disabused of the idealism of the sixties and seventies, times during which many individuals had the noble intentions of self-sacrifice and devotion to the social good. The decade of greed and self-absorption was well under way, and *Habits of the Heart* explored the attitudes that underlay it. Hailed critically, the book was updated and republished in 1996. In concluding the book, the authors told us:

> We will need to remember that we did not create ourselves, that we owe what we are to the communities that formed us, and to what Paul Tillich called "the structure of grace in history" that made such communities possible. We will need to see the story of life on this earth not as an unbroken success but as a history of suffering as well as joy. We will need to remember the millions of suffering people in the world today and the millions whose suffering in the past made our present affluence possible.

Unfortunately, however, this is generally not the way Americans think about their circumstances. Instead of being mindful of our good fortune and appreciating our communities, some of us harass our neighbors, whether regarding fences, swimming pools, or noise. We bedevil people because we don't like them or just want to bedevil them, or because they stutter, or because we think they've slighted us, or simply to get them to pay attention to us. Then, if we think they have infringed our rights, we will battle them, even into the courthouse. Such incivility may be the luxury of a wealthy, safe, settled country.

But after the way Americans reacted to the events of September 11, 2001, speculation abounded that perhaps things had changed. There was a sense that 9/11 was a watershed event because it brought terrorism—in this case, acts of violence wrought by foreigners—to American soil. We were no longer isolated and safe. The attacks also disrupted the economy considerably. We all heard, however, the many stories of selflessness and heroism arising out of the horrific events. There also seemed to be a different mood: We had discovered that we had come together, after all, as Americans who were proud of their country, and we weren't going to bow down to the acts of cowardly terrorists. There was virtual unanimity in the sense that we could pull together both to help out the victims and to bring the terrorists to justice. Despite some regrettable cases, we were almost self-conscious in our attempts to treat Arab Americans with the respect generally afforded to all American citizens. Congress even seemed united in a show of bipartisan sentiment to pull together behind the president to help win this new, strange battle. One had the sense that, despite the horror of the attacks, we had rediscovered what it was like to be one people and were determined to continue treating each other with a new sense of respect.

But within a year of 9/11, that spirit had already seemingly started to fade. We still had road rage, parents berating their children's teachers, and battles over cigarettes and cell phones. Our political campaigns were as negative as ever. Had we slipped back to the way we had been? Although it's hard to quantify such matters objectively, it feels that way. We have begun to lose the sense of connection that we felt we had rediscovered.

On this point, Robert Putnam has extensively researched, documented, and decried the disintegration of America's social structures in his acclaimed *Bowling Alone: The Collapse and Revival of American Community*.[19] The book is a worthy follow-up to *Habits of the Heart* in its exploration of America's slide into individualism. He traced the decline in membership in a large number of social institutions. His overriding metaphor is the precipitous decline in membership in bowling leagues with a simultaneously steady rise in the number of people actually bowling. We are a country, essentially, of people who go bowling alone. It is not a difficult step to take to suggest that this lack of connection among Americans could itself be a significant cause of increasing incivility: If we are not connected to our neighbors, then what's the point of bothering to treat them with respect?

We would do well to remember how it felt immediately after the terrorist attack on the World Trade Center. In fact, we should try to remember what the *real* crisis felt like. Petty things didn't matter—who cared if someone cut you off in traffic? Or, for that matter, who cared if you were five minutes late because you consciously chose not to cut someone off? Life felt more positive when we both tolerated and showed respect for the other person. We might remember what we felt: We have much more in common as Americans than we realized. As we are one people, we should strive to act like it.

We should hope and work to make 9/11 a truly watershed event in terms of the perspective that it brought us. It should have made us see what was important—that we were all citizens under one broad roof—and realize that many other matters were of no importance at all. We should remember that the other person is a citizen, too, and strive to forgo the uncivil act, the unnecessary behavior that causes pain or discomfort for that other person. We should, in realizing that we are all one people, also try to give that other person a break: Forgive the insult and the thoughtless act. We should respect each other as neighbors, as friends, as colleagues, as partners, because we now know that no matter what small inconveniences any of those people can cause for us, there are those who would willingly wreak murder and chaos on us all, even at the expense of their own lives. So we ought to stick together, respect each other, and take care of each other.

Of course, pulling together as a community in the war against a national enemy raises its own broad issues of civility. What of the quiet neighbor of a different ethnic group who isn't as quick to retrieve his emptied garbage cans as we might expect? Do we regard him with a suspicion born of past events or respect his right to lead his life in whatever manner he chooses? These individual dilemmas mirror the larger issues that our country faces: how to preserve our history and spirit of diversity and immigration, protect the rights of the accused, and otherwise maintain our open society while protecting it from very real threats. The answers aren't as simple as we would like them to be.

That doesn't mean, however, that we shouldn't strive for a more civil way of living, to remember that there are more important things than our own individual needs and to look instead to the common good. We do have other, greater problems than whatever seeming outrage it is that our neighbor has just committed with his backyard swimming pool. It's not merely terrorism, either. We shouldn't forget that our country is facing serious issues over the environment, the economy, and our country's place in the world. Our own place in the neighborhood or in the office is insignificant in comparison. We should attempt to grow into the kind of American that we would want everyone else to be: someone who respects others' rights, considers the common good, forgives the petty insult, and obeys the rules; in short, someone who behaves civilly.

Let's return to Gomez and Hug for a further, final step. One would like to have thought that, after 9/11, Hug wouldn't have behaved as he did, idealistic as it may sound. Assuming that he had, though, how could the dispute have had a happier ending, some more amicable resolution? Neither of the counsel involved recalls Hug's apologizing to Gomez; indeed, both thought such an act highly unlikely in the context of the litigation.[20] And one can't imagine Hug's apologizing once the settlement papers were signed, either, considering his earlier attitude toward Gomez.

Yet—and this is asking for Hug to have been a different person—how far might an apology have gone to mollify Gomez? Given Hug's words and actions, it probably would have had to be quite an apology to have had any effect. Still, it would have been worth a try. One of the counsel in *Gomez* handles a number of cases involving employment discrimination and constitutional rights violations. In his opinion, a good number of these sorts of disputes, involving individuals who have been treated discourteously by others, could be resolved at an early stage with a sincere apology.[21] It makes good sense. Unfortunately, it apparently didn't happen for Gomez. Nor did it likely happen for any of the persons whose lawsuits are discussed in this book.

We should strive to remember that we are one American people with common interests, threats, and problems that we must address as a society. When one loses sight of those principles, incivilities are bound to occur. The law expects it, and in living together in one crowded society, it is finally inevitable. But when one of us commits an incivility, one should accept the responsibility and even apologize. Defuse the situation. Give the other person the chance to back off. It is the civil thing to do.

To live humbly with those concepts in mind is to begin the process of living in a more civil, caring, respectful society. If we can think and act accordingly, what a much more pleasant country we will have in which to live, as well as a country that expends its time, energy, and resources on things that truly matter. We will no longer be seeking civility but living it.

INTRODUCTION

1. Nickerson et al. v. Hodges et al., 84 So. 37 (La. 1920).

2. *Id.* at 38.

3. *See, e.g.,* Leroy Rouner, ed., *Civility* (Notre Dame, Ind.: University of Notre Dame Press, 2000), and essays therein, 13, 23, 78, 94, 116, 172. For a history of the term and changing notions of civility, *see* James Schmidt, "Is Civility a Virtue?" 17–39, and Lawrence Cahoone, "Civic Meetings, Cultural Meanings," 40–64, in Rouner, *Civility*. For a description of the dangers associated with the overemphasis on "civility" or "tolerance" in the education context, *see* Edwin J. Delattre, "Civility and the Limits to the Tolerable," 151–67, in Rouner, *Civility*.

4. For a discussion of how civility falls between the arenas of law and individual freedom, *see* Rouner, *Civility*, 2.

5. One book on the subject is Leon James and Diane Nahl, *Road Rage and Aggressive Driving: Steering Clear of Highway Warfare* (Amherst: Prometheus Books, 2000.) *See* also an entire Web site devoted to it, at http://www.drdriving.org (visited 3 November 2000).

6. Even the mobile phone companies, anxious to put the best face on things, have issued

sets of rules. *See, e.g.,* http://www.liptom.com/trnmyinfo/general/etiquette.html (visited 3 November 2000).

7. Jeff Pearlman, *Sports Illustrated,* "At Full Blast," http://cnnsi.com/features/cover/news/1999/12/22/rocker (visited 6 June 2000).

8. Rouner, *Civility,* 2, and essays therein, 73–74, 78, 145, 148. *But see* Alan Wolfe, "Are We Losing Our Virtue? The Case of Civility," 126–141, in Rouner, *Civility.*

9. Mark Caldwell, *A Short History of Rudeness* (New York: Picador USA, 1999).

10. Rouner, *Civility,* 240. *See also* Wolfe, "Are We Losing Our Virtue? The Case of Civility," 139, in Rouner, *Civility.*

11. *See, e.g.,* Rouner, *Civility.*

12. *See, e.g.,* Judith Martin, *Miss Manners' Guide to Excruciatingly Correct Behavior* (New York: Atheneum, 1982).

13. Judith Martin, *Miss Manners Rescues Civilization* (New York: Crown, 1996). She recently issued an "updated and revised" version, *Miss Manners: A Citizen's Guide to Civility* (New York: Three Rivers Press, 1999). The later version differs from the earlier mainly in that it is shortened and slightly rearranged with some different headings. As the older version is more complete, we will cite that one.

14. Martin, *Miss Manners Rescues Civilization,* 75.

15. *See, e.g.,* the foundation's Web site, http://www.fce-community.org (visited 26 October 2000).

16. M. Scott Peck, *A World Waiting to Be Born* (New York: Bantam Books, 1993).

17. *Id.,* 32.

18. *Id.,* 53–54.

19. *Id.,* 14.

20. *Id.,* 112.

21. Stephen L. Carter, *Civility* (New York: HarperCollins, 1998). It should be noted that Carter's work has drawn criticism. Rouner, *Civility,* and essays therein, 6, 127–30, 182; Jay Tolson, *Civnet[journal],* July–August 1998, http:www.civnet.org/journal/issue8/rvjtol.htm (visited 3 March 2001).

22. Carter, *Civility,* xii.

23. *Id.,* 11.

24. Other commentators have noted that the definitions of civility and civil society originally referred to a domain outside of the religious and political realms. Schmidt, "Is Civility a Virtue?" in Rouner, *Civility,* 26.

25. Carter, *Civility,* 223.

26. W. Page Keeton, ed., *Prosser and Keeton on the Law of Torts,* 5th ed. (St. Paul: West Publishing Co., 1984), 1–3.

27. However, one set of facts could give rise to both a tort and a crime: Dan hits Paul with a baseball bat; Dan is liable for a civil battery and a criminal battery as well.

28. Nickerson et al. v. Hodges et al., 84 So. at 39 (La. 1920).

CHAPTER 1

1. Henry C. Wheelwright, ed., *Rules of Civility for the 21st Century from Cub and Boy Scouts from across America* (Washington, D.C.: Stone Wall Press, 2000), 27. There are

a number of reproductions of the now-famous rules of civility that George Washington copied out as a schoolboy. As our topic deals with whether and how civility has changed or declined in American society, perhaps it's useful to cite this source, which includes the interpretations of the rules by a number of Boy and Cub Scout troops from around America. It is unfortunately unclear from this volume, however, how they would apply Washington's rules to the Scouts' adamant refusal to allow gays to act as scoutmasters. And the rules aren't just for Cub Scouts; incivility was of such concern to the president of Hamilton College that he gave a copy of the rules to each member of the class of 2002 on their matriculation. Rouner, *Civility*, 3.

2. John Updike, *Couples* (New York: Fawcett Crest, 1968), 74.

3. Such a friendly scenario could lead to more innocent horseplay, the results of which could themselves still be a battery. *See, e.g.*, Lambertson v. U.S., 528 F.2d 441 (2d Cir. 1976). Another complicated area of the law is that one regarding the implied consent that participants in a sporting contest give to the dangers inherent in playing the sport. For an interesting summary of many cases from a number of jurisdictions, *see* Dotzler v. Tuttle, 449 N.W.2d 774 (Neb. 1991). As the law regarding friendly horseplay that unintentionally goes awry and injuries sustained in sporting events is not relevant to our discussion of civility, we won't get into those matters.

4. Martin, *Miss Manners Rescues Civilization*, 153–55.

5. *See, e.g.*, Dylan Thomas, *Under Milk Wood*, in which Mr. Pritchard is allowed by Mrs. Ogmore-Pritchard to smoke one pipeful of "asthma mixture," which he must take "in the woodshed, if you please." (London: Dent, 1978), 14.

6. *See, e.g.*, King County, Washington, Code §§ 12.50.010–.50. Section .030 prohibits smoking "in all county work and common areas, whether in enclosed individual or shared office spaces."

7. McCracken v. Sloan, 252 S.E.2d 250 (N.C. App. 1979).

8. McCracken v. Sloan, 252 S.E.2d at 252.

9. McCracken v. Sloan, 252 S.E.2d at 252.

10. *Citing* Dean William Prosser, *Handbook of the Law of Torts*, 4th ed. (St. Paul: West, 1971), 37.

11. Carter, *Civility*, 11.

12. McCracken v. Sloan, 252 S.E.2d at 252.

13. Pechan v. DynaPro, 622 N.E.2d 108 (Ill. App. 1993).

14. Leichtman v. WLW Jacor Communications Inc., 634 N.E.2d 697 (Ohio App. 1994).

15. Leichtman v. WLW Jacor Communications Inc., 634 N.E.2d at 699, *citing* Roscoe Pound, *An Introduction to the Philosophy of Law* ([citation omitted by court], 1922), 169.

16. Leichtman v. WLW Jacor Communications Inc., 634 N.E.2d at 700.

17. William Flynn, Esq., telephone conversation with the author, 19 November 1999.

18. A similar situation occurred in Hennly v. Richardson et al., 444 S.E.2d 317 (Ga. 1994). There the plaintiff could not bring her claim for battery arising out of having smoke blown in her face because it was in an employment setting, so her alleged injuries

would have been compensable only under the worker's compensation law. The dissent in the case noted the sad facts of the plaintiff's having her supervisor blow smoke in her face despite knowing that she hated it and was unable to do anything about it due to her inferior position.

19. Also alleged were the intentional infliction of severe emotional distress and slander. These torts are taken up in chapters 6 and 10, respectively.

20. Snyder v. Turk, 627 N.E.2d 1053 (Ohio App. 1993).

21. Michael Murry, Esq., conversation with the author, 1 November 2000.

22. *Id.*

23. Keeton, *Prosser and Keeton on the Law of Torts*, 5th ed., § 9.

24. *Id.*, citing C. J. McKean in Respublica v. De Longchamps, Pa. 1784, 1 Dall. 111, 1 L. Ed. 59.

25. *Id.* at 10.

26. Hough v. Mooningham, 487 N.E.2d 1281 (Ill. App. 1986).

27. For the record, the dissent believed that the majority had fouled up by allowing Hough to have proceeded under other theories, those of negligence and willful and wanton misconduct. The proper cause of action, which for the purposes of our discussion we assume was what everyone meant all along, was battery.

28. Hough v. Mooningham, 487 N.E.2d at 1287.

29. Squyres v. Phillips, 285 So.2d 337 (La. App. 1973).

30. *Id.* at 339.

31. Phillips also raised as a complete defense to the battery claim that she had been acting in self-defense. In the right circumstances, Phillips might have won. If one is attacked, one may certainly respond in one's own defense, and one will not be liable for injuries dealt out for that "battery." However, the court concluded that, not only was there insufficient evidence that Phillips had acted in self-defense, but the evidence was that Phillips had started the fight. Self-defense to a claim of battery implies a full-blown affray: a barroom brawl or a response to a mugging. Those situations involve relationships that are far removed from any consideration of civility, so we have not taken up the issues presented by self-defense.

32. Again, those other torts, slander and the intentional infliction of emotional distress, covered in chapters 10 and 6, respectively, do allow plaintiffs to sue for mere words in certain specific situations.

CHAPTER 2

1. For all of the rules that Jeff and Marie discuss, *see* the Sexual Offense Prevention Policy (SOPP) at http://www.Antioch-college.edu/survival/html/sopp.html (visited 28 August 2002).

2. *See, e.g.,* Craig Briskin, "Antioch College: Sexually Correct or Just Right?" first published in "HUPD Blues," November 1993, http://www.digitas.harvard.edu/~perspy/issues/2000/retro/antioch/html (visited 23 February 2001); James Hannah, "Ohio College's Sex-Consent Rules, Derided By Some, Boost Recruiting," *Philadelphia Inquirer*, 15 January 1995, p. A11.

3. Dr. Regina Sewell, Educator-Advocate for the Sexual Offense Prevention Program of Antioch College, conversation with the author, 22 February 2001.
4. SOPP, "Consent," section 4.
5. *Id.*, section 6.
6. Martin, *Miss Manners Rescues Civilization*, 180.
7. *Id.*, 181.
8. Caldwell, *A Short History of Rudeness*, 240.
9. Alex Comfort, *The New Joy of Sex* (New York: Crown Publishing Group, 1991).
10. John Gray, *Men Are From Mars, Women Are From Venus* (New York: Harper Trade, 1992).
11. Martin, *Miss Manners Rescues Civilization*, 180–81.
12. Dr. Regina Sewell's other statements regarding the workings of the SOPP in this paragraph are also taken from the conversation cited in note 3 above.
13. Hannah, "Ohio College's Sex-Consent Rules, Derided By Some, Boost Recruiting."
14. Dr. Regina Sewell.
15. *Id.*
16. Just to take all of this a number of steps further: Under the facts as originally stated, Marie had no way of knowing that Jeff would find her kiss offensive and could argue that the offensiveness couldn't have been evident to the ordinary person. Similarly, under the common law, Marie might be able to argue that Jeff's actions indicated his implied consent to her approach, thus nullifying any assault or battery claim. While, under the common law, Marie can in some cases rely on the consent implied in the situation, the SOPP requires her to seek explicit consent. The SOPP seems to have been drafted on the premise that there had been too much reliance on implied consent when none existed.
17. Keeton, *Prosser and Keeton on the Law of Torts*, 44–45.
18. Reed v. Maley, 74 S.W. 1079 (Ky. App. 1903). The same result obtained in a later case, Davis v. Richardson, 89 S.W. 318 (Ark. 1905).
19. Clack v. Thomason, 195 S.E. 218 (Ga. 1938).
20. *Citing* Atkinson v. Bibb Mfg. Co., 178 S.E. 537 (Ga. App. 1935).
21. Newell v. Whitcher, 53 Vt. 589 (1880).
22. Years later, the court in Reed v. Maley recognized the existence of the overt act in Newell.
23. Keeton, *Prosser and Keeton on the Law of Torts*, 61, *citing* Samms v. Eccles, 358 P.2d 355 (Utah 1961).
24. Farpella-Crosby v. Horizon Health Care, 97 F.3d 803 (Former 5th Cir. 1996).
25. At trial the jury found that Ms. Farpella-Crosby's complaints to Horizon Health Care's human resources department about Blanco's behavior constituted adequate notice to the employer so that it became liable for Blanco's actions. The Fifth Circuit refused to reverse that finding on appeal. Obviously, Ms. Farpella-Crosby would rather have the chance to pursue a recovery against a corporation than an individual, the scope of whose assets was doubtful.

26. Farpella-Crosby, 97 F.3d at 809.
27. *See, e.g.*, Beardsley v. Webb, 30 F.3d 524 (4th Cir. 1994). Of course, one could recover under Title VII for an offensive touching as well if it otherwise created the cause of action for sex discrimination.
28. Martin, *Miss Manners Rescues Civilization*, 164–65.
29. *Id.*, 163.
30. Kathleen K. v. Robert B., 150 Cal. App. 3d 992 (Cal. App. 1984).
31. Griswold v. Connecticut, 381 U.S. 479 (1965).
32. Barbara A. v. John G., (1983) 145 Cal. App. 3d 369 [193 Cal. Rptr. 422] (hg. den. Sept. 29, 1983).
33. Kathleen K. v. Robert B., 150 Cal. App. 3d at 997.
34. *See, e.g.*, Hogan v. Tavzel, 660 So.2d 350 (Fla. App. 1995); BN v. KK, 538 A.2d 1175 (Md. 1988). *But cf.* Berner v. Caldwell, 543 So.2d 686 (Ala. 1989), in which the male defendant claimed to have had no knowledge that he himself had been infected, and thus was given a verdict in his favor on the intentional torts of battery, assault, misrepresentation, and fraud. The plaintiff could still go forward on her claim against him for negligence, which is, in essence, a failure to act with reasonable care toward others. The defendant, however, had the nerve to file a claim against the plaintiff for defamation! The court's opinion noted only that the defamation claim was still pending.
35. SOPP, "Preface."
36. Carter, *Civility*, 180.
37. *Id.*, 102.
38. Peck, *A World Waiting to Be Born*, 109.
39. Carter, *Civility*, 223–25.
40. Martin, *Miss Manners Rescues Civilization*, 165–66.

CHAPTER 3

1. John L. Diamond, Lawrence C. Levine, and M. Stuart Madden, *Understanding Torts* (New York: Matthew Bender, 1996), 371, *citing* Restatement of Torts § 157. By "real property" we mean land, or real estate, as opposed to "personal property," which is any other, portable property. The only notable collision between the two categories is property known as "fixtures," that is, personal property that has become so affixed to the land that the law considers ownership of it to follow ownership of the real estate. An example is a toolshed.
2. Keeton, *Prosser and Keeton on the Law of Torts*, 67.
3. *Id.*, 70.
4. Hasapopoulos v. Murphy, 689 S.W.2d 118 (Mo. App. 1985).
5. *Id.* at 121.
6. Michalson v. Nutting, 175 N.E. 490 (Mass. 1931).
7. Hasapopoulos, 689 S.W.2d at 119, n. 1.
8. Melnick v. CSX, 540 A.2d 1133 (Md. 1988).

9. Smith v. Holt, 5 S.E.2d 492 (1939).
10. *See, e.g.*, Paul J. Miller, "Cutting Through the Smog: The 1990 Clean Air Act Amendments and a New Direction Toward Reducing Ozone Pollution," http://www.Stanford.edu/group/ELJ/v12-miller.html (visited 2 November 2000).
11. Melnick, 540 A.2d at 1137, *citing* Sterling v. Weinstein, 75 A.2d 144, 147 (D.C. 1950).
12. Whitesell v. Houlton, 632 P.2d 1077 (Haw. App. 1981).
13. *Id.* at 1079.
14. Our other tropical state, Florida, follows the Massachusetts rule. Gallo v. Heller, 512 So.2d 215 (Fla. App. 1987).
15. Melnick, 540 A.2d at 1138.
16. *Id.* at 1138, *citing* Michalson v. Nutting, 175 N.E.2d 490, 491 (Mass. 1931).
17. Patterson v. Oye, 333 N.W.2d 389 (Neb. 1983).
18. *Id.* at 391.
19. Beals v. Griswold, 468 So.2d 641 (La. App. 1985).
20. *See generally* Keeton, *Prosser and Keeton on the Law of Torts*, 67–69.
21. Angelo Codevilla, *Character of Nations: How Politics Makes and Breaks Prosperity, Family, and Civility* (New York: HarperCollins, 1997), 133.
22. *Id.*
23. *Id.*, 134.

CHAPTER 4
1. Diamond, Levine, and Madden, *Understanding Torts*, 371.
2. Keeton, *Prosser and Keeton on the Law of Torts*, 617.
3. *Id.*, 619–20.
4. Diamond, Levine, and Madden, *Understanding Torts*, 370.
5. People v. Cifarelli, 454 N.Y.S.2d 525 (N.Y. Crim. Ct. 1982).
6. *Id.* at 527.
7. *Id.* at 527, *citing* People v. Markovitz, 423 N.Y.S.2d 996, 999 (N.Y. Crim. Ct. 1979). The Markovitz court cites some interesting examples from history: "disorderly inns or ale-houses, stage-plays, unlicensed booths and stages for rope-dancers, mountebanks and the like, are public nuisances and may upon indictment be suppressed and fined," *citing* 4 Blackstone's *Commentaries*, 167.
8. In some circumstances, a public nuisance *could* be a civil tort action, in addition to a criminal case. Keeton, *Prosser and Keeton on the Law of Torts*, 618.
9. People v. Cifarelli, 454 N.Y.S.2d at 527.
10. *Id.*, *citing* People v. Markovitz, 423 N.Y.S.2d at 996, 999.
11. Gorman v. Sabo, 122 A.2d 475 (Md. App. 1955).
12. *Id.* at 477.
13. *Id.*
14. *Id.* at 479.
15. Carter, *Civility*, 38 *et seq.*
16. *Id.*, 41.

17. *Id.*, 42.
18. David Halberstam, *The Fifties* (New York: Villard Books, 1993). Halberstam also takes up the subject of Levittown and its implications, 131–43.
19. *Id.*, 114.
20. Peck, *A World Waiting to Be Born*, 176.
21. Slaird v. Klewers, 271 A.2d 345 (Md. App. 1970).
22. One reading the case will see that the court added a second condition that must also be satisfied before the court will find a nuisance: The inconvenience must diminish the value of the property materially. However, neither the trial court nor the court of appeals addresses the point, perhaps because the other condition, that the inconvenience must seriously interfere with the ordinary comfort and enjoyment, wasn't met. A plaintiff has to prove both, so missing on one makes the other moot.
23. *Id.* at 347.
24. Hornsby v. Smith, 13 S.E.2d 20 (Ga. 1941).
25. *Id.* at 22, *citing* Bush v. Mockett, 145 N.W. 1001 (Neb. 1914), *quoting* Barger v. Barringer, 151 N.C. 433 (N.C. 1909).
26. Hornsby, 13 S.E.2d at 24.
27. *Id.* at 25.
28. *See* note 15 above.

CHAPTER 5
1. Hay v. Stevens, 497 P.2d 362 (Or. 1972).
2. This litigation occurred in the early 1970s, before the advent of serious environmental awareness.
3. Stevens v. Hay, 519 P.2d 1040 (Or. 1974).
4. Hay v. Stevens, 530 P.2d 37 (Or. 1975).
5. *Id.* at 39, citing Dean William Prosser, *Handbook of the Law of Torts*, 4th ed. (St. Paul: West, 1971), § 87 at 578. Footnote to the quotation omitted by the court.

CHAPTER 6
1. Wilson v. Pearce, 412 S.E.2d 148 (N.C. App. 1982).
2. *See generally,* Keeton, *Prosser and Keeton on the Law of Torts*, 55–59.
3. *Id., citing* Wilkinson v. Downton, [1897] 2 Q.B.D. 57.
4. *Id.* at 63–64.
5. Wilson v. Pearce, 412 S.E.2d at 152, n. 1, *citing* West v. King's Dept. Store, Inc., 365 S.E.2d 621 (N.C. 1988).
6. Wilson, 412 S.E.2d at 153.
7. *Id.*
8. Harris v. Jones, 371 A.2d 1104 (Md. App. 1977), *aff'd*, 380 A.2d 611 (Md. App. 1977).
9. Harris v. Jones, 371 A.2d 1104 (Md. App. 1977).
10. *Id.* at 1111–12.

11. Harris v. Jones, 380 A.2d at 615, *citing* Chief Judge Calvert Magruder, *Mental and Emotional Disturbance in the Law of Torts*, 49 HARV. L. REV., 1035 (May 1936).

12. *Id.* at 1053.

13. RESTATEMENT (SECOND) OF TORTS § 46 cmt. d (1965). The Restatements of the various areas of the law is a publication of the American Law Institute that attempts both to set forth existing law and to comment on it.

14. *See* note 11.

15. Zalnis v. Thoroughbred Datsun Car Co., et al., 645 P.2d 292 (Colo. App. 1982).

16. *Id.* at 293.

17. *Id.*

18. *Id.* at 294, *citing* RESTATEMENT (SECOND) OF TORTS § 46 cmt. f (1965).

19. The case had arrived at the appeals court on an appeal of the trial court's grant of motion for partial summary judgment on the intentional infliction claim. There had been no action, apparently, on the slander claim, which could have arisen out of any of Trosper's statements, including his assertion that Zalnis had been engaged in a sexual relationship with one of his salesmen—who, by the way, would have an interesting slander claim of his own against Trosper, the racist epithet aside.

20. In some cases, age disparity can make a difference. *See, e.g.*, Delta Finance v. Ganakos, 91 S.E.2d 383 (Ga. App. 1956), in which an adult tried to intimidate an eleven-year-old girl into opening the door so he could repossess her television set. Certainly the implied position of power that accompanied his superior age went to the court's determination that the defendant's actions had been outrageous.

21. Ford v. Isdaner, et al., 542 A.2d 137 (Pa. Super. 1988), *allocatur denied* 554 A.2d 509 (Pa. 1988).

22. Ford v. Isdaner, et al., 542 A.2d 138.

23. Kazatsky v. King David Memorial Park, Inc., 527 A.2d 988 (Pa. 1987).

24. What the supreme court actually said in Kazatsky was that "because the evidence adduced in this matter does not establish a right of recovery under the terms of the provision as set forth in the Restatement, we again leave to another day the question of the viability of section 46 in this Commonwealth." Kazatsky v. King David Memorial Park, Inc., 527 A.2d 988, 989 (Pa. 1987). The court refers to the RESTATEMENT (SECOND) OF TORTS, § 46. Thus the majority in Ford appears to have read Kazatsky correctly.

25. Ford, 554 A.2d at 509 (Pa. 1988).

26. Carter, *Civility*, 102.

27. *Id.*, 100–101.

28. *Id.*, 101.

CHAPTER 7

1. Salvo v. Edens, 116 So.2d 220 (Miss. 1959).

2. *Id.* at 221.

3. *Id.* at 221–22.

4. *Id.* at 222, *citing* § 1059, vol. 1A recompiled, Mississippi Code of 1942.

5. For the application of another anti-dueling statute, *see* Zayre of Virginia v. Gowdy, 147 S.E.2d 710 (Va. 1966). There, a teenaged girl accused by a security guard of stealing a swimming suit sued the department store under Virginia's anti-dueling statute, now Title 8.01, Civil Remedies and Procedure, § 8.01–45. The court affirmed a verdict in her favor, holding that words conveying a charge of criminal offense involving moral turpitude were insulting under then-section 8–630.

6. Salvo v. Edens, 116 So.2d at 223–24.

7. Title VII, 42 U.S.C.S. § 2000e *et seq.*

8. Cariddi v. Kansas City Chiefs Football Club Inc., 568 F.2d 87 (8th Cir. 1977).

9. Martin, *Miss Manners Rescues Civilization*, 230.

10. Howard Goodman, "Penn Dumps Speech Code and Plans a New Approach," *Philadelphia Inquirer*, 17 November 1993, p. A1.

11. Howard Goodman, "Water Buffalo Bias Case Dropped," *Philadelphia Inquirer*, 25 May 1993, p. A1.

12. *Id.*

13. Deborah Leavy, *Philadelphia Inquirer*, 28 May 1993, p. A31.

14. Goodman, "Water Buffalo Bias Case Dropped."

15. *See* http://www.upenn.edu/osl/openexp.html (visited 16 November 2000).

16. Martin, *Miss Manners Rescues Civilization*, 231.

17. Carter, *Civility*, 164.

18. *Id.*, 70.

19. *See* http://www.state.ct.us/cmac/policies/netiqu.htm (visited 25 May 2000).

20. *See, e.g.,* Charles Bermant, *Seattle Times*, 17 October 1999, http://www.seattletimes .com/news/technology/html98/inbo_19991017.html (visited 25 May 2000).

21. Joseph M. Saul, "E-Mail Etiquette: When and How to Communicate Electronically," *Information Technology Digest* 5 (8 April 1996), http://www.itd.umich.edu/ITDigest/0496/feat04.html (visited 25 May 2000).

22. One of the authors was copied on an E-mail from one (clueless) business adversary to another, in the midst of heated negotiations that eventually ended in a failed deal, in which he concluded with a ":-)" and told her that though they'd been writing so much, they hadn't met, so sometime he ought to attach a picture.

23. Kenneth S. Stern, "Hate and the Internet," http://www.ajc.org/pre/internet3.htm (visited 30 May 2000).

24. *Id.*

25. 18 U.S.C. § 245(b).

26. Act of April 11, 1968, Pub. L. No. 90–284, Title I, § 101(a), 82 Stat. 73.

27. Stern, "Hate and the Internet."

28. O'Sama M. Khouraki, *New University Newsletter*, http://www.newu.uci.edu/archive/1998/winter/980216/n-980216-trial.html (visited 30 May 2000).

29. *Id.*

30. *See, e.g.,* http://www.state.ct.us/cmac/policies/netiqu.htm.

CHAPTER 8

1. *The Seattle Times*, 14 November 2000, p. A18.
2. Caldwell, *A Short History of Rudeness*, 240.
3. Von Lusch v. Board County Commissioners, 302 A.2d 4 (Md. App. 1973).
4. Von Lusch v. Board County Commissioners, 330 A.2d 738 (Md. App. 1975).
5. Von Lusch v. State, 368 A.2d 468 (Md. App. 1977).
6. Von Lusch v. State, 356 A.2d 277 (Md. App. 1976).
7. Von Lusch v. State, 368 A.2d 468 (Md. App. 1977).
8. Von Lusch v. State, 387 A.2d 306 (Md. App. 1978).
9. Von Lusch v. State, 356 A.2d at 282.
10. Von Lusch v. State, 387 A.2d at 307.
11. Commonwealth v. Strahan, 570 N.E.2d 1041 (Mass. App. Ct. 1991), *rev. denied*, 576 N.E.2d 685 (Mass. 1991).
12. General Laws c. 269, § 14A, as amended by St. 1978, c. 379, § 3.
13. Commonwealth v. Strahan, 570 N.E.2d at 1043. Strahan was also convicted of trespass and appealed that conviction as well. The court of appeals affirmed that conviction. As it doesn't bear on the telephone law aspects of the case, we have omitted discussion of it.
14. *Id., citing* State v. Patterson, 534 S.W.2d 847, 850 (Mo. App. 1976). In Patterson, the mayor of Bunker, Missouri, pop. 447, was initially convicted of making "repeated telephone calls" during a seven-week period "for the sole purpose of harassing" Ms. Lough, who was the city clerk. All of the calls but one related to city business, and the main subject was Ms. Lough's refusal to return the town's accounts to city hall. Patterson's conviction was reversed on the grounds that he did not make the calls "solely to harass" Ms. Lough. At some point, Mayor Patterson was impeached and removed from office by the Board of Aldermen, but the next city election rewarded him with the highest number of votes. Nevertheless, the Board refused to allow him to take office as mayor. This case, obviously, was about more than a number of phone calls.
15. Von Lusch v. State, 387 A.2d at 310.
16. Caldwell v. State, 337 A.2d 476, 478–80 (Md. App. 1975).
17. *Id.* at 483.
18. *Id.* at 484.
19. MD. ANN. CODE art. 27, § 121B. The statute, originally enacted effective 1 October 1993, has been recodified as § 3–802 (2002).
20. MD. ANN. CODE art. 27, § 121A(c), originally enacted in 1986, has been recodified as § 3–803 (2002).
21. Pall v. State, 699 A.2d 565 (Md. App. 1997).
22. Greg Miller and Davan Maharaj, "N. Hollywood Man Charged in 1st Cyber-Stalking Case," *Los Angeles Times*, 22 January 1999, p. A1.
23. *Id.*
24. Greg Miller, "Man Pleads Guilty to Using Net to Solicit Rape," *Los Angeles Times*, 29 April 1999, p. C5.

25. *Id.*
26. Miller and Maharaj, "N. Hollywood Man Charged in 1st Cyber-Stalking Case."
27. CAL. [PENAL] CODE § 646.9(a) (West Cum. Supp. 2003).
28. CAL. [PENAL] CODE § 646.9(g) (West Cum. Supp. 2003). (Verbal means both written and oral. No doubt the drafters of the statute intended "verbal" to mean "oral," but we all know where good intentions lead.)
29. CAL. [PENAL] CODE § 646.9(h) (West Cum. Supp. 2003). To round out our Maryland theme, that state's legislature also now has a cyberstalking statute. Originally enacted 1 October 1998, it was recently recodified as MD. ANN. CODE § 3–805(b) (2002) and reads as follows: "A person may not use electronic mail with the intent to harass: (1) one or more persons; or (2) by sending lewd, lascivious, or obscene material."
30. "Southland Focus," *Los Angeles Times,* 23 July 1999, p. C2.
31. CAL. [CIV.] CODE § 1708.7 (West Cum. Supp. 2003).
32. Miller, "Man Pleads Guilty to Using Net to Solicit Rape."
33. A recent case from Michigan illustrates how scary it can be. U.S. v. Baker, 890 F. Supp. 1375 (E.D. Mich. 1995), *aff'd sub nom* U.S. v. Alkhabaz, 104 F.3d 1492 (6th Cir. 1997). There, two young men traded E-mails detailing their fantasy of kidnapping and killing a woman. Alkhabaz was arrested on a charge of violating 18 U.S.C. § 875(c), which prohibits interstate communications containing threats to kidnap or injure another person. (His correspondent, "Arthur Gonda," had been, as of this writing, neither identified nor located.) Alkhabaz was acquitted on the grounds that he and Gonda were not communicating "true threats"—that is, they were only fantasizing together and had not actually threatened a prospective victim.

   In another case under 18 U.S.C. § 875(c), U.S. v. Kammersell, 196 F.3d 1137 (10th Cir. 1999), Matthew Kammersell logged onto America Online (AOL) and sent an instant message to his girlfriend. She was employed at an AOL service center. The instant message contained a bomb threat; Kammersell had hoped that AOL would allow her to leave early so that the two of them could go on a date. Kammersell was convicted of communicating threats via interstate communications. He argued on appeal that because both he and his girlfriend were in Utah, there was no interstate communication, and thus no crime under the federal law. The United States Court of Appeals for the Tenth Circuit held that because all AOL instant messages go through its server in Virginia, the instant messages do constitute interstate communications. The conviction was upheld.

CHAPTER 9

1. MD. ANN. CODE art. 27 § 20.
2. State v. West, 263 A.2d 602 (Md. App. 1970).
3. *Id.* at 603.
4. *Id.*
5. U.S. CONST., amend. I. The First Amendment by its terms limits the acts of the U.S. Congress, but, many fights ago the U.S. Supreme Court made it clear that the Four-

teenth Amendment makes the First Amendment, among others, applicable to the states and their legislatures. Section 1 of the Fourteenth Amendment states in part: "No State shall make or enforce any law which shall abridge the privileges and immunities of citizens of the United States; nor shall any State deprive any person of life, liberty, or property, without due process of law." U.S. Const., amend. XIV.

6. Ala. Code § 13A-12-131 (1975).

7. Baker v. Glover, 776 F. Supp. 1511 (M.D. Ala. 1991).

8. Miller v. California, 413 U.S. 15, 24 (1973).

9. Cohen v. California, 403 U.S. 15 (1971).

10. *Id.* at 20.

11. Chaplinsky v. New Hampshire, 315 U.S. 568, 572 (1942).

12. *Baker*, 776 F. Supp. at 1715, *citing* Cohen, 403 U.S. at 20.

13. The court cautioned, however, that its holding was limited to this bumper sticker. Mr. Baker hadn't asked the court to find the statute itself unconstitutional on its face, but merely as to this bumper sticker. The statute could possibly be used to prohibit other, truly obscene speech, and it could even be used to ban other bumper stickers.

14. Cohen, 403 U.S. at 21.

15. Alex Roth, "Profanity Lands Man in Hot Water," *Detroit Free Press*, 24 December 1998, p. 1A.

16. MCL 750.337, MSA 28.569.

17. Roth, "Profanity Lands Man in Hot Water."

18. *See* Appellant's Brief, People v. Boomer, Circuit Court No. 99-6546-AR.

19. *Id.*

20. *Id.*

21. People v. Boomer, 655 N.W.2d 255 (Mich. App. 2002).

22. Mitch Albom, "Old Laws Won't Save Us From Ourselves," *Detroit Free Press*, 13 June 1999, p. 1E.

23. *Id.*

24. For a discussion of how offensive speech is a matter of civility and morality and not illegality, *see* Robert B. Pippin, "The Ethical Status of Civility," in Rouner, *Civility*, 103–17.

25. Americans do tend to understand and accept that there is a trade-off between the ability to speak one's mind and speaking civilly. *See, e.g.*, Alan Wolfe, "Are We Losing Our Virtue? The Case of Civility," in Rouner, *Civility*, 136.

CHAPTER 10

1. *See, e.g.*, Paul Palazzo, *The Seattle Times*, 29 May 2000, p. F1.

2. Keeton, *Prosser and Keeton on the Law of Torts*, 773.

3. Diamond, Levine, and Madden, *Understanding Torts*, 419–22.

4. Keeton, *Prosser and Keeton on the Law of Torts*, 772.

5. Funderburk v. Bechtel Power Corporation, 698 P.2d 556 (Wash. 1985).

6. Keeton, *Prosser and Keeton on the Law of Torts*, 773.
7. Norman Smith, Esq., conversation with the author, 7 December 2000.
8. Donovan v. Fiumara, 442 S.E.2d 572 (N.C. App. 1992).
9. The court noted that North Carolina had done away with the commonly recognized fourth type of statement, that imputing unchastity to a woman, by statute in 1975. *Id.* at 580.
10. N.C. GEN. STAT. § 14-177 (1999).
11. *Id.*
12. Donovan, 442 S.E.2d at 576.
13. *Id., citing* Moricoli v. Schwartz, 361 N.E.2d 74 (Ill. App. 1977).
14. *Id., citing* Steffan v. Aspin, 62 U.S.L.W. 2309–2310 (D.C. Cir. Nov. 16, 1993). The Department of Defense policy toward gays has, of course, evolved since into its present-day "Don't ask, don't tell" stance. *See* 10 U.S.C. § 654 (1993).
15. *Id., citing* Williams v. Freight Lines, 179 S.E.2d 319, 323 (N.C. 1971).
16. West v. King's Dept. Store, Inc., 365 S.E.2d 621 (N.C. 1988).
17. *See* chapter 4.
18. Donovan, 442 S.E.2d at 580, *citing* Moricoli, 361 N.E.2d at 76.
19. *Id.* at 580.
20. Horowitz v. Baker, 523 N.E.2d 179 (Ill. App. 1988).
21. How far is too far? The Illinois courts give us some good examples. In Costello v. Capital Cities Media, Inc., 445 N.E.2d 13 (Ill. App. 1982), *aff'd in relevant part after later appeal*, 505 N.E.2d 701 (Ill. 1987), a newspaper editorial had characterized a politician's flip-flop on taxation as "lying leadership," and the statement was held actionable per se. Likewise, in Erickson v. Aetna Life & Casualty Co., 469 N.E.2d 679 (Ill. App. 1984), referring to a chiropractor's treatment as "unreasonable and unnecessary" was actionable per se. On the other hand, in Valentine v. North American Co. for Life & Health Insurance, 328 N.E.2d 265 (Ill. 1974), calling an insurance agent a "lousy agent" was mere name-calling. So, in Skolnick v. Nudelman, 237 N.E.2d 804 (Ill. App. 1968), referring to someone as a "nut," "mishuginer," and "screwball" were all mere name-calling. Maybe calling someone a liar and referring to a chiropractor's unnecessary treatment are much closer to statements of fact than calling someone a lousy insurance agent. Calling someone a screwball, though, surely amounts only to name-calling. Even one of the most touchy of insults, to call someone a racist, has been held to have been overworked to the point of being sanitized and is now considered mere name-calling. *See, e.g.*, Stevens v. Tillman, 855 F.2d 394 (7th Cir. 1988), *cert. denied*, 489 U.S. 1065 (1989).
22. Lampkin-Asam v. Miami Daily News, Inc., 408 So.2d 666 (Fla. App. 1981), *rev. denied* 417 So.2d 329 (Fla.), *app. dismissed*, 459 U.S. 806 (1982).
23. Lampkin-Asam, 408 So.2d at 667–68.
24. New York Times v. Sullivan, 376 U.S. 254 (1964).
25. Long v. Arcell, 618 F.2d 1145 (5th Cir. 1980).
26. Lampkin-Asam v. Miami Daily News, Inc., 408 So.2d at 667, fn. 1, *citing* Gertz v. Robert Welch, Inc., 418 U.S. 323, 329–40 (1974).

CHAPTER 11

1. *See, e.g.*, the National Coalition on Television Violence at http://www.nctvv.org (visited 11 December 2000).

2. Funderburk v. Bechtel Power Corp., 698 P.2d 556 (Wash. 1985).

3. Even well-regarded experts are not necessarily effective. In a trial in which one of the authors assisted, the other side's expert accountant was clearly well trained as a witness. He sat up straight in the witness chair, smiled at the lawyer who questioned him, and then, to answer, turned ostentatiously in his chair to address the jury directly. The jurors literally leaned back and away from him, put off by the well-practiced but unwanted invasion. In a trial of some national notoriety, that of Wilmington, Delaware, lawyer Thomas Capano, for the murder of the governor's appointments secretary, Anne Marie Fahey, a well-known psychiatrist had been engaged by the state. He took the witness chair carrying a large wooden hat that he placed on the railing in front of him. Capano's lawyer, delighted by such a show just as his cross-examination of the witness was to begin, called special attention to the hat. The shrink was apparently clueless enough to be pleased, and the jury was obviously invited to notice what was either a sign of ego or just quirkiness, neither of which would enhance his credibility.

4. Hasapopoulos v. Murphy, 689 S.W.2d 118 (Mo. App. 1985).

5. Wash. R.P.C. 3.2.

6. Wash. R.P.C. 3.4(d).

7. Miss Manners has reported the perceived increased incivility in the legal profession. Martin, *Miss Manners Rescues Civilization*, 240–42.

8. Barrie Althoff, "The Ethics of Incivility," http://www.wsba.org/barnews/ethicsand thelaw/ethics-incivility.htm (visited 11 December 2000). As to intentionally misstating understandings, Wash. R.P.C. 4.1(a) states, "In the course of representing a client a lawyer shall not knowingly; (a) Make a false statement of material fact or law to a third person."

9. Paramount Communications Inc. v. QVC, 637 A.2d 34 (Del. 1994).

10. Principe v. Assay Partners, 586 N.Y.S.2d 182 (N.Y. Sup. Ct. 1982).

11. In the Matter of Stanley, 507 A.2d 1168 (N.J. 1986).

12. Althoff, "The Ethics of Incivility."

13. *See, e.g.*, guidelines for professional courtesy adopted by the King County, Washington, Bar Association Board of Trustees at http://www.kcba.org/guidelin.htm. (visited 11 December 2000).

14. Guidelines for Conduct of the American Bar Association's Litigation Section, http://www.abanet.org/litigation/litnews/practice/guidelines.html (visited 11 December 2000).

15. *Id.*

16. Carter, *Civility*, 92.

17. Wash. R.P.C. 2.1.

CHAPTER 12

1. Ackerman v. Kaufman, 15 P.2d 966 (Ariz. 1932).
2. Ackerman v. Southern Arizona Bank & Trust Co., 7 P.2d 944 (Ariz. 1932).
3. Ackerman v. Southern Arizona Bank & Trust Co., 7 P.2d 945 (Ariz. 1932).
4. Both cases at 7 P.2d 946 (Ariz. 1932).
5. Keeton, *Prosser and Keeton on the Law of Torts*, 889; Diamond, Levine, and Madden, *Understanding Torts*, 413.
6. *See, e.g.*, 42 U.S.C. § 1988(b) (2002).
7. Ackerman v. Kaufman, 15 P.2d at 968.
8. Something that doesn't appear from the record in this set of cases is what happened to the first injunction that Kaufman received, in case number four listed above. Presumably, that was a valid judgment. The next time Ackerman filed suit, Mr. Kaufman ought to have been able to walk into court with the order from the prior court and get a dismissal, at least, if not a contempt order for Ackerman. But that first injunction doesn't appear to have come into play at all.
9. O'Toole v. Franklin, 569 P.2d 561 (Ore. 1977).
10. *Id.* at 563.
11. *Id.* at 564, *citing* Prosser, *Handbook of the Law of Torts*, 851, § 120 (4th ed. 1971).
12. Keeton, *Prosser and Keeton on the Law of Torts*, 889.
13. Minasian v. Sapse, 145 Cal. Rptr. 829 (Cal. App. 1978).
14. *Id.* at 832.

CONCLUSION

1. Pantaleon Florez, Esq., conversation with the author, 26 February 2001. The court's opinion is silent on a number of fairly important facts that counsel in the litigation were kind enough to provide. Where applicable, their contributions will be noted. Otherwise, the facts stated are those in the court's opinion.
2. *Id.*
3. Pantaleon Florez, Esq.
4. Hug v. Gomez, 645 P.2d 916 (Kan. App. 1982).
5. *Id.* at 919, *citing* PIK Civ.2d 14.01 (1977).
6. *Id.* at 919.
7. This is from the court's opinion. Neither counsel could remember any litigation between the two, and it seems unlikely that there was any. Pantaleon Florez, Esq.; Terry E. Beck, Esq., conversation with the author, 26 February 2001.
8. Zalnis v. Thoroughbred Datsun Car Company, et al., 645 P.2d 292 (Colo. App. 1982).
9. Hug v. Gomez, 645 P.2d at 922.
10. Terry E. Beck, Esq.
11. *Id.*
12. Martin, *Miss Manners Rescues Civilization*, 232.
13. *See* "A Guide to Mediation and Arbitration for Business People," http://adr.org/rules/guides/AAA0035-0900.htm (visited 3 March 2001).

14. *See* http://www.nafcm.org (visited 1 March 2001).
15. *See, e.g.,* Trina Grillo, "The Mediation Alternative Process: Dangers for Women," YALE L.J. 100(6) (199): 1545–1610; Susan Silbey and Austin Sarat, "Dispute Processing in Law and Legal Scholarship: From Institutional Critique to the Reconstruction of the Juridical Subject," DENV. U. L. REV. 66 (1989): 437–98. For a response to Professor Grillo, *see* Joshua Rosenberg, "In Defense of Mediation," 33 ARIZ. L. REV. 167 (1991).
16. Grillo at 1589–90.
17. Grillo at 1599.
18. Robert N. Bellah, Richard Madsen, William M. Sullivan, Ann Swidler, and Steven M. Tipton, *Habits of the Heart: Individualism and Commitment in American Life* (Berkeley and Los Angeles: University of California Press, 1996).
19. Robert D. Putnam, *Bowling Alone: The Collapse and Revival of American Community* (New York: Simon & Schuster, 2000).
20. Terry E. Beck, Esq.; Pantaleon Florez, Esq.
21. Pantaleon Florez, Esq.

Robert N. Bellah, Richard Madsen, William M. Sullivan, Ann Swidler, and Steven M. Tipton. *Habits of the Heart: Individualism and Commitment in American Life*. Berkeley and Los Angeles: University of California Press, 1996.
The book was an instant classic when first published in 1985. The authors make their case about how traditional American individualism has led to a sense of isolation. The authors' interviews with ordinary Americans portray a willingness and need for individuals to reconnect with a larger society. Though not generally supported by statistical analysis, the book makes interesting reading for the layperson.

Mark Caldwell. *A Short History of Rudeness*. New York: Picador USA, 1999.
Caldwell, a literary critic on the faculty at Fordham University, provides a historical approach to incivility. His thesis is that notions of etiquette began to crumble long before the end of the twentieth century due to the changing demographics of class. In fact, he posits, the ground is constantly shifting as mores and social positions change. He supports his version of history with numerous examples from decades past.

Stephen L. Carter. *Civility*. New York: HarperCollins, 1998.
A law professor at Yale, Carter nevertheless takes a broader approach. He argues that civility began to erode with the similar erosion in Americans' sense of belonging to a

cohesive society, which he says occurred in the 1960s. He advocates a return to civility through the institutions upon which America was built: family, school, and, most important to Carter, church.

P. M. Forni. *Choosing Civility: The Twenty-Five Rules of Considerate Conduct.* New York: St. Martin's Press, 2002.
Professor Forni, who teaches civility and Italian literature at Johns Hopkins University and comments on civility for National Public Radio, has issued his essential twenty-five rules for behavior. In a concise, compact manner, he also considers the reasons behind the current lack of civility and why it matters that we behave. He takes up criticism, complaining, responsibility and blame, and praise, among other topics.

Giovinella Gonthier and Kevin Morrissey (contributor). *Rude Awakenings: Overcoming the Civility Crisis in the Workplace.* Chicago: Dearborn Trade Publishing, 2002.
Gonthier, a former ambassador, explores the problem of incivility in the workplace from a business standpoint. Incivility, she argues, negatively affects productivity, and, therefore, profitability. She begins by exploring the changes in technology and workplace diversity and how they created a new world with new challenges to civility. Her audience is managers who must deal with impoliteness and the bottom-line issue that she argues it is.

Judith Martin. *Miss Manners Rescues Civilization.* New York: Crown, 1996.
Miss Manners is at her delightful, insightful, common-sense best, taking on all arguments that etiquette is something to be scorned and avoided. Her most important argument is that etiquette provides a set of rules with which everyone can feel comfortable and that finally provides more freedom because it does not carry the weight of law. However, she notes that, unfortunately, the law has had to take over where etiquette has failed, notably in the area of discrimination.

M. Scott Peck. *A World Waiting to Be Born.* New York: Bantam Books, 1993.
While Peck, like Gonthier, explores incivility in the corporate world, he approaches it from the standpoint of the individual's narcissistic impulses that result from his having "a hole in the mind," that is, the inability to see himself as part of a larger whole. Peck takes a more spiritual approach than Gonthier, too, by arguing that one must submit oneself to a higher authority in order to achieve this greater consciousness. Peck's workshop ventures, through his Foundation for Community Encouragement, are the background for his thesis.

Robert D. Putnam. *Bowling Alone: The Collapse and Revival of American Community.* New York: Simon & Schuster, 2000.
Putnam's metaphor is the precipitous decline in membership in bowling leagues with a simultaneously steady rise in the number of people actually bowling. He argues that this decline has led to a lack of connection among Americans. In an attempt to provide an agenda for reversing the trends he finds, Putnam concludes by issuing a series of challenges for the beginning of the twenty-first century. To educators, to employers and employee groups alike, to America's urban and regional planners, to the faith-

based communities, to the media, to the leaders of our cultural institutions, and last to our politicians and government officials, he suggests specific goals for finding ways to ensure that Americans are provided the means and opportunities to reconnect with each other, to rediscover what they have in common, and to recreate the American community.

Leroy Rouner, ed. *Civility.* Notre Dame, Ind.: University of Notre Dame Press, 2000.

Dr. Rouner, Professor of Philosophy, Religion, and Philosophical Theology at Boston University, edited a collection of essays dealing with civility on a number of levels. The contributors are academics in a wide variety of disciplines: philosophy, education, psychology, sociology, and political science, among others. The authors define civility, as both a civic and a philosophical matter; they explore it in its religious and social contexts; and they explain civility as a matter of manners.

Henry C. Wheelwright, ed. *Rules of Civility for the 21st Century from Cub and Boy Scouts from across America.* Washington, D.C.: Stone Wall Press, 2000.

George Washington's recently rediscovered and now-famous Rules are given a twentieth-century gloss by Cub and Boy Scouts. Some of the insights are surprising, and not just precious or innocent. The Rules themselves are not presented in Washington's order but are divided into themes such as respect, impatience, fairness, criticism, and, a virtue also in short supply in American society, brevity.